THE GREAT CALIFORNIA DESERTS

Other books by W. STORRS LEE

The Sierra
Canal Across a Continent
God Bless Our Queer Old Dean
The Strength to Move a Mountain
Yankees of Connecticut
Green Mountains of Vermont
Town Father
Bread Loaf Anthology (EDITOR)
Footpath in the Wilderness (EDITOR)
Stagecoach North
Father Went to College

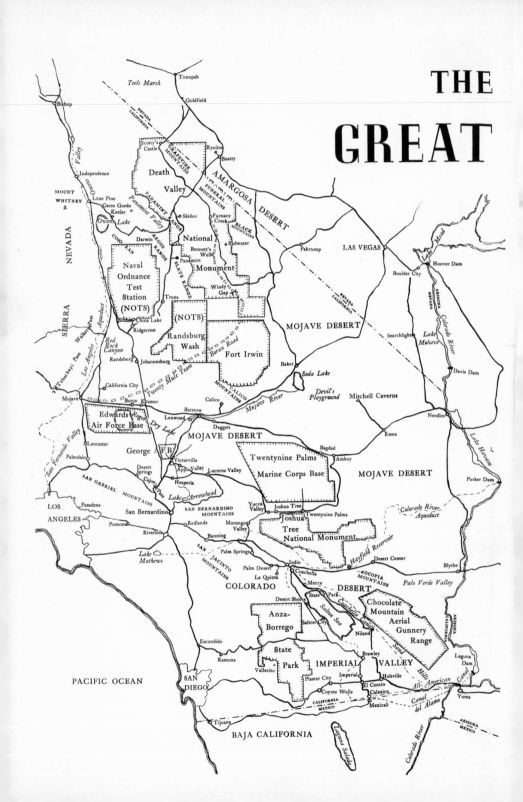

THE

GREAT

CALIFORNIA DESERTS

by W. STORRS LEE

Illustrations By EDWARD SANBORN

G. P. Putnam's Sons   New York

© *1963 by* W. STORRS LEE

Library of Congress Catalog
Card Number: 62-18285

MANUFACTURED IN THE UNITED STATES OF AMERICA

TO

Bill, D. Phil.

ACKNOWLEDGMENTS

FOR assistance in the preparation of this book, I express appreciation to the following Californians: Lieutenant Joseph H. Adams, Public Information Officer, Fort Irwin; Mr. and Mrs. Lee J. Anderson, Covalda Date Company, Coachella; Mrs. Frank Bennett, President, Historical Society, Palm Springs; Colonel Charles A. Brown, Director of Information, Edwards Air Force Base; Mr. Rolla E. Chandler, Bureau of Land Management, Dept. of Interior, Riverside; Colonel James G. Chestnut, Office of Chief of Information, U. S. Army, Los Angeles; Mr. A. B. Christman, Technical Information Dept., U. S. Naval Ordnance Test Station, China Lake; Mr. Eugene L. Conrotto, Editor, *Desert Magazine*, Palm Desert; Major Ruth M. Dudley, Office of Information, Edwards Air Force Base; Miss Betty Franklin, Librarian, Academy of Motion Picture Arts and Sciences, Los Angeles; Captain R. M. Hartman, Information Office, Eleventh Naval District, San Diego; Mr. Ted Loeff, Literary Projects Co., Beverly Hills; Mr. Bruce Minard, prospector, Cantil; Mr. Ralph S. Minor, metallurgist, and Mrs. Minor, Lafayette; Sergeant Clifford R. Morrison, U. S. Marine Corps Base, Twentynine Palms; Mr. Don McNeilly, Manager, Chamber of Commerce, Palm Desert; Mr. Cecil B. Smith, Mojave Industrial Action Committee, Mojave; Mr. Roger Stinchfield, Supervisor, Mitchell Caverns State Park, Essex; also to Mr. Howard Cady and Mr. Thomas C. Wallace of G. P. Putnam's Sons; to the library staff of the University of California; to the publishers, listed under QUOTATION SOURCES, who kindly granted permission to quote from copyrighted works; and especially to my wife Mary Louise Lee.

CONTENTS

THE GREAT CALIFORNIA DESERTS

I
BIG, BARREN, BEAUTIFUL BACK YARD

THE auctioneer looked like an auctioneer and acted like one. His arms were in constant motion, his head wagged, his hands talked. He was in total command of his audience, arrogant, flaunting, glib. The voice was an auctioneer's. It boomed and blustered. But the jargon that came with the voice was a parody on an ancient trade; here was a salesman trying to get across to bidders in a crowded Los Angeles auditorium the honest worth of what he was selling. He did not belaud his wares, he derided them; he did not cadge and cajole; he jeered at the indulgence of his audience.

"What am I offered for this parcel, ladies and gentlemen?" he trumpeted with a hint of sarcasm. "What am I offered? Five acres, and all sand. Uncle Sam appraises it at ten dollars. But I don't wanna cheat you. Cactus and rattlesnakes go with it, but no water. It's crawling with rattlers. No oil, no gold; government hangs onto the mineral rights. Cactus and greasewood are all you'll ever harvest on it. Five acres of the saddest-looking desert north of the Mexican border. Forty miles from nowhere. Cost you a fortune to bring in water. What am I bid? Ten dollars an acre, says the government. Who wants to lead off with—?"

"Five hundred dollars!" screamed a lady in the middle of the jam-packed hall.

Nobody laughed.

"Five hundred?" gasped the auctioneer. "Remember it's cash on the barrel. The lady says five—"

"Five fifty," interrupted a gentleman in the rear in a wilted blue sports shirt.

"Six hundred," roared a solid-looking citizen in the front row.
The auctioneer shook his head in bewilderment. "Understand
what you're bidding on, ladies and gentlemen," he warned. "This
ain't suburban real estate. It's desert wasteland. Nobody's holding
out on any information. You can spot it on your maps. No water
nor promises of water. The rattlers and the cholla come free. It's
not worth—'"

"Six hundred and fifty," broke in the woman who had first
mentioned five. And there was desperate determination in her
voice. She knew what she was buying.

"Sold! Sold to the lady for six hundred and fifty dollars,"
barked the auctioneer abruptly, as if he were afraid someone
might jump the figure still higher. "Step up with the cash, lady.
Next parcel."

"They're crazy," the auctioneer confided to his clerk in an
almost inaudible aside.

Crazy or not, the Angelenos wanted title to that desert. The
next plot—even more remote—went for $500, another particu-
larly undesirable piece for $450, and one questionable homesite
for $700. Parcel after parcel was snatched from under the auc-
tioneer's hammer at prices 100 to 500 percent over the appraised
value. Land-poor Uncle Sam was unloading thousands of arid
acres in cadaverous Mojave Desert, and the public was reacting
as though it were the Garden of Eden.

Beginning in 1941, chunks of desolate Western land had been
placed on the market under the Small Tracts Act by the Bureau
of Land Management, Department of the Interior. For a fee of
$25 a homesteader could file on a plot, and after three years, if
enthusiasm had not lagged, he could take permanent possession.
But there was a catch in the deal. A structure of some kind had
to be erected on the site and made to look as though it were lived
in. Few buildings had gone up on these isolated plots.

Then in 1957, in a reversal of its old policy, the bureau decided
to waive the residence requirement and auction off the unwanted
Mojave sand to the highest bidder—cash, one claim to a customer.
But there could be no advance fanfare, no advertising. That was
against the working principles of the bureau. So the whole business was turned over to a practiced auctioneer. By tactfully pre-

senting his problems to the newspapers, he managed to get a few incidental press notices.

For the opener he rented the Los Angeles American Legion Hall, seating capacity 700, hoping for a large enough audience to fill the front rows. But neither the auctioneer nor the bureau had reckoned on the craze for desert terrain that had spawned since World War II. Instead of a few dozen stragglers, the hall was mobbed. Armies of prospective buyers, with their neighbors and kin, descended upon the place. Traffic was tied up for blocks. When the auditorium was filled, men and women fought for standing room, for space in the aisles and the lobby. Twelve hundred people were clamoring for admission.

Police were summoned to unsnarl the traffic and contend with the elbowing throng. Los Angeles had fire laws that could not be disregarded. Firemen were called out to help clear the aisles. "Let's call the whole thing off until we can get a larger hall," proposed bureau officials, after consultation with the auctioneer, the police and the firemen.

Somehow word of the contemplated postponement began to circulate among the audience, and pandemonium ensued. Officials were booed and heckled. People who had seats kept them, and the overflow that had been forcibly ejected continued to mill around outside. Finally a compromise was reached: the first 50 tracts would be offered to those who had seats; the next 50 to standees. Before the uproarious evening was over 100 tracts had been put on the block and 96 sold.

Such was the response to the first public offering of the Mojave lands on March 18, 1957. It was an eye opener to the Bureau of Land Management. In one evening they had been given an astonishing object lesson on the hunger of Californians for desert space.

The salesmen were better prepared for the eight auctions that followed, one a week during the rest of March, through April, and into May. Instead of the American Legion Hall, the huge Embassy Theatre was engaged. Still there was no advertising, but week after week the theatre was crowded. By May 15, nine hundred parcels of dehydrated desert had been offered for sale and 895 of them had passed from government ownership to private ownership, at outlandish figures. The location did not seem to matter. They could be near Palm Springs or at Deadman Lake, twenty miles from Daggett or on Lost Horse Mountain, in Apple Valley, near Lake Arrowhead or Thousand Palms. Large or small, rock strewn or snake infested, accessible or inaccessible, the parcels were snatched up.

As fast as the Bureau of Land Management could complete surveys, other auctions were scheduled. They were moved from the Embassy Theatre to the American Legion Stadium at El Monte, where real crowds could be assembled. For a three-day sale in September 1959, two thousand, two hundred tracts were put on the block; on July 16, 1960, one thousand, six hundred and fifty. In 1962 almost four thousand were listed and they were going faster than ever in a direct-sale program.

The sales were symbolic of the new eagerness to find a place in the desert sun. Suddenly the enormous area of parched, barren, almost rainless Sahara that forms the back yard of greater Los Angeles had boomed into the fastest-growing resort area in the United States—15,000 square miles of Mojave, stretching from the Tehachapi, San Gabriel and San Bernardino mountains all the way across the state to Arizona; and to the south, 8,000 more square miles of what popularly carried the name of Colorado Desert until much of its expanse was turned green by the irrigation of Imperial Valley or other reclamation projects.

No, the unoccupied land was not all for sale. The back yard also included vast stretches that could never be sold, like the Joshua Tree National Monument where more than a half-million acres of rare yuccas are preserved for all time as a public haunt; a comparable acreage of painted desert in Anza-Borrego State Park, east of San Diego; the seared badlands of Death Valley, almost 2,000,000 acres in extent; besides the hundreds of square miles fenced off by the Army, the Navy, the Marines and Air Force for proving grounds, flying fields, missile experiments, training and storage. To Californians, regardless of the ownership, it was all pridefully lumped together as "The Desert"— their desert, and the possessory spirit sometimes seemed to exceed state bounds and lap over into Nevada, Arizona and Mexico.

The dates and honeydews coming from fabulous Imperial Valley probably cinched the first argument in favor of seeking a Western-style escape to Arabia. If the sand and dried silt of Imperial could be made to yield fortunes, other areas could be turned to good account too. Further incentive was added by the rise of Palm Springs from a little sanitarium village, with a 1925 population of less than a hundred souls, into a sprawling society oasis; Hollywood had hallowed that ground, and disciples of Hollywood wanted to sun themselves on like soil.

Then, in the late thirties, word got around that there was unabashed beauty in the desert. An Easter tour to see the beds of primroses, verbena and poppies was the thing. Tourists were beginning to find that there were other attractions in the desert besides ugly ghost towns and the relics of those "fierce, shy, profane, sun-drenched derelicts"—the miners. A more sophisticated glamor was based on appreciation of desert silence, crisp, star-spangled nights and the shoulder tan.

World War II interfered. Gas-coupon dispensers did not look kindly upon desert joy-riders, and regardless of the starting point, it took a lot of gasoline to get to Skidoo, Mecca or Bagdad. Yet, in a way, the War opened the desert as it had never before been opened. The military discovered that the dry terrain and crystal overhead were ideal for all kinds of land and sky maneuvers, as well as for cheap open-air storage of battle paraphernalia; and quick delivery of supplies could be made to the Coast by either rail or plane.

Countless thousands of recruits saw the Great American Desert for the first time while in uniform. They did not always feel that their tours were under the most desirable auspices, and few of them developed any feverish affection for the open spaces of Camp Irwin, Dunlap or Muroc Air Base. But curiously enough, when the war was over, ex-sergeants and lieutenants wanted to come back with their wives and kids for another look at the setting. Many of them stayed on. And the military had become so attracted to the desert that they stayed, anyway, and expanded.

On December 7, 1941, Barstow—where the Marines had established something like a beachhead—was a harsh desert crossroads town. Through-motorists drew up at a gas station, had their tanks and water jugs filled, and hurried on without delay toward Mojave or Needles. There was not much at Barstow that could invite delay. Twenty years later, thanks largely to the Marines, the Santa Fe Railway and the Mojave River, Barstow had grown into a youthful city, ranging over so much territory that a circuitous freeway, sweeping far around the metropolis, was needed to fend off the traffic.

More dramatic was the transformation along a secondary road

between Indio and Palm Springs. There in the rugged San Jacinto foothills, during World War II, soldiers trained under General Patton at the Tank Proving Grounds. No sooner had the tanks disappeared than a shrewd real-estate syndicate moved in, drilled for water, and struck an artesian gusher. In a few months the area had turned green and the fetching name of "Palm Desert" was on the map. Paved streets were laid out around broad fairways and a fabulous clubhouse worthy of comparison with anything at Palm Springs. Patton's Proving Ground, considered valuable a few months before only for the roughing up that tanks could give it, was selling for $25,000 an acre, and $100,000-dollar residences were going up on it.

Lockheed Aircraft and other plane companies started moving more and more of their operations into Palmdale, and employees were just one jump behind to inspect housing developments anywhere within a radius of thirty miles. Other aircraft companies, which had been hugging the Pacific or paying ever-mounting taxes on San Fernando real estate, began exploring the desert and found it hospitable and relatively cheap. A swiftly developing electronics industry learned that low desert humidity gave more accurate control over sensitive instruments, and joined the march to inland sites.

The parade of householders, fed up with smog and Los Angeles traffic jams, pushed steadily eastward. There they found year-round sunshine, clean air, open spaces, easy access to recreation facilities, cheap building and a new way of life. They liked it. The publicists called it "patio living," "sun living," "ranch living," "fairways living." And Walt Disney inadvertently proved to be the master publicist of all when he introduced millions to the charm and romance of *The Living Desert*. That big, bad, beautiful back yard was rapidly being pre-empted.

Sociologists could make convincing assertions that "the life," as much as the industrial transplantations, accounted for the population shift. Desert converts, like those who participated in the mob excitement at the Los Angeles auctions, usually began as weekenders. They struck out for places such as Owens Lake on the dry side of the Sierra, the Salton Sea, Red Rock Canyon, or almost any patch of soil where they could stretch out and find sanctuary.

At Glendale, at Pasadena, at Santa Ana and Burbank, every Friday night the weekenders loaded into cars and headed east.

They soaked up sun at their hide-outs and dreamed for two days of the swimming pools, patios and air-conditioned family rooms they would have one day when the desert was covered with Palm Springs and Palm Deserts. Often there was a trailer in tow, more often a boat. They sped around the tepid, salty waters of a desert lake all day Saturday and were up at dawn on Sunday for more of the same. Then, late Sunday afternoon, they edged into the bumper-to-stern traffic lanes that led back to smog and metropolitan congestion. And each trip left them with a stronger conviction that they did not want to go back to the city.

"Here in this mountain fastness, where at night the desert wind roars across the cliffs and at dawn the desert sun comes up out of a vast silence of gray and gold and the mystery of dim, shadowy leagues, we have found peace and solitude and settled content," sighed a convert who had escaped with his family to the solitude of Ghost Mountain permanently. "We moved to the desert because we were tired. We arrived all at once at the realization that we were not equal to the job of coping with modern, high-power civilization. We longed for peace and the whisper of the clean wind across unspoiled wilderness.

"There is that about the desert which is fierce. There is nothing soft about Ghost Mountain. In the beginning, fiercely it fought us. Just as in the end, with a warmth equally fierce, it took us to its heart. The wind and the sun fought us. The searing heat of the summer fought us. And the pack rats and the pocket mice and the centipedes and the snakes and the scorpions and the tarantulas all resisted our intrusion. It was a fight every foot of the way. We have rooted down slowly and firmly. You can't hurry the desert . . . But the terror and uncertainty that we knew in the cities is gone forever."

Typical of the modern pioneers who sought more than mere peace and contentment in the desert were Lee and Ruth Anderson, raised on farms in Michigan and New Jersey respectively. The Andersons happened into Coachella Valley in 1920, when it was still mostly an expanse of sagebrush, mesquite and sand dunes—with a few oases devoted experimentally to date palms and miscellaneous farm crops. They had no remotest thought of turning into sand farmers. But the desert cast its spell on Lee Anderson. He tasted the dates and decided then and there that anything as good as those dates he had to have a hand in growing.

For a beginning he had exactly $600 and a modest grubstake

from his father-in-law. Every dollar of his savings went into land and palm shoots—which could not be counted on to yield a big bumper crop for a decade. To tide his family over those lean years, he planted cotton, onions, sugar beets, sweet corn, peas, soy beans, grapes, pecans, on the side. His wife and children joined him in the fields. They did all the work on twelve acres themselves until they could afford Mexican help.

Anderson kept buying more cheap desert land, grubbing out the mesquite, leveling and planting it. No Michigan or New Jersey farmers ever worked harder. And the labor paid off hand somely. By 1944 the original 12 acres had multiplied to 550, and Anderson had the satisfaction of turning down an offer of $1,225,-000 for his ranch. His palm groves were producing 2,000,000 pounds of dates a year.

Hard times struck after World War II. The demand for dates dropped; the price dropped. Politics, heavy competition and tight bank financing crept into date production. The federal government stepped in with restrictions on Mexican labor and new marketing orders, requiring that for every 100 pounds of whole dates shipped out, 39 pounds be converted into some combination product.

Anderson was forced to give up much of his acreage, but the desert had such a grip on him he could not give up his sand pioneering. He pioneered in crop variation; pioneered in helping to bring Colorado River water to Coachella Valley; pioneered in natural organic farming; pioneered in introducing new date products until his mail-order business included over a hundred different items, ranging from date confection and date butter to dried date chips for TV snacks and the survival kit.

"The greatest thing to bring to the desert is vision," claims Anderson. "You've got to keep looking ahead, got to keep making adjustments, got to keep growing. Unless you're continually pushing the desert back, sooner or later it will swallow you up."

Vision as expansive as the Andersons' was tardy in reaching the California desert. A few early visionaries did note the fertility of the lands which the Colorado River had once overflowed, but they did not get very excited about it. "Too thick to drink, not thick enough to plow," was the common appraisal of the river, and as far as the rich, dry soil was concerned, the Indians were welcome to keep it.

Far from visualizing either an agricultural or residential future for the desert, the first transcontinental wayfarers saw it only as a perilous obstruction. Twentieth-century grangers and escapists have indeed taken impressive risks in establishing themselves on the sands, but the risks are all trivial compared to the gambles of their precursors, who considered themselves fortunate if they could retain life, sanity and a few of their possessions while making the crossing.

There were no roads, and such trails as existed were unmarked and unreliably mapped. Prospectors in search of raw mineral wealth, or emigrants in search of the easiest route to an overadvertised California Paradise, were the principal travelers, and few of them completed the trek without suffering purgatorial agonies. The desert was the curse of the continent—an even greater curse than the frigid heights of the Rockies and the Sierra Nevada.

"Desolation beyond conception," it was labeled by William Lewis Manly, as tough a tramper as ever journeyed from coast to coast. "Away out in the center of the Great American Desert, with an empty stomach and a dry and parched throat! It is not in my power to tell how much I suffered."

Men of science, poking into the desert on professional missions, shared a similar sentiment. TWENTY MILES FROM WOOD, TWENTY MILES FROM WATER, FORTY FEET FROM HELL—GOD BLESS OUR HOME read the sign left behind by a party of geologists, after spending Christmas Day at Saratoga Springs.

Laymen who set out across the desert and lived to tell of their ordeals mocked at the maniacs who wanted to scour the parched hills and valleys for gold or other valuables. No sane man would enter the desert if there were any way of avoiding it, they swore. In the most irrational dreams, no one conceivably fancied that there would one day be a wild scramble for possession of desert acres as a home and retreat.

On a 1,000-mile reconnaissance, as late as 1902, the revered mineralogist and desert promoter George W. Parsons was appalled by the number of graves and skeletons being found on the barren wastes—the remains of wanderers who had perished in the frantic search for water. It was Parsons who launched a one-man campaign for the erection of simple, inexpensive signs to direct travelers to the nearest water source, though it might be 10, 25 or 30 miles distant. He roved up and down California, pleading his cause, and kept up a steady flow of appeals to Washington, urging Congress to take action.

His most telling propaganda was a single, graphic paragraph which highlighted the peril of roadless, waterless desert travel: "Noon. Into the unshaded wilderness the mounted sun pours its intolerable rays, making the thin air dance. Myriad infinitesimal shadows lie shrunken under the clumps of brush. Even the gray-backed lizards have ceased their darting and sought shelter from the midday blaze. Nothing moves. Nothing disturbs this desolation of silence but a lost man, crazed, bareheaded, semiblinded, moaning for water, water in that scorched and barren waste. Anguish of thirst, the like of which may be only once endured, has drawn back his lips, and the sun has cracked and baked them. His blackened tongue protrudes. Crouched in the desert, there drifts to his dying ears the music of splashing waters; to his dimming eyes appears a perfect vision of fountains and marble fonts and fern-embowered shade—and oh, it is so near. Leaping, uttering delirious sounds, stopping to divest himself now of one frayed garment, now another, naked he runs to cast himself into this Eden of moisture, into his palace of shadows—and stumbles into the Paradise of the grave."

Of course Parsons was accused of being melodramatic, but any desert vagrant knew very well that he was not overdoing the scene. Thanks to the untiring promoter, the signs were erected and gradually the toll in casualties diminished, although the signs failed to shorten the trails to the nearest spring. All too often, lost, demented gold grubbers could not make the last miles.

"It was awful when Rhyolite and the other towns was goen strong," alleged Bill Corcoran, a professional who had done enough grubbing and prospecting to know. "There's those graves all over the valley and there's lots of people died out there we don't know about. The weather just dried them out and these sandstorms come. The greenest kids in the world would come out to Rhyolite and get a pack outfit and go out in the desert. They wouldn't know how to pack a boorow, or even tie them up. The boorows would come back into town and then we would go out looken for the men. Sometimes we found them.

"You wanna remember they was no roads in the valley then and it was a lonesome place even if they was a hundred prospectors foolen around in the hills. Thirty or forty days you wouldn't see a soul. And those fools not knowen better would be packen around the valley in the summer. In the daytime. Out in the sun. They was so many found dead that you couldn't pay any attention to them. Most of them ran outa water.

"Some of them that was found dead duren the boom days was fellars that had been in the valley long enough to know better. Bill Ryan. Bill was an old prospector up to the Keane Wonder Mine. Bill had been up in Rhyolite on a big drunk and he come down to the Keane Wonder and from there he started to Furnace Creek. I guess he knew he was goen to die because he lay down close to the road so someone could find him. He died between the time the wagon left Furnace Creek in the mornen and when I come across the valley that night. I stepped on Bill in the dark. Like to scared me to death. I thought it was a mattress and I lit a match. And there was his eyes staren up at me. God! It was horrible to look at. His whiskers sticken up at me!"

Bill himself admitted that he came within a snicker of going the way of his whiskered friend Ryan: "Three days wanderen around outa my head, with angels flyen alongside a me pouren water out of a silver pitcher into a silver bowl. I could hear the rustle of their wings and the splashen water. I could see more water than I ever knew was on earth before. Water was runnen in all directions, and I could hear it rainen plainer than it ever rained when I was myself. I'll never come closer to dyen and not go. I musta fell down all over the country; I busted my ribs and cut my head on the rocks and threw away my shirt and one shoe and didn't know it. When they found me I couldn't talk, my tongue and throat was swollen so. In those three days I was wanderen around the desert I went down from one hundred and eighty-five pounds to one hundred and twenty-six. Sixty pounds in three days was what I lost. That's some dryen out."

For all ambulatory invaders of the Mojave, the Colorado, Death Valley and the dry wastes between the crisscross of mountain ranges, the one injunction repeated again and again was: "Get the desert behind you as quick as you can. Keep moving— and fast." But the prospectors did not take kindly to injunctions. They liked people to mind their own business and not keep giving advice; they valued their independence. Off and on for fifty years before anyone thought much about taming the desert, they were its only human tenants of any consequence, and they were there to stay on their own terms, as long as there was lucre to lure them. By 1902, when George Parsons' was the one voice in the wilderness pleading for lifesaving water signs, they had long since established a *laissez-faire* attitude toward any kind of salvation, as well as a tradition that held in contempt all injunction, all entreaty, all law and order. They were an ornery tribe.

In the nation-wide stampede toward Sacramento and the Sierra, after Jim Marshall had turned up the yellow flecks in Sutter's Creek on January 24, 1848, many of the Argonauts tried to take short cuts across the desert. Half dead from thirst, starvation and terror, they had fumbled their way through passes and dry gulches of the desert ranges within a stone's throw of richer gold and silver diggings than they were ever to find in the Sierra, but no one then had advertised the desert wealth. They were hellbent for another destination, and it was not until later that they learned what they had passed up. So the desert gold rush came late, and the scavengers who headed back toward Death Valley and its droughty environs usually made the trip for their health, as outcasts, rustlers and highjackers trying to keep out of range of the long arm of lynch law. The society they created east of the Sierra was in keeping with their characters. Theirs was the first desert society.

Names were enough to type them: Alkali Bill, Pike Wilson, Three-finger Jack, Mono Jim, Seldom Seen Slim, Duke of Nebraska, Slim Ludwick, Diamondfield Jack, Doc O'Toole, Truthful Tom, Shorty Harris, Panamint George, Curley Graham, Fraction Jack Parker, Slim March, Stuttering Parker, Peavine Johnny. There were thousands more like them. Rarely did any of them elect to retain his given name, and if so, it was used with derision or with strong suspicion that it was really an alias. "Slim" was the most common sobriquet, for it fitted a lean, lithe majority and the Abe Lincoln look so many possessed. There were few Shorty Harrises or Peavine Johnnies.

The gold towns inland from Sacramento were rugged and tough, but none of the goings on at Downieville, Angels Camp or Hangtown were quite up to the standard set in the Death Valley region. This was the real hangout for the trigger-happy, the round-the-clock card sharps, and those who weren't dependent on well-water, as long as the whisky held out.

Whisky could compensate for all the shortages and discomforts of Death Valley. And the extent of that compensation can still be

25

witnessed in the mountains of broken glass they left behind in
the ghost towns. Saloons were the town halls, courts and capitals
for the desert domain. Empties accumulated in such quantity at
cross-trail camps that they were used to line the walls of dugouts
into which vagrants crawled for midday shelter from the sun. Entire houses were sided and sheathed with bottles laid on the hori-
zontal.

"This is the thirstiest trail on record," teetotaler Parsons observed soberly after covering twenty-seven miles of desert terrain
near Death Valley in 1902. "The trail was well marked with dead
soldiers—empty bottles of those gone before not *in* spirit, but
with spirit. Arithmetic failed me after a count of the first five
hundred."

Worthy of a full chapter in the history of bacchanalianism was
the first Death Valley cocktail party, just over the Nevada border.
A teamster, knowing something about the laws of alcoholic supply and demand in the region, procured a vanload of the stuff
at Rhyolite and headed south. Whatever his destination, he never
reached it. Prospectors seemed to sniff the cargo afar off and descended upon the wagon in droves. Finally the mule skinner
climbed down from the wagon and set up a bar on the trail.

"Drinks were supposed to be four bits," recounted one of the
waylayers, "but the bartender kept whatever you gave him. That
bartender didn't have time to make change. He was busy. He just
kept what money he got, and if you didn't have any money, you
drank anyway, so I guess it all come out pretty even. My, but they
got awful drunk around that wagon."

In the midst of the bout a prospector from a nearby cabin
made the mistake of boasting that he had just packed in a case of
reasonably fresh eggs, and suddenly everyone developed a hankering for punch. The eggs were confiscated and a few watering
buckets substituted for a punch bowl. Into the buckets went the
eggs and whisky, with proportionate quantities of rum, gin, wine
and beer for flavoring.

"You grabbed a dipper," recalled the benefactor who had reluctantly sacrificed his eggs, "and when you had a chance, you
stuck it in one of the buckets and drank whiskey and gin and beer
and eggs, all mixed up. Even the egg shells. You drank them, too.
My God, it was awful. Afterwards I wished I had my eggs back."

Water was scarce in the Death Valley mining towns. Men died
for lack of it.

Even in this society of rebels and revelers, however, it was recognized that there had to be some order and community sense,
and as the occasion arose they created their own rules and regu-
lations—though the results were seldom committed to paper.

Once in awhile, when a shady character became too obstreper-
ous for his own good or the common good, he was quietly put
out of the way. At Skidoo a reckless nonconformist was strung
up without benefit of public trial, and after the body had hung
for a suitable interval as an example to the iniquitous, it was per-
functorily buried. But the rites were hardly over when reporters
from more civilized country turned up to cover the event. They
had caught wind of this administration of Skidoo justice and
were naturally disappointed to learn that their arrival was too
late for the pictures they wanted.

The town fathers assembled at a local bar to commiserate with
the journalists, and a few drinks helped to convince them that
they were missing out on some first-class publicity. So the accom-
modating officials disinterred the body, rehung it for the photog-
raphers, posed for pictures, then ordered the corpse restored to
its resting place.

Strictly private squabbles were settled privately in the desert,
and if the facts later had to be aired, the affair could be readily
presented as another accidental tragedy—with witnesses to provide essential testimony. But the usual expedient for getting rid
of a public nuisance was a simple ritual of excommunication. A
group of self-appointed kingpins openly approached the offender,
said as little as possible, and casually handed him a filled canteen.
It was his ticket to the desert. He understood, departed unhur-
riedly, and never returned.

A trickle of water was all that separated life and death. Nowhere in America was the margin between the two so narrow. In
a land where everyone was on the move, where neighbors were
neighbors for a few months at most, where friendships were tran-
sitory and one stranger as suspect as another, there was amazingly
little reverence for life, and less reverence for death. A neighbor
or passing acquaintance who met an untimely end was given a
burial of sorts, with minimum display of grief and scriptural
reference. In fact, the ceremony was more commonly seasoned
with banter rather than solemnity, and the grave marker per-
petuated the spirit of the occasion:

Died July 31, 1887

We didn't know this gent's name.
A proper burying he got the same.

or

Here lies Symanthie Proctor
Who ketched a cold and wouldn't doctor.
She couldn't stay, she had to go.
Praise God from whom all blessings flow.

   The short-lived town of Calico kept a poetaster busy for almost
a decade composing suitable epitaphs for its hillside graveyard:

Here lies Slip McVey.
He might be here today
But bum whisky and a bad gun put him away.

1882

Beneath this stone, a lump of clay,
Lies Nora Young
Who on this 21st of May
Began to hold her tongue.

1881

Joe F. Kelley
Saloon-Keeper

This one is on me.

Here rests Sadie Arbuckle.
Her demise was
Noted by many men.
Her reputation can
Be quoted by those
Who knew her when.

1882

Joe Crabbe

When I am dead and in my grave
No more whiskey will I crave,
But on my tombstone shall be wrote
They's many a jolt went down his throat.

The lighthearted attitude toward death persisted right down to the days when the first automobile tourists began to invade the Mojave and Death Valley about 1910 or 1912, as exemplified in one of Death Valley Scotty's favorite yarns.

"Yar, I was out prospectin'," he liked to ruminate, "when I come across an old man an' woman. They'd driv up in their auto and the damn thing had broke down. They hadn't et or had a drop of water fer two days. Must've been all of a hundred and fifty miles from anywhere.

"Well, I had my burros, but I give 'em what water and grub I had and started back to get help. Then I got to thinkin'. Time I got back them two would be dead. And they'd sure have suffered to beat hell. Took me quite a spell to figure out what to do."

In telling his story to shocked and spellbound tourists in after years the leathery prospector drolly expatiated on the seriousness in the predicament of the old couple and the hard choice he had to make in relieving them somehow of the frightful agony they inevitably faced. He explained how he couldn't bear to let them die that way. It was not charitable. Then he customarily paused, as if there were no more to tell.

"But what did you do?" someone invariably cued him after a long moment of suspense.

"Oh," he'd reply in slight irritation, conveying to his rapt listeners the impression that they ought to know the answer, "there wasn't any choice. Went back an' shot them, of course. Th' only Christian thing to do."

To survive the abuse of California desert during the years when it was first being probed, one had to be a little zany and philosophical, as well as callous. It was America's most formidable torture chamber. The hot winds were unfriendly, the rough footing was unfriendly, the white piercing light was unfriendly, the Indians, the snakes and the bayoneted cactuses were unfriendly. And the friendship of Argonauts who held a prior claim on the land was not anything that could be counted on.

It was a crazy, deceptive country of wild contrasts and incongruities. In a land of no water, the noon sun turned the lower layers of atmosphere into a refracting agent and created vast lakes and rivers, convincing in every detail, as blue as the ocean of sky that was being reflected. Topsy-turvy images of rocks or shrubs took on the likeness of ships and sails and islands in the expanse of water; along the shore line were wharves and small craft, and in the distance a town complete with chimneys and church spires.

More often on the bleached desert there appeared a tiny oasis with luxuriant vegetation and shimmering palms, a welcome sight to any old-timer and a bit of paradise to the uninitiated. It was not a case of a man deranged by thirst and the heat, seeing things. Those images looked as real as the real thing, even to experienced desert plodders. They fooled the best of them. Yet when a neophyte made the dash to the shores or shade, the water had a way of quickly receding, evaporating, and becoming just another endless stretch of barren waste. Another mirage—one of the most unkind taunts of an unfriendly land.

Heat, drought, deceptive distance and mirages were not the only abominations. At higher altitudes in winter the creeping chill of night could easily match the scorching sun of full day. Or a gaunt, yellow cloud could appear unheralded on the horizon, swiftly envelop everything in sight, and bring on a hurricane of wind and sand—wind against which no man could stand, and a hail of sand pellets that could blast the skin off an unprotected face in half an hour.

Then there were curious dust devils that swirled across the desert—frequently a half dozen of them at a time—funnels of superheated air, boiling skyward from the floor of the wasteland and carrying with them every movable dead shrub within reach; ominously winding, twisting, wavering as they advanced, and finally disintegrating as mysteriously as they had started.

Nor was the desert always dry. A black cloud could loom up over a mountain height, and in a few minutes dump a year's supply of water on three square miles of terrain. It came in a deluge, inches of it, and woe unto the human who happened to be in the path of an ancient channel. With a roar and rumble, the brown water rolled down a canyon, sweeping away everything before it. There was no escape for man, beast or object in the right of way. And within an hour the streambed could be as empty as before the cloudburst, the water miraculously gone, and the only reminders of its passing, the debris left stranded along the banks.

While topographic engineers were making surveys of the Grapevine Mountains in 1895, they entered an unnamed canyon that had recently been flushed by such a flash flood. Fresh layers of talus and mud were impacted along a new high-water mark below the mouth of the canyon, and there were tangles of dead wood, cactus and sagebrush, too firmly matted to be torn out. Half buried in silt, they found, too, the body of a man who had been caught in the wash. In his pocket was a letter addressed to "Titus," so as a memorial to the disfigured casualty, the unnamed gulch was at once spotted on the topographic maps as Titus Canyon. The name still stands.

Yet another canyon a short distance away might remain high and dry for a decade, with never a trickle running down it. Minor landmarks noted in the stream bed one spring could be undisturbed ten springs later.

In a blind arroyo tucked into Sheepshead Mountain, prospector Charlie Walker once came across a mysteriously deserted camp that appeared to have been abandoned in great haste at least a week or two before, perhaps longer. No freshet had poured down it in many months. Charlie knew that guessing at lapse of time was pretty futile, for without damaging downpours or marauding animals, things like bedding and bottles and tinned food could last almost indefinitely in the dry air.

A hunk of half-cooked dried bread rested in the Dutch oven; the inevitable catsup bottle and dishes were still in place on a packing-box table; cans of codfish and corned beef had been left out as though they were intended for the next meal; a saddle sat on a nearby boulder. Wind had rent the canvas tent, but the poles stood in place, and between them were two cots made up with bedding and pillows.

Confident that he had uncovered the makings of a first-class murder mystery, Charlie at once appointed himself detective. For two days he scoured the area, looking for some clue. There were no signs of struggle, no bloodstains, no bodies, no bones or coyote tracks. He gave up and moved on to town, where he was unable even to interest the sheriff in his mystery. There had been no reports of missing miners and the law was too busy to help invent a calamity case. So Charlie remained in charge.

Tenaciously he continued making inquiries, and endured a good bit of ribbing for his obsession. Months later, while expounding at length on his case at a restaurant in Beatty, a huge man lumbered up to him and jeeringly broke in: "Sheepshead Mountain? That was my camp."

Charlie all but upset the table in scrambling to his feet. A ready hand was on his holster. At last he had a suspect claiming ownership to the camp of the murdered men.

"Sit down. Sit down," the suspect calmly proposed. "Yar, that was our camp all right. Partner and I, we weren't gettin' nowhere at prospectin'. Going a little giddy with the heat and the quiet. So one day while we was fixin' breakfast, we jest took it into our heads, quick like, to light outa there fer Rhyolite and try our hand at faro. Planned to come back next day, but we hit a streak of crazy luck, cleaned up a pile, more'n we'd made at prospectin' fer a year. We decided 'twant worthwhile goin' back to that camp at all—ever. What you see at the camp was jest as we left it."

"But when—?" burst in Charlie.

"Oh, let's see," puzzled the big man, tipping back his hat and scratching his thin gray hair. "I can tell you exactly. Come March, that was jest twenty-two years."

It was the last time Charlie Walker ever tried to compete with the sheriff in playing detective.

Even the driest parts of the Mojave, the Colorado Desert and Death Valley, however, do get rain—an over-all average of perhaps three or four inches of it in a year, but spotty and unpredictable. Bagdad, California, once went without a drop for thirty-six months, while in the San Gabriel Mountains a fall of 1.02 inches was recorded in a single minute, and another desert gauge registered 2.47 inches in three minutes.

As in other desert regions as far apart as the hot interior of Australia, the white Sahara and the frigid Gobi, plants do grow, animals prosper, and a little rain descends. And because of that sporadic rain the very bounds of California desert are in dispute. In fact, no two authorities can be brought to agree on exactly what constitutes a desert or the proportion of the planet covered by it. Figures vary from a precise 19 percent to a more liberal estimate of one-third.

Meteorologists simplify the dilemma by maintaining that a desert is any place where evaporation exceeds precipitation. Botanists think of deserts as regions of widely spaced, peculiarly specialized vegetation. Economists, geologists and real-estate barons rely on their own definitions. The only rule of thumb that everyone has agreed to is that a desert has to have a rainfall of less than ten inches a year; dryness is the predominant attribute.

The 26,314,000 acres of California dry lands easily qualify under almost any definition, and they comprise over a quarter of the state's land area. There are barren flats, broad alkali beds, broken ranges of dry mountains, acres of volcanic rubble, great outwash fans, square miles of sand dunes, parched plateau country, sweeping bottom lands and occasional oases—a sample of just about every surface texture found in unwatered wastes anywhere.

Some of the world's ugliest deserts are man made, through tampering with watershed, rerouting of rivers, and cutting off distant forest reserves. A good example lies at the eastern foot of the Sierra Nevada in Owens Valley, but Westerners have conquered much more desert than they have created. While arid lands are expanding in other parts of the globe, in California they are receding.

In any case, Californians can not be held responsible for the deserts within the state boundaries. Nature has to accept the blame. Ample moisture to water the whole Mojave blows in from the Pacific, but it does not get there. The Coast Range and the High Sierra block the air stream so completely that moisture from the ocean is wrung out of the clouds before it reaches the land that needs it most. Boosting the storms over the mountains is one of the few forms of irrigation that engineers and meteorologists have not yet tackled.

Although high temperature does not make a desert, it is one of the popularly expected attributes, and the southeastern reaches of California have it. Thermometers thrust into the topsoil of Death Valley in midsummer have registered an incredible 190° —only 22° below the boiling point. The highest official air temperature ever recorded anywhere on the globe was 136° in Azizia, Lybia. Greenland Ranch, California, places as a close second with 134°.

But a single superheated day does not constitute a simmering summer or make the hottest place on earth, declares the eminent Polish meteorologist Dr. W. Gorczynski. After making long-term statistical comparisons among torrid spots like the oasis of In-Salah deep in the French Sahara, Jacobabad in the desert of upper India, Azizia and Bagdad, Iraq, the scientist impartially asserts, without qualification, that none of these is "the hottest spot on the planet." Says he: "The highest thermal honors go to America's Death Valley." It is a dubious distinction.

All deserts have common characteristics, but the American prototype has one almost unique feature—the profusion of cactuses. Cactaceae are little known in the sand stretches of the Old World. In California they are as much a part of the desert as "bad men," cowboys, dry lakes, chili con carne, tourist courts and the irrigation ditch. Cactuses are distinctly an American institution, and although Mexico is their happiest habitat, north of the border they have been favored largely with Yankee names: niggerhead, grizzly bear, Joshua tree, Spanish dagger, beaver tail, fishhook, hedgehog, prickly pear and a dozen others. In turn they are grotesque, beautiful, utilitarian and a bane of desert existence.

One that has retained its Mexican name, the cholla, richly bristling with cushions of inch-long thorns, has proved to be the greatest pest of all. Declared George Parsons waggishly: "The cholla certainly stands at the head of the cactus family for ability to enter the epidermis of the human family upon the most slender invitation." And it even succeeded in poking its way into a once-popular stanza:

> The devil was given permission one day
> To select him a land for his own special sway,
> So he hunted around for a month or more
> And fussed and fumed and terribly swore.
> But at last was delighted a country to view
> Where the prickly pear and mesquite grew;
> An idea struck him, and he swore by his horns
> To make a complete vegetation of thorns.
> He studded the land with prickly pear
> And scattered the cactus everywhere,
> The Spanish dagger, sharp-pointed and tall,
> And at last the Cholla to outstick them all.

With or without the intrusive cholla, California desert sports the weirdest collection of natural improbabilities on the face of the United States. Next to tall stories, the Mojave and its environs produce more borax than anything else, but the list of incongruities is so ample that no one needs to expand it by fabrication.

In this parched area there have actually been shipwrecks, and full-blown waterspouts have not infrequently been sighted. Here, streams in normal seasons become smaller the farther they flow, and campers have to climb for water—as well as excavate their firewood. There are lake beds that look as though they had been pumped dry only day before yesterday, though they have been empty for a million years. The ground becomes so hot that even rattlesnakes and scorpions die in the sun, and a thirsty burro is reported to have been scalded by a gush of steam and near-boiling water when he gnawed through a rusted water pipe on the desert floor.

It is a land where rain often evaporates before it quite reaches the ground; where one animal—the kangaroo rat—lives out its life span without ever swallowing a drop of water; where there are mountains of borax and beds of table salt more than a third of a mile deep; where the lowest land in North America—Bad-water's 280 feet below sea level—is within sight of the highest point in the United States, south of Alaska—Mount Whitney's towering 14,495 feet; where half-ton boulders, called "skating rocks," mysteriously move along the desert floor at Race Track under some natural power that has never been explained.

It's a land where in less than fifty years the worthless waste-land of Imperial Valley became the most productive vegetable garden in the world; where the expanse of lava extrusions and igneous debris is so vast that geologists liken it to the surface of the moon, and the National Aeronautics and Space Administration sends its moon-suited spacemen there for workouts in the craters; where a modern prospector, never off the bottle long enough to be troubled with D.T.'s, swears that he has seen lizards with feathers and snakes with ears, and knows of one isolated spot where the vibration from earthquakes is almost continuous; where the "bad men" of one generation became so glorified in the next—through fiction, movies and TV—that if all the created characters were to move physically into the desert, the popula-tion would be multiplied by thirteen.

This is the land that has suddenly become so coveted, the boomingest resort region in America, and it is being peopled so swiftly that one responsible authority predicts: "By the year 2000 the Mojave will probably be as thickly settled as the San Ber-nardino-Redlands area is now."

"Invest in the desert! Get a homesite today before it's too late!" is the big pitch. And there is something to it, for prime Mojave land that no one would look at ten years ago now sells for $20,-000 an acre. That can be compared with the $1.25 per acre at which millionaire Albert M. Johnson was permitted to purchase 1,529 acres around his castle in Death Valley in 1938—through special act of Congress. And everyone then thought that the gov-ernment was robbing a good citizen.

However, it isn't for speculation alone that the desert land is being snapped up. People have grown to love it with a passion, in the same way that a sailor falls in love with the sea, a plainsman with his flat horizon, a New Englander with his rolling carpet of green. "The first five years are the hottest," say the converts. After that, nothing can draw them away.

The desert is many different things to as many people. They love the vast, blue open sky, the grandeur of far mountains, the caressing warmth of the winter sun, the spring flowers, the cactuses, the mirages and queer-shaped lakes, the dry wind, the painted canyons, the sweeping contours of outwash fans, the roving dust devils, and even the heritage of the bad men.

"Like mountains, forests and seas, the desert is one of the permanent homes of the human spirit," observes critic, teacher and naturalist Joseph Wood Krutch. "The idea as well as the fact of the frontier exercised an enormous influence upon our development. And the desert is today the last remaining frontier. But it is not merely a frontier. It also has a message of its own.

"The mountains, the valleys and the plains spoke of limitless opportunity and exhaustless resources. They invited to action, development and exploration. Because Americans are an active people, they are now asking for the desert. The most difficult of all regions to exploit may also be turned to practical use. They may in time triumph over it completely. What is the desert good for? Perhaps the answer is just 'Good for contemplation'—for that attitude of mind which invited the Arabs to think of the stars and the Hebrews to think of God. It would be just as well if we in our turn thought more about both."

II
NEITHER WATER NOR GRASS—NOTHING

FOR twenty-two years, between 1908 and 1930, California was haunted by a mysterious desert detective. Alone or with his "Watson," he sleuthed the wastelands from Yuma to San Bernardino, prying into canyons, pushing his way through mesquite thickets, inspecting long-abandoned water holes and dried stream beds. Wherever he went he had questions—and few answers for those who wanted to know what he was up to. He was multilingual and seemed to be just as much interested in the local testimony of a Mexican field hand or vagrant Indian as of a condescending ranchero.

"Desert" detective was perhaps too narrow a designation, for he did not limit his investigations to barren regions. The reconnoitering carried him north as far as San Francisco Bay, southward to Arizona, and deep into Mexico. But the Mojave and the Colorado deserts seemed to be the nucleus of his activity.

One year he would be driving a tin lizzy, another year a dust-layered Dodge or an old Studebaker, but regardless of the make or model, he and his driver managed to navigate it over tracks and trails that were not meant for any gas-propelled vehicle.

Nor did he always travel by car. He was seen unobtrusively slipping on and off coaches at flag stops of the Southern Pacific. He went on horseback, by mule, on foot; once in a motorcade that included a Dodge truck loaded with a highly inflammable ninety gallons of gasoline. But he usually traveled lightly. No tripods and instruments such as the geologists and government engineers lugged into the desert. His principal accessory was a notebook—that indispensable notebook—along with a folder of maps, a manuscript, a camera and, of course, a canteen.

It was the notebook that made him suspect. In it he was constantly jotting entries as he rode along. To the bafflement even of his driver, he would be quietly making notes, occasionally referring to his maps and comparing them to the landscape, when he would suddenly order a halt, and with camera, canteen—and notebook—vanish beyond a cactus-covered wash for half a day.

Over the years, anecdotes about him were passed from one locality to another. Could such an affable character really be a secret agent? He gained a reputation for getting into predicaments from which he found it awkward to extricate himself and car. Far from any highway, someone would come upon him mired in a stream bed that had been visited too recently by a flash flood, bogged in innocent-looking quicksands, or stalled in the middle of a river he was courageously trying to ford. He always accepted these embarrassments with composure, and welcomed the driver of a span of mules that came to his rescue, as if he had been expected.

But not infrequently the mishaps occurred beyond the reach of immediate aid. Once he waited out an overnight emergency as guest of a *vaquero* and his wife, sleeping "on the soft side of an adobe brick floor"; on another occasion he found it necessary to walk fourteen miles in blistering heat for help; on still another he spent an entire night carrying boulders to build a road that would get his car out of the sludge.

Broken springs, blowouts in desolate places, empty radiators on waterless stretches, were all part of the torment he took so philosophically. Nothing fazed him. At Beatty's Ranch, one morning in 1921, the heat was too much even for his car; at sunrise the thermometer registered 114°. So he left the flivver behind and set out for Coyote Canyon on horseback. He could take it, if the car could not.

Not content with a single, meticulous search of a region, he returned again and again—as many as eight times to some trails that failed to yield the evidence he was seeking. In 1930, when the probing was finished to his satisfaction, he had retraced every foot of the journeys made a century and a half before by an explorer named Juan Bautista de Anza, and that Mexican pioneer had at last been elevated to the place he deserved in American history.

The detective was Herbert Eugene Bolton, distinguished historian, professor and librarian at the University of California.

Over a period of a quarter century Dr. Bolton sampled in kind most of the trials the great Anza encountered on his journeys, and brought to light a frontiersman more notable in the development of the West and Southwest than any Daniel Boone of the East.

"I think it safe to say," ventured the historian modestly, "that no pioneer routes of such great length in any country's history have ever been so thoroughly explored and identified as I have explored and identified these. Anza traveled twice and back from Mexico City to Monterey (once to Suisun Bay), a distance of more than ten thousand miles. Between these points I have retraced exactly or approximately his entire journeys."

Until the history detective dug up the details, Anza was a neglected figure in the school texts. Dr. Bolton established him for all time as a great patriot and empire builder, the forerunner of men like Lewis and Clark, Frémont, the forty-niners and the whole Westward-Ho throng. The panorama of cities surrounding the Golden Gate stands as his monument.

It was Anza who persuaded the Mexican Government, in the early 1770's, that an overland supply route across the desert to the Pacific was essential, that the California coast should be colonized without delay, and that he was the man to lead the way. Nor was there anything immodest about his proposal. He was well qualified for the job—"a man of heroic qualities, tough as oak and silent as the desert from which he sprang"—a third-generation frontiersman whose grandfather had served for thirty years on the Sonora border, whose father had fought Indians and been killed by the Apaches, who himself had engaged gallantly in suppressing savage uprisings, and in hand-to-hand combat killed a famous Indian chief.

Anza had already plotted the most feasible route across the treacherous California deserts and given it a trial run before he took on the assignment of leading the first colony from Mexico to form a settlement at San Francisco. The band of settlers numbered 136. To accompany them was a contingent of just over 100 soldiers, muleteers, *vaqueros,* priests, servants, interpreters—and Lieutenant Don José Moraga, destined to become one of the most distinguished names of the Bay region. They assembled at Tubac, the northern outpost of Spanish civilization in present-day southern Arizona, on Sunday October 22, 1775.

"Nolite timere, pusillus grex," Fray Pedro Font solemnly

quoted from the Gospel according to Saint Luke after mass on that final day before departure—"Fear not, little flock." Father Font was to accompany the emigrants. Like Anza, he too had traveled widely in the American deserts and knew better than his congregation what they faced in their historic pilgrimage.

"You must show perseverance and patience in the trials of the journey," he counseled, "yet consider yourselves happy and fortunate that God has chosen you for such an enterprise. Your travels across the Colorado Desert to Monterey can be likened to the journey of the Children of Israel through the Red Sea to the Promised Land.

"I entreat you to show kindness to the heathen on the way. God will mete out punishment if they are mistreated or scandalized, in the same way that He meted out punishment to the Israelites for their excesses. And punishment will also come upon you if you murmur at the commander or his orders, as the Israelites murmured against Moses, failing to render him due obedience. If you conduct yourselves as good Christians, I assure you of the help of God and our patroness the Most Holy Virgin of Guadalupe. Your joys will be mixed with trials, but quit yourselves as true followers of the Virgin, and God will bestow upon you the benefits of this life, the joy of eternal rest in the Promised Land and in the true fatherland of glory."

At eleven o'clock next morning the 30 families of colonists bid farewell to civilization and set out into the unknown—an expedition stretching out for almost half a mile. Four scouts took the lead, with Anza close behind; then, flanked by the soldiers, rode the main body of men, women and children—mostly children, 115 of them. Lieutenant Moraga and a squad of soldiers made up the rear guard; and last came the impressive train of some 450 horses, mules and extra mounts, with a herd of 355 cattle. By comparison, Thomas Hooker's more celebrated little expedition from Massachusetts to Connecticut was a mere holiday parade.

The very first night on the trail brought an ominously harrowing incident. Señora Felix died in childbirth. And a painful death it was. But her boy survived, and Father Font assured his shocked disciples that the healthy birth was indeed a good omen.

It took a full month to cover the three hundred miles between Tubac and the confluence of the Gila and Colorado rivers near Yuma. In that month, as Font had predicted, the emigrants suffered most of the miseries known to the Children of Israel. And to the list of Biblical discomforts was added an epidemic of dysentery from polluted water. None was spared, not even the animals. Anza all but relinquished his duties as commander, to serve as full-time physician and veterinarian. Sick and dying horses were left behind, but the ailing men and women somehow kept on the march. Father Font himself was stricken and in utter distress crawled like an animal into the brush along the trail where he could suffer for a night in solitude. But he was on his feet at dawn. He had to say Mass before the procession could get under way.

A muleteer deserted and headed for home, but he was shortly captured and publicly administered such a thrashing that neither he nor any other member of the company was ever again tempted to try that way out of their woes. There was no turning back. And every mile of that first three hundred was filled with the terror of a possible Apache attack. Anza could count on the friendship of the Pima and Yuma Indians, but the Apaches were relentless enemies.

Night after night they were short of water and pasturage for the hundreds of animals. One whole day was lost in rounding up stock which strayed away in search of feed, and when the starving cattle were finally located they were so enraged at being driven away from their patches of grass that they turned on the herders and "charged like wild bulls."

The glistening white of alkali flats blinded the people. It was like being forced to stare continuously into the sun. Along the river bottom of the Gila they had to beat their way through a tangle of brush and cactus and were tormented beyond endurance by the thorns that lacerated arms and faces and worked into their clothes.

This was only a prelude. West of Yuma, after fording the dangerous Colorado, they knew that their real troubles would just be starting. Ahead were the forbidding deserts of California, the terrible heat and the long *jornadas* without water. It was the one stretch that Anza most feared. Two years before, he had become lost in the sands and all but perished. He had found no route through the desert and made instead a detour deep into Mexico to circumvent the dunes. Now he wanted to avoid taking that long detour.

Scouts were sent ahead to try once more to find a passage. They returned jubilantly, after four days of wandering, to announce that they had found a passage. Spirits soared. This would mean shortening the total distance by days.

But at this point the Colorado Desert brought off one of its rarest tantrums. The emigrants had come prepared for scorching heat. It was now December. Instead of heat, an arctic cold wave swept down upon the dunes—"weather such as the oldest Indians had never experienced before."

Thanks to the Christian affection that had been stirred in the Indians of the region by generations of missionaries from Spain, tribal chiefs did what they could to relieve the sufferings of the wayfarers. They helped gather firewood and build shelters; they brought quantities of fish. In return for token ornaments, they came bearing stores of maize, beans, squash and watermelons— "More than two thousand watermelons of enormous size," claimed Anza. "Indeed, we threw watermelons away and left them because we had nothing in which to carry them."

Occasionally the arrival at an Indian encampment was like a triumphal entry. At one village a thousand cheering natives formed mile-long columns for the colonists to march through— the squaws in one line, the braves in the other. Anza had a handout of beads or tobacco for every one of them, and accepted their deference and childlike cordiality in good faith. Not so the Reverend Father. "All their affability, which is due more to the gifts of beads than to their gentleness, might easily be converted to arrogance whenever an attempt is made to reduce them to the catechism," he admonished.

To Father Font's more fastidious tastes, the savages were thoroughly repulsive. "Near the tent of the commander a beef was killed for today, as is done every six days," he recounted. "I was seated with the commander near the beef, taking chocolate. The Indians became such a mob and were so filthy because of their vile habits, that we could not breathe, and there was no way by which to get away from them."

Nevertheless, Anza knew how to handle his hosts; he urged them to dance for the entertainment of the Mexicans, joined their festivities himself, gave his soldiers free rein to enjoy themselves with the all-too-willing red maidens, distributed spirits liberally, and in retaliation received a scornful reprimand from his padre. "Anyone who gets drunk sins," stormed Font, "and anyone who contributes to the drunkenness of others also sins. Only ignorance can absolve him of his guilt, and you were not ignorant of the intemperance of these people when they have *aguardiente*."

But these evenings of occasional letdown offered scant compensation for the distress brought on by that long cold wave that gripped the Colorado Desert during the winter of 1775. After leaving Yuma, the company had followed the course of the Colorado River for a few days, then cut north, skirting the present Mexican border, and plunged into the desert.

Anticipating that the meager wells would never provide sufficient water for the entire caravan at one time, Anza broke it into three divisions, spaced about a day apart, and went ahead with the first. It was not until December 12 that he led his group into the Imperial Valley region. There, indeed, they had expected to find a climate comparable to what they were accustomed in Mexico. Instead, most of them saw snow for the first time in their lives.

Near the site of Plaster City to-be, he made the first camp north of the border. "We halted at the only site where there was firewood and pasturage," Anza explained, "because fuel was extremely necessary as a protection from the severe cold, and to await the rain which was threatening from all directions."

His weather eye misjudged the lowering clouds. At daybreak the first snow squall hit the shivering men, women and children. It passed on, but the white sierras in the distance were deeply blanketed in white—a grim foreboding of what was to come. The real snowstorm did not strike until the following morning. Over the desert, where it never snowed, a veritable blizzard swept down from the northwest, "with fierce and extremely cold wind, which continued the entire day." No march was possible against the pelting sleet and wind. Huddled around tiny brush fires, the company remained in camp all day on December 14, and for nearly a week following.

The storm continued without letup until eleven o'clock that night, when at last the clouds dissipated and a moon broke through. To peasants who had never before seen snow, there was nothing beautiful about the eerie scene, as bright as day. It was more like a shroud of death. To make matters worse, the cold wave tightened and the wet snow froze solid. On the slippery crust all were compelled to join in the desperate scavenging for sage and greasewood to keep the campfires aglow.

"The people were crippled by the storm," Anza admitted, in

stark understatement. Just after noon of the 15th, the second division stumbled into camp, frostbitten and worn out. The blizzard had caught them in a much more exposed place. Five saddle animals had perished from cold and fatigue and as many men had barely been saved from freezing to death. One in a state of shock had been brought around only after he was bundled in blankets and thawed out in a circle of bonfires.

The next day, still stalled in the drifts, they discovered that they were not alone in the desert. There were hostile Indian bands in the hills; they had made a sneak raid during the night and driven off the loose horses. Soldiers were dispatched to follow them in the snow trail, with explicit instructions not to injure the thieves. The animals were recovered without a battle, but for men who were already at the limits of their endurance it meant an exhausting round trip of nearly twenty-five miles.

Not until the third day after the great storm did the last division appear, and its members had suffered the most severe hardships of all. Many had been seriously frostbitten, and one officer's ears were so badly frozen that he was left totally deaf. Four pack animals had died and six other played-out beasts had to be abandoned along the way.

The animals, like the people, had been nurtured on the hot plains of Mexico and could not become acclimated so quickly to the unprecedented chill of Imperial Valley. Quivering cattle were gaunt, lame and half starved. On the desert marches they had been forced to go without water for as long as four days, yet when taken to water, dazed beasts turned away and preferred to browse for brush and leaves. Ten head had been lost from exhaustion on December 14, and the toll mounted daily after that. The dead animals were dressed and butchered for jerky and salt beef, but, noted Anza, "The meat is unpalatable because of its scent, color and taste. These animals have become so scrawny and lean that they have no resemblance to those which started the journey."

In the morning round-up on December 20, after a frigid night, three saddle animals and five head of cattle were found frozen. Worse, crazed by thirst and cold, a herd of fifty had stampeded during the night, doubling back on the trail toward their last watering place. Four herders were sent after them, and when they did not return, a group of guards was sent to rescue the herders. Three days later the men staggered back to report that the cattle had stampeded into a swamp and died there—all fifty, and the mounts of the herders had fared badly too; all had given out but one.

The loss of fifty cattle in a single calamity—the cattle on which they depended for sustenance on the road—was the most crushing blow Anza had yet experienced. Aware that he would be held accountable by his superiors and possibly charged with negligence, he penned a wordy defense: "The foregoing loss cannot be charged to want of attention and care. This is proved by the lack of such loss previous to this fatal event. Although other cattle have played out for causes unavoidable on such a march, yet they have been brought with the greatest care possible, even to the extent that they have not been abandoned until they have died of inability to move. With this in view, at the time when I began the journey, I provided seven men to devote themselves solely to caring for the cattle, watching and striving for their best management. In the journeys which have been made, they have been left behind or sent ahead according to circumstances. And finally, no effort whatever has been spared to prevent any kind of misfortune, although in spite of this I have had this disaster, as distressing to me as it is irreparable."

The dwindling of the stock was all too apparent to the colonists. A kind of hysteria crept over the men and women. The snow, as much as the thought of diminishing herds, terrorized them. They had been born in a *tierra caliente*. Before they left, no one had so much as hinted of snow and ice. Were they being led into a trap? If it was like this in the desert, they reasoned, the snow would be over their heads farther north.

The commander did his patient best to disabuse them of their fears. He was confused himself by the tricks of a deceptive desert and had not yet learned that the usual weather of California was unusual. Confidently he promised the bewildered throng that they would soon come out into the warmth and sunshine of the coast lands; the ordeal would not last much longer.

It was a long-shot guess, but he was right. By the end of the month the badlands and snow were behind them, and the people could see for themselves the lush green of San Joaquin Valley.

That mass march across the Colorado Desert was never again quite equaled. The emigrants lost close to half their cattle and a large proportion of their pack animals, but they made the incredible journey with the loss of only one life—Señora Felix.

In fact, by the time they reached San Gabriel Mission on January 4, the roster of 115 children had increased to 118. Three were born en route.

There were detours, delays and discouragements ahead, but the hardest part of the journey was over. In April, Anza turned over the command of the expedition to Lieutenant Moraga at Monterey, and two months later—on June 27, 1776—the band of colonists called a halt at a lagoon called Dolores, within sight of the Golden Gate. The Pilgrim Fathers of San Francisco had arrived.

Anza led the first and last organized Mexican colony across California desert, and he was one of its most notable explorers, but others had been investigating the lay of the barrens for many years before him. From time immemorial, tribes of Indians had known routes into the desert, routes extending from east of the Great Basin all the way to the Pacific, and as poorly paid scouts, they showed many a groping white man the way.

Hernando de Alarcón, commander of the fleet that was supposed to support Coronado's land expedition, was probably the first European to catch a glimpse of the desert, when he sailed up the Colorado River in 1540. His was a close race with Melchior Diaz, who crossed Arizona that same year, forded the Colorado, and presumably pushed for some distance west.

But after Alarcón and Diaz, the desert was left alone by white men for more than a century and a half. Contenders for land in the Americas were kept busy with more strategic engagements. Spain, meantime, established New Spain, with Mexico City as its capital. Slowly, through the efforts of its military and missionary arms, it reached out north, south, east and west.

To assist with the frontier expansion in the north, a distinguished mathematician and astronomer, Father Eusebio Francisco Kino, arrived in New Spain in 1681. He was shortly appointed royal cosmographer to accompany a colonial expedition into Lower California, but Father Kino was more interested in the souls of Indians than in cosmography, and there were a larger number of souls to save on Sonora and Arizona than in Baja California—which he insisted on thinking of disrespectfully as "the largest island of the world."

Kino wandered north to more challenging vineyards. In his billowing Jesuit robe he traipsed up, down and across the Sonora,

the Colorado and Mojave deserts, and by 1699 was convinced that California was not an island after all. En route he preached and prayed among the Indians, created a network of missions extending across southern Arizona and northern Mexico. Husbandry and economics interested him too. Sold on the idea that the Indians stood a better chance of promotion to eternal life if they could raise the standard of their earthly life, he started building ranches and more ranches—always within hearing of the clanging mission bell. Before he was through he had a string of nineteen enormous ranches covering hundreds of thousands of acres and was the cattle king of America.

Often he had to choose between his religious duties and his responsibilities as rancher. "On arriving at the great *rancheria* of the Rio Colorado," he confided, in 1700, "more than a thousand persons assembled together to welcome us. Soon more than two hundred others came, and the following day more than three hundred from the other side of the very large-volumed Rio Colorado, swimming across it. We made them many talks about our holy faith, which were well received, and they thanked us for them with very tender and loving words, both in the Pima language and in the Yuma.

"These talks, ours and theirs, lasted almost the whole afternoon and afterward till midnight, with very great pleasure to all. They begged of me to stay with them, if only one or two days, saying that many people were coming from up the river and from down the river. But I dared not linger, lest I fail to collect the cattle for California, as I had been charged, and as the branding time was near at hand."

Father Kino faced his calling realistically. He could return later for the roundup of Indian proselytes, but the cattle roundup could not be postponed. From all his enterprises the great padre could easily have become a millionaire, but never did a Spanish peso of the profit go into his own pocket for private gain.

Modest, gentle, self-effacing, ascetic, he devoted his entire wealth of energy to lifting the lot of the desert Indians. He was "merciful to others but cruel to himself." For rest he habitually chose the floor or the ground; never could he be persuaded to sleep in a bed. His food was eaten without salt or sweetening, and was seasoned only with bitter herbs to make it more distasteful. Among a bibulous people, the only wine he ever drank was to celebrate Mass.

The physical punishment he inflicted upon himself would have killed ten lesser men. Day after day for a solid month he would travel 25 miles or more on horseback. Racing from ranch to mission, from Mass to emergency, he often traveled 50, 60 or 80 miles between dawn and sundown, stopping for a baptism here, extreme unction there, a word of encouragement to a wavering fellow priest, or a crisp warning to a Pima chief. Impossible day's journeys of even 105 and 130 miles through the heat of Sonora wastelands were not impossible for him. And between other pressing engagements he conducted no less than forty expeditions across the desert country.

Kino set a very high standard for the long line of padres that were to follow him. Spain and the Catholic orders helped to maintain that standard, for during those decades men of superior wisdom and intellect, as well as of sectarian devotion, found their calling in the broad wilderness of the Southwest.

There was philosopher Miguel José Serra, for example, born on the Mediterranean island of Majorca, Doctor of Sacred Theology, and for fifteen years a professor of philosophy in the college at Palma. When he took the cloak he changed his name to Junípero, and in 1749 accepted assignment to Mexico City. From there he went north to found a line of missions along the Pacific Coast and become "the patron saint of California."

Nor was he a stranger to the desert. When he plodded through it in the spring of 1769, heat and thirst were the least of his afflictions. He had a gangrenous foot and a painfully ulcerated leg which crippled him so badly that he had to be lifted bodily onto his horse. At Loreto his friends begged him not to attempt the trip. "When I saw him with his swollen foot and leg with the ulcer," sympathized a colleague, "I could not keep back the tears, as I thought of how much he had still to suffer on the rough and difficult trails." He survived the trip through the western extremity of the Colorado Desert, accompanied only by a servant and two guards, and went on to fame and greater glory as president and founder of a dozen missions.

There were contemporaries like Father Francisco Palóu, who in 1773 set up the cross in the desert to mark the boundary between Baja and Alta California, and later helped to organize the mission at San Francisco; Father Font, the critical friend and companion of Anza; Father Fermin Francisco de Lasuen who succeeded Serra; and tireless Father Francisco Garcés, native of

Aragon, who also accompanied Anza on many of his expeditions.

Garcés became the Christian exemplar and Galahad for the whole southwestern desert region and the white pathfinder in the Mojave. He kept alive the Kino tradition and carried it further, giving up all the civilized amenities for the Indian way of life, in order that his converts might more readily accept his gospel.

Claimed Font, with a touch of irony, after leaving him to his destiny among the capricious Yumas: "Father Garcés is so well fitted to get along with the Indians and to go among them that he appears to be an Indian himself. Like the Indians he is phlegmatic in everything. He sits with them in the circle, or at night around the fire, with his legs crossed, and there he will stay musing two or three hours or more, oblivious to everything else, talking with them with much serenity and deliberation. And although the foods of the Indians are as nasty and dirty as those outlandish people themselves, the Father eats them with great gusto and says that they are good for the stomach and very fine. In short, God has created him, as I see it, solely for the purpose of seeking out these unhappy, ignorant and rustic people."

Among all the Catholic frontiersmen from Europe, Garcés—next to Kino—was perhaps the greatest. His contribution in opening a direct route from Arizona to the Coast, through the Mojave, was most notable. Rarely in his writings did he allow himself to give more than a hint of what he had to endure on his expeditions. For the record he would gratefully acknowledge Indian hospitality, including "the great abundance of acorn porridge wherewith we relieved the great neediness that we had." He mentioned near tragedies in cryptic understatment: "At a passage in the river the mule mired down, and wetted was all that he was carrying"; and described a life-and-death emergency as something commonplace: "I traveled two leagues west southwest and halted in an arroyo in an uninhabited *rancheria;* the rain, the cold and hunger continued, for there were no roots of tule to eat and the remaining *rancherias* were afar. In which emergency I determined that my companions should kill a horse to relieve the necessity. Not even was the blood thereof wasted, for indeed there was need to go on short rations to survive the days that we required to reach the next *rancherias.*"

Yet for all his sacrifice, Father Garcés met a terrible end at the hands of the people he loved—clubbed to death by his best

friends, the Yumas, who had to reap a vengeance for the treachery of other white men.

The Spaniards, both lay and cleric, were the real pioneers of
the California deserts. The names of towns, mountains and canyons they left on the map accent that fact. Their successors, the
Yankees, followed the trails with zeal and long-suffering, but
they lacked the unworldly devotion and selfless purpose of the
padres and the Anzas.

In the vanguard of invaders from the East came the trappers,
and in all likelihood the earliest arrived anonymously and departed anonymously—if they made a getaway alive. They were
not welcome. A major incentive for Anza's expedition had been
to colonize the bay area before the Russians got a toe hold there;
British and French had to be crowded out too; and any trespassing American ran the risk of immediate arrest, if he lacked the
proper credentials.

Trappers seldom had any credentials. To be sure, they were
not particularly interested in desert; the beaver they were looking for were in the mountains. But they were a nosy clan, sometimes prone to jump to the conclusion that the shortest route
to a new fur country might be by way of the desert. They reached
the desert by miscalculation, or in dire distress sought succor at
the missions. And there were accidents.

Late in the summer of 1808, some twenty miles east of the
Colorado River, a long pack train of Mexican traders intercepted
two empty-handed trappers from Missouri. The train was headed
for Los Angeles; the trappers, so they said, were headed for Santa
Fe. They identified themselves as James Workman and Samuel
Spencer of St. Louis, and were astounded to learn that they were
more than 500 miles from Santa Fe, rather than the 10 or 15 they
had reckoned. Never were two hardened woodsmen more hope-
lessly lost.

Persuaded by the caravan commander that two ragged, unarmed, unprovisioned men had no chance of getting anywhere
near Santa Fe on foot, they joined the company, reversed their
direction, and headed instead for the Coast. The tale they had
to tell that night at the bivouac was as implausible as it was
bloodchilling.

More than a year before, on April 25, 1807, they had set out
from St. Louis with a party of 18 others, equipped with the usual
rifles, traps, pistols, awls, axes, knives, kettles, blankets and extra

horses, and captained by a hardy frontiersman, Ezekiel Williams. Williams had been studying the report of the Lewis and Clark expedition and had convinced himself that he could find an easier pass through the Rockies to the headwaters of the Columbia.

En route to that far destination, they had trapped with phenomenal success on the upper Missouri River until driven south by the Sioux. They gave up the ambitious plan to reach the Columbia and moved farther south. While on a buffalo hunt on the Yellowstone, 5 of the company were killed by the Blackfoot Indians. On the headwaters of the Platte, 5 more fell to the Crow Indians and all their horses were stolen. A scared group of 10 cached their furs and escaped to the upper waters of the Arkansas. There 7 more lost their lives.

Captain Williams, Workman and Spencer were the three survivors. With all the dodging of Indians, they were now thoroughly confused in their geography, and after a few more days of wandering they decided it was time to head for home. But in what direction? The captain was sure they were on the Red River and was determined to descend it. Spencer and Workman contended that they were due north of Santa Fe and that the sensible maneuver was to find the Rio Grande and get to the nearest outpost of civilization as soon as possible—Santa Fe.

They agreed to disagree and thereupon parted company. Williams headed down a river that turned out to be the Arkansas; by canoe and on foot, Spencer and Workman fought their way down the Colorado until they came to a well-marked ford. There they abandoned the river and started overland for Santa Fe. Even when informed of their whereabouts by the Mexican traders, they were reluctant to believe that they had not actually descended the Rio Grande.

The Apaches were on the warpath, claimed the traders, so the two fugitives accepted the proffered protection of the pack train and next day started across the hot Mojave—twenty days from San Gabriel.

"The season was dry and the company had often to perform long and toilsome journeys before they could reach water," reported the trappers years later. "In one or two cases the distance from one watering place to another was not less than one hundred miles, and very often from thirty to fifty. The surface, too, was a bed of sand, which furnished nothing to sustain the mules. Between stages where grass and water can be had . . . the country is almost as desolate as the Sahara of Africa. If a caravan breaks its regular chain of stages, their toils and sufferings are very severe. These caravans are often very large, numbering sometimes several thousand horses and mules, which sweep away all the grass near the route and leave the earth bare . . . Bones of animals lost by caravans were scattered about in great profusion. After crossing the Colorado, the company traveled for many days until they reached the Spanish towns on the Pacific."

In view of the hospitable company that had taken them under their wing, the Missourians were not arrested, but they were unimpressed with their hosts on the Coast. "The inhabitants of California are not very refined and enlightened people," they certified. "Indeed they are but little above the Indians. It is the policy of their religious rulers to keep them in this condition to perpetuate their wealth, power and influence."

Workman and Spencer eventually found their way back to the refinement and enlightenment of St. Louis. Possibly they were the first natives of the United States to make the overland journey across the desert to Spanish California; possibly the whole story was an invention. It was too good not to be true; too neatly composed to be entirely acceptable.

There was no question, however, about the authenticity of an equally trying Mojave excursion made by Jedediah Smith twenty years later. He, too, set out from the American fur emporium, St. Louis, and, as part proprietor of the Rocky Mountain Fur Company, was recognized as one of the country's most celebrated trappers. Eager to explore new hunting terrain in the Rockies, he and fifteen veterans roamed the headwaters of river after river in Utah and Arizona during the summer and early fall of 1826, with little to show for it. Their luck had played out. Beaver were scarce everywhere.

In a desperate plight, with supplies exhausted and their mounts crippled, they stumbled into an Indian encampment on the edge of the Arizona Desert. Strike out for California, advised the Indians after they had sympathetically sized up the situation; your white brethren have plenty of supplies.

Smith was already far beyond the point of no return, unless his supplies could be replenished. Besides, he was never one to turn down a gamble and a new adventure. He accepted the advice, the corn and withered pumpkins presented by the Indians, and was on his way.

"I traveled a west course fifteen days over a country of complete barrens," he wrote to General Clark, then Superintendent of Indian Affairs at St. Louis and already famous for his expedition with Meriwether Lewis, "generally traveling from morning until night without water. I crossed a salt plain about twenty miles long and eight wide; on the surface was a crust of beautiful white salt, quite thin. Under this surface there is a layer of salt from a half to one and a half inches in depth; between this and the upper layer there is about four inches of yellowish sand."

In retrospect that was all Smith had to report to General Clark about one of the most grueling trips ever made across the Mojave from Needles to Cajon Pass. He arrived at San Gabriel Mission on November 27, 1826, to be summoned at once to the governor general at San Diego and placed under surveillance. In the eyes of Mexican bureaucrats, Smith and his untidy companions were Yankee spies in cahoots with the Spaniards, who had just been deposed. But after weeks of restriction and cross-examination the trappers were summarily expelled from California and ordered to return to the United States by the same route they had come.

The Fathers at San Gabriel were more charitable. With good Christian generosity they reoutfitted the aliens, gave them their benediction, and sent them happily on their way. But Jedediah Smith had seen enough of the Mojave. He had no desire to repeat the desert ordeal, disregarded the instructions of the governor general, and traveled north to make history by being the first to break a trail over the High Sierra.

Far less fortunate in their treatment by the Mexicans were eight other Americans who were led under guard, a year and a half later, into the office of the same governor general at San Diego, on March 27, 1828. They were the remnant of a trapping company which had once consisted of 120 men, with a train of over 300 mules and horses, back in the River Platte country.

"Who are you?" snarled the governor maliciously.

A bearded Kentucky colonel, Sylvester Pattie, reached a grimy, unsteady hand into the pocket of his tattered hunting jacket, produced a crumpled paper, and placed it on the governor's desk. It was his passport, issued in Santa Fe.

"Forgery!" denounced the governor, scarcely glancing at the dirty document and tearing it into bits. "To the guardhouse with them all."

It was no ordinary guardhouse to which Sylvester and his companions were ushered. Each was taken to the solitary confinement of an airless, flea-ridden cell from which there was no possible escape.

This was the Mexican reception for trappers who had come —like Jedediah Smith—begging for supplies, after two years of battling with Indians, dismal luck at trapping, and decimation of the company. But it was the desert crossing that had been most cruel. Sylvester's son James, who was one of the members, later described the worst days of it.

"We hurried on through the drifted sand in which we sank up to our ankles at every step," he wrote. "The cloudless sun poured such a blaze upon it that by the scorching of our feet it might have seemed almost hot enough to roast eggs in. What with the fierce sun and the scorching sand and our extreme fatigue, the air seemed soon to have extracted every particle of moisture from our bodies. In this condition we marched on until nearly the middle of the day without descrying any indication of water in any quarter.

"We attempted to chew tobacco. It would raise no moisture. We took bullets in our mouths and moved them around to create a moisture to relieve our parched throats. Our tongues had become so dry and swollen that we could scarcely speak so as to be understood. In this extremity of nature, we should perhaps have sunk voluntarily, had not the relief been still in view on the sides of the snow-covered mountains.

"We resorted to one expedient to moisten our lips, tongue and throat, disgusting to relate, and still more disgusting to adopt . . . The application of this hot and salt liquid seemed rather to enrage than appease the torturing appetite . . . Having availed ourselves to the utmost of this terrible expedient, we marched on in company a few miles further.

"Two of our companions here gave out and lay down under the shade of a bush. Their tongues were so swollen and their eyes so sunk in their heads that they were a spectacle to behold. We were scarcely able, from the condition of our mouths, to bid them an articulate farewell. We never expected to see them again, and none of us had much hope of ever reaching the mountain . . . The excessive and dazzling brightness of the sun's rays so reflected in our eyes from the white sand that we were hardly able to see our way before us."

Miraculously, a few of them did reach the mountains and water the next day, and the stronger summoned the energy to return and revive those who had been left behind.

"More hotter as hell," was the appraisal of the desert given by the Pennsylvania Dutchman in the company. "It should be named the teyvil's plain. None but teyvils could live on it." And James Pattie himself concluded with more restraint: "It seemed a more fitting abode for fiends than any living thing that belongs to our world. During our passage across it, we saw not a single bird, nor the track of any quadruped, or in fact anything that had life, not even a sprig, weed or grass blade, except a scrubby kind of tree, resembling a prickly pear and covered thick with thorns. The prickly pears were in such abundance that we were often puzzled to find a path so as neither to torment our feet or our bodies with the thorns of these hated natives of the burning sands."

And the reward for the eight men who had endured that touch of hell-fire was confinement in Mexican prison cells. Sylvester Pattie died in his, and the others were released only after weeks of torture. Yet even reports of such treatment could not scare Americans from taking the southern route.

Five years later, in 1833, Joseph Reddeford Walker, completing an extensive western expedition in the interests of the Missouri fur trade, avoided the Pattie abuse by brazenly going to headquarters at Monterey with an introduction from a Yankee sea captain who did business with the governor. That introduction made all the difference. His Excellency was delighted to grant Walker permission to do all the hunting and trapping he wanted, as long as he did not engage in trade with the Indians or trap on their lands.

The restriction was immaterial to Walker, for he had already trapped the forbidden territory, crossed the Sierra from the east, roamed freely down the California valleys, and was primarily interested in getting the guarantee of unmolested exit from Mexican jurisdiction.

He got his clearance, and in a few weeks was on his way back east, trailed by a company of 52 men, a pack train of 315 horses, 47-beef for provisions and 30 dogs. His Indian guides led him over a new Sierra trail—Walker Pass—and from the eastern foot of the mountains he hoped to cut north to the Humboldt Basin. It was the best route he could choose under the circumstances, but still a poor one, for he reached the northern fringe of the Mojave just at the beginning of the dry season. The Sierra crossings had given him a hard time; the deserts gave him a harder one. Before he reached Humboldt Basin he had lost 64 horses, 10 beef cattle and 15 dogs.

Hardest to take were the death throes of the pet mongrels. "These dogs," commiserated Zenas Leonard, scribe for the expedition, "when death threatened to seize them, would approach the men, look them right in the face with the countenances of a disturbed person, and when no help could be offered, would commence a piteous and lamentable howl, drop down and expire."

For days men and beasts alike were without water. "Our thirst far exceeded any description," Leonard moaned, and seldom was he at a loss for appropriate words to describe any situation. "At last it became so intense that whenever one of our cattle or horses would die, the men would immediately catch the blood and greedily swallow it down."

A blistering wind swept down from the north, so fierce that the cattle balked at facing into it, and with it came a blizzard of sand. The animals had to be kept on the move, for if they were allowed to pause for a moment they would immediately drop from exhaustion, and no amount of coaxing would bring them to their feet. They had to be poked and prodded and shouted at. And as they slowly plodded into the hot storm they stirred up stifling clouds of sand that obscured the surroundings, obscured themselves, and blinded the herders.

When the wind ceased, Walker ordered a night march, but the cattle strayed off in the darkness, and even Walker lost his bearings in the effort to round them up. By morning light they discovered that the sand had cut into the hoofs and hocks of the animals. They were lame and bleeding. A halt had to be called and half a day spent in fashioning "moccasins" from the hides of dead cattle to bind onto the hoofs of the beasts.

"Our situation at present seems very critical," wrote Leonard at the end of that harrowing day. "A dull, gloomy aspect appears to darken the countenances of every member of the company. We are now completely surrounded with the most aggravating perplexities—having traveled two long days' journey into the plain and no idea of how far yet to its termination, and from the manifestations of many of our most valuable stock, we are well convinced that they cannot endure these hardships much longer . . . When our forces collected together, we presented a really forlorn spectacle. At no time while crossing the Rocky Mountains or the Sierra Nevada did our situation appear so desperate."

It was the instinct of the thirsting animals that saved Walker's party. On the next night march, when all hope of survival was waning, the horses and cattle suddenly became unmanageable. Frantic efforts of fifty-two men could not check their insistence on turning off to the side. Finally the riders had to let them go. The slow-moving procession turned into a stampede. With unfaltering determination, the animals made a two-mile dash to "a beautiful stream of fresh water." The crisis was over and sweet pasturage was found next morning.

John C. Frémont, who managed usually to find something attractive in every California panorama, could see the desert only as a glaring scar, on his notable excursion of 1844. He was stunned by the ugliness of his first view of Mojave from the height of a mountain pass, where everything behind was lush and green. "There," exclaimed his Indian guide, pointing to the barrens and badlands, "there are the great *llanos; no hay agua; no hay zacate—nada*. Neither water nor grass—nothing. Every animal that goes out there dies."

Frémont learned that the Indian's assessment was not seriously exaggerated. "It was indeed dismal to look upon," he agreed, "and hard to conceive so great a change in so short a distance. One might travel the world over without finding a valley more fresh and verdant, more floral and sylvan, more alive with birds and animals, more bounteously watered than we had left behind in San Joaquin: here within a few miles a vast plain spread before us, from which the boldest traveler turned in despair."

He descended the Mojave River, which to his amazement, "instead of growing larger, dwindled away, as it was absorbed in the sand." The man who was loath to find fault with anything in California complained about the drifting sand, the gales, the burning sun, the dry gullies—and what all four did to his prize animals. He was appalled by the quantities of horse skeletons which littered the roadway and surrounded his camping places, shocked on finding the corpses of two human casualties, and made miserable by *jornadas* of 40 and 60 miles without water.

"The most sterile and repulsive desert we have ever seen," he called it. "Although in California we met with people who had passed over the trail, we were able to obtain no correct information about it. The greater part of what we had heard was found to be only a tissue of falsehoods. The rivers that we found on it were never mentioned, and others particularly described in name and locality were subsequently seen in another part of the country. The road was described as a tolerably good sandy surface, with so little rock as scarcely to require the animals to be shod; and we found the roughest and rockiest road in the country, which nearly destroyed our band of fine mules and horses."

Yet in all this catalogue of desert tribulation, distributed over a period of three centuries, no ordeal could quite match that of the San Joaquin Company. That company, composed of 107 wagons, some 200 people and more than 500 horses and oxen, left Salt Lake the first of October, 1849. On Christmas Day, three months later, 27 wagons reached the floor of Death Valley, and of the 27, only one ever left it.

But these overlanders represented the start of a new era in desert traffic. The Treaty of Guadalupe Hidalgo had been signed on February 2, 1848. Hostilities with Mexico had ended. California was part of the United States, and of equal importance to the destiny of the nation, gold had been discovered there—just nine days before the treaty was ratified.

The gold rush was on, and the Mojave was about to assume new geographical significance. Next to the mighty Sierra Nevada, the miles of hot sand stood out as the most formidable blockade to the new national bonanza.

III
RICHEST MINE IN ALL CALIFORNIA

UNTIL a frazzled detachment of the San Joaquin Company rolled into Death Valley to celebrate the Christmas season of 1849, no civilized man had ever before inspected the place or heard of it. The valley was nameless. Looking over the dry waste, one of the stragglers suggested that at last they had found "the Creator's dumping ground, where He had left the worthless dregs after making the world, and the devil had scraped these together a little."

Yet within a few months after the last members of the company had dragged themselves out of the "dumping ground," Death Valley was infamously famous. Quite by accident, the survivors had set the stage for spreading the gold rush from the Sierra foothills to the Panamints and the Grapevine mountains. That first group of Death Valley tourists was to become one of the most publicized of all the thousands of overland parties.

The San Joaquin Company itself was a product of mere chance. Late in the summer of 1849, a heterogeneous throng of forty-niners began to congregate outside Salt Lake City. There, in frustration, they stalled and backed up. It was too hot to proceed across the salt sands of Utah and too late to continue on the northern route leading to the Sierra Nevada; the California range would be deep in snow by the time they could reach it.

Altogether the milling crowd represented the leftovers, misfits and late starters from a much greater multitude that had been more foresighted in planning the transcontinental trek. They had little in common, except their inaptitude as frontiersmen and their impatience to get to the Western diggings, though intermingled were a few happy-go-lucky irresponsibles who saw the whole venture as a lark and did not give a damn whether they reached California that year or the next. For them it was a jaunt rather than a serious journey. They could chuckle at the prudence and precaution of families who had loaded into prairie schooners all their earthly possessions, babes in arms and half-a-dozen young children.

Most of that Salt Lake gathering had started from home towns in the Middlewest or East as loosely knit organizations of friends and neighbors. Squabbles over inconsequential cargo had already undone fast friendships, and the neighborly spirit had lost its cement.

The Wades from Illinois, for instance, with their three children, were at odds with everyone and sufficient unto themselves, as were the Earhart brothers, the Ryniersons, the Philipses and the Grangers. The Bennett family still maintained a speaking relationship with their long-time friends the Arcanes, but there were signs of strain after a young fellow named William Manly, short on provisions and transportation, was philanthropically accepted into the Bennett clan as handy man and scout. The Reverend J. W. Brier preferred to keep his family entirely aloof. He did not want his children contaminated by the common herd. He busied himself by giving erudite lectures on education and theology to anyone who would listen, let his wife drive the team and do the necessary lugging of the children, and when the family ran out of bread and bacon he trusted in the efficacy of prayer for replenishment.

Customarily a company starting out for the West adopted a corporate name, with laws and bylaws to which all members swore allegiance. Before reaching Salt Lake some of these had disbanded. Other organizations had lost their organization, but individuals clung to the names, mostly for sentiment's sake. Such were the Buckskins, the Bug-Smashers, and the Mississippi Boys, the Hawkeyes, the Georgians, the Wolverines, and the Jayhawkers.

As if in answer to some of Parson Brier's supplication, along came the solution to all the collective problems. A veteran bushwhacker and Mormon elder, Captain Jefferson Hunt of Salt Lake City, was about to leave for the new western outpost of the Latter-day Saints at San Bernardino by a back trail. He would pilot the whole crowd down the valleys of Utah and Nevada to Cajon

Pass and San Bernardino, avoid the big snows, and keep out of the very shadow of the dreaded Sierra. Wagons had never used the route, but he was sure they could make it. Ten dollars per wagon was his fee—modest enough, everything considered, and it would net a tidy sum for the guide, if the owners of all 107 wagons anted up.

The proposition was quickly accepted, and at last the stalled mob could get under way. Old organizations might retain their identity if they chose, but all marched under the banner of the San Joaquin Company, facetiously punned into "the Sand Walking Company." In a burst of revived enthuiasm they set out.

The high spirits lasted just two days. Then a dissenter named Smith began circulating a map and pointing out that Hunt was taking them all the way around Robin Hood's barn to get them to the gold fields. He knew of a short cut that would eliminate weeks of travel. In fact, his map showed more details than any chart the Mormon elder had for his route. Every camp, every watering place, the steep grades and the grazing grounds were all clearly spotted. Anyone could follow it. The Reverend Brier took one look and was convinced that Hunt had sold them a bill of goods. He joined Smith in a campaign to put the Mormon in his place. Within a day a general secession movement gained ground.

"Never heard of your trail," muttered Hunt when the document was finally unfolded for his inspection. "There's no road through that country. I swear no white man's ever been over it."

This was clear evidence of what a dolt they had taken on as guide. Around the campfires that night there were rallies for Smith and there were rallies for Hunt. The argument continued as they moved slowly along the trail that led toward a fork where everyone would have to make a decision.

Hunt was in a spot, but he expressed his views frankly. He knew that attempting the cutoff was sheer folly. However, they had hired him as guide and he would take them any way they insisted, with one reservation: if even one family chose his route, he felt obligated to them.

The test of strength came at the fork a few days later. Seven wagons out of 107 followed the Mormon—and all of them got through to San Bernardino without serious difficulty. An even 100 took the cutoff, and for three days the secessionists congratulated themselves over and over again on the wisdom of their choice. It was the most level travel they had experienced. Then the fun began. The cumbersome covered wagons reached Poverty Point in the Wasatch Mountains, and the road ended at the edge of a steep precipice. Drivers drew up and looked into a canyon that even a sure-footed mule could not descend.

For two days, scouts scoured the area in search of a pass. No luck. One by one, families sheepishly withdrew and turned back to catch up with Hunt. But not the stubborn Briers, the Bennetts and the company of 36 Jayhawkers. There were knockdown, dragout fights between partners who could not come to agreement on the itinerary or on an equitable division of their common property. Spans of matched horses and oxen were broken, food and furniture haggled over, one wagon was sawed in half to satisfy partners who were determined to part company.

When the Jayhawkers finally found a way to circumvent the canyon, 27 wagons were left. Come what may, they would cut their own trail to the Coast. Smith's map was no better than Hunt's charted route.

Blindly the 27 continued on a cutoff, and in the following weeks there was scarcely a day that they did not encounter obstacles as formidable as Poverty Point cliff. No effort was made to stay together. The energetic Jayhawkers usually took the lead, but if another group hatched a hunch that they could outmaneuver the Jayhawkers and beat them through a pass, they went their separate ways.

Trial and error was the rule. On a zigzag course, parties would overtake each other, only to separate again without an exchange of words. A group that pushed into a canyon one day and came to a blind end, cheerfully doubled back the next. Followers noted the tracks and went through the same lost motion. Paths crossed and recrossed. Gradually desperation from hunger, thirst and fatigue turned good men into fiends.

They wrangled and brawled. They stole from each other. They contracted skin diseases and dysentery. They pilfered Indian caches of food, then cursed the savages for their retaliatory raids. When scrawny oxen died they devoured the vile flesh, sucked tainted marrow from the bones, chewed the intestines, even boiled the horns and gnawed at them.

Wagons, as well as oxen, gave out. The Jayhawkers were the first to abandon their transportation. The Briers, who happened to be with them at the time, foolishly followed their example.

"Finding the oxen would carry packs well, the company loaded the necessaries on the cattle and burned everything else with the wagons," wrote Mrs. Brier. But she admitted, "It was a fatal step, as we were about 500 miles from Los Angeles and had only our feet to take us there."

The culmination of all the woes came as they approached Death Valley at Christmastime. "On the rim of Death Valley," continued Mrs. Brier, "poor little Kirk, my eldest boy, aged nine, gave out, and I carried him on my back, barely seeing where I was going, until he could say, 'Mother, I can walk now.' Poor little fellow! He would stumble on over the salty marsh for a time and then again sink down crying, 'I cannot go any farther.' Then I would carry him again.

"Many times I thought I would faint, as my strength would give out, and I would stumble to my knees. The little ones would beg piteously for a drop of water, but we had none to give them. At times we would see mirages of lakes and streams, and would press forward over salty marshes only to find them a delusion."

Mrs. Brier broke down only once. That was in camp when someone who had butchered an ox, mercifully gave her a few slices of liver to cook for her starving children. She set the choice meat down to stir the fire. When she reached for it a moment later it was gone. Someone had stolen it.

In Death Valley the situation was hopeless. Food was all but gone. The animals were spent. Personal belongings had long since been thrown away. Men, women and children alike were scarecrows. And the best Yuletide sentiment they could conjure up was an agreement that from that point on it was every man for himself. Singly or in pairs the Jayhawkers took off, carrying on their backs the last of their dried ox meat, and they were not inviting anyone to travel with them, particularly Brier, his wife and yowling children.

The pastor disregarded the admonition and followed anyway, his wife and sick children trailing behind. A few others, after resting up at Furnace Creek and sensing that they were only inviting death by remaining in the valley, abandoned their teams and tramped on in the same general direction.

All were completely deceived by the mountain ridges. Their map did not show the secondary ranges east of the Sierra. While crossing the Amargosa Desert of Nevada, they had been sure that they would descend into Owens Valley at the foot of the Sierra

Nevada as soon as they got through the Funeral Mountains. Instead, they had entered Death Valley. They did not know that beyond the valley was the Panamint Range and another desert, beyond that the Argus Range, more dry washes and mesas, the Coso Range and still more parched country before they could reach Owens Valley.

In their desperation they overlooked the obvious fact that the successive mountain ridges all ran more or less north and south, and the sensible thing to do was to follow down one of the valleys and get out of the mountains. The tongue-tied Wade family did that sensible thing. Without an adieu to anyone, they quietly headed south, came out on the Mojave Desert, followed the Mojave River upstream to Cajon Pass, and their troubles were over. Theirs was the only wagon among the 27 to reach its destination.

Troubles were far from over for a group of 15 that remained at Tule Spring in Death Valley—the Bennetts, the Arcanes, Manly and a handful of others. The 4 teamsters for the Bennetts and Arcanes had deserted and gone off on the Jayhawker trail, leaving their employers helplessly immobilized. But their scout Manly was of sterner stuff. He knew that it might cost him his life, but he could not leave the Bennetts to certain death. Moreover, he persuaded John Rogers, a friend he had made on the way, to remain too.

Manly had proved himself to be a guide and forager of the first order. He had traveled all the way from St. Albans, Vermont, by stages, earning his way as a trapper. He was tough and intelligent. Only out of loyalty to the Bennetts had he consented to take the cutoff. Once on it, he had done his best to help them out of their predicament. Daily he had roamed ahead, climbing mountains to survey the landscape, eying the horizon, plotting the most feasible road. Altogether on his circuitous scouting ventures he had tramped four times the mileage of anyone else.

"It is not in my power to tell how much I suffered on my lonely trips," he confessed, "trips lasting sometimes days and nights, that I might give the best advice to those of my party. I believed that I could escape at any time myself, but all must be brought through or perish, and I knew I must not discourage the others. I would tell them the truth, but I must keep my worst apprehensions to myself, lest they lose heart and hope and faith ... And perhaps I had not seen the worst. I might be forced to watch men and women and children choke and die. Alone I wept aloud, for I believed I could see the future, and the results were bitter to contemplate."

As though Manly had not already done enough, the Bennetts and Arcanes now looked to him for one last chivalrous service— lacking the faintest notion of the peril involved. Would he take Rogers with him, make a survey of the whole region ahead, search out a good wagon route to the San Fernando Valley and come back to lead them over it? Going and coming, his scouting expedition might take as long as ten days, they reckoned, and there were just about enough scraps of food to tide them over, without killing too many more oxen. They would wait for him where they were. Perhaps he could bring back help and supplies for the journey out.

Manly had a superior sense of geography, had seen the lay of the land ahead from a mountain crest in the Panamints, and knew how naive the proposal was. But it was a challenge. He accepted it and convinced Rogers that he should join him. They packed the dried meat from an entire carcass of beef on their backs and were off.

Instead of ten days, it was almost a month before the scouts returned. In those weeks they endured hardships that few human beings had ever been subjected to. Manly suggested that it was like a trip into purgatory. Again and again they faced inevitable death from thirst and starvation. For days both were ill, but they kept moving. A pulled knee tendon crippled Manly; he hobbled on with the help of an improvised crutch. They lived on such delicacies as grass and crow. And, miraculously, they reached a ranch in San Fernando Valley where they found sympathy, food and two pack animals.

The return to Death Valley was almost as painful as the exodus. Along the way they were obliged to leave their one horse to die at the foot of a sheer canyon wall, though they succeeded in coaxing a mule up it after building a narrow shelf for the animal to climb. Unable to carry all the supplies secured at the ranch, they cached them in pits. But one token of the bounty of San Fernando Valley they carried to the end—an orange for each of the Bennett children. The fruit had been presented by Manly's Mexican hostess at the ranch, with explicit instructions to deliver it to the children.

Only the Bennetts and the Arcanes had managed to retain faith in their scouts and wait out the long weeks in Death Valley.

The rest had moved on—several to their deaths. Manly and Rogers had come across some of the bodies.

And now to get the survivors out! Take the oxcarts over the mountains? Utterly impossible. But saddles might be made for the oxen so that the women and children could ride them. Manly ordered it.

"Good-bye, Death Valley," Mrs. Bennett uttered as they looked back from the summit of the Panamints a few days later. The unnamed desert had been named. The label stuck.

On March 7, 1850, Manly led the last of the survivors out into green San Fernando Valley, and expressed the sentiment of all: "We were out of the dreadful sands and shadows of Death Valley, its exhausting phantoms, its salty columns, bitter lakes and wild, dreary sunken desolation . . . a horrid Charnel house, a corner of the earth so dreary that it requires an exercise of the strongest faith to believe that the great Creator ever smiled upon it. If the waves of the sea could flow in and cover its barren nakedness . . . it would indeed be a blessing.

"We had crossed the North American Continent, and were basking in the warmth and luxuriance of early summer . . . Our lives had been given back to us. And we thought not of the gold we had come to win."

But others were not so quick to forget that lure.

Back in the Panamints one of the surviving Jayhawkers had a minor accident. No two chroniclers of the event could ever agree on details of the event, but presumably Jayhawker Towne was the victim. Worn out by his travail, he stumbled on the rock-strewn trail and dropped his rifle. Languidly he got to his feet, rubbed his scraped shin, picked up the rifle and struggled on. He had tramped for miles before he discovered that the sight for his weapon was missing. The gun was worthless without the sight. He remembered the fall and knew exactly where he had stumbled. Back over the miles he went. He had no other choice.

There, sure enough, right where he had taken the spill was his gun sight. He stooped to pick it up, but instead picked up first a chunk of rock that caught his eye. The silver ore was unmistakable. He pocketed both the gun sight and the rock, then scrambled up the cliff to look for more of the stuff. For the first time in weeks he forgot his fatigue, his pangs of hunger and his great need for water. He had discovered a mine—a rich one.

Pockets bulging with evidence, Towne jubilantly hurried on to catch up with his mates. He was wise enough to get far out of range of his find before he broke the secret. He would have to split the profits too many ways if they all took it into their heads to go back for verification. But once they had reached a safe distance he talked and talked. In fact, he talked for ten years. No one doubted that the Jayhawker had found a superb mine in the Panamints. It was even given a name—the Gun Sight Mine—and the name was freely bandied about. But during all those years he could persuade neither himself nor his friends to head back to that scene of God-awful death and desolation.

It was not until 1860 that anyone became very much interested in Death Valley again. The grimness of it, as pictured by scattered Sand Walkers, was enough to frighten people away. Then suddenly, after a full decade, the publicity they had given to the whole area east of the Sierra began to pay off.

The Jayhawkers and Sand Walkers could not be given all the credit for the new interest at that particular time; diggings on the west side of the mountains were playing out, and Argonauts were looking for other fields to conquer. The Nevada bonanzas had proved that there was plenty of gold and silver farther inland. And the greatest notoriety of all was being given to the inland side of the Sierra by fugitives from minetown justice who were finding wonderful hide-outs there, and getting rich on the side. Word was circulating generally that there was gold in that desert country, as well as phantoms, thirst and skeletons.

One man who had fallen hard for the Gun Sight Mine story was an Oroville, California, physician, Darwin French. The idea of all that unclaimed silver going begging had been preying on his mind for years. Finally, in the spring of 1860, the bug got the best of him. He dismissed his patients, locked his pill cabinet, rallied a dozen fellow Orovillians for company and set out for Death Valley. All of them, particularly the doctor, should have known better than to consider such an expedition in summer, but prospecting was an ailment that could not be cured by prescription or emetic. It had to be allowed to run its course, and they had an incurable case of it.

French and his followers left Oroville on their thousand-mile jaunt magnificently equipped. They had all the tools that vet-

erans of the trade considered indispensable, and enough additional impedimenta to put them high in the rank of gentlemanly amateurs—even telescopes and transits—and a train of mules and horses that made them look as though they were starting on a crusade.

The expedition did virtually turn into a crusade to honor the ambitious doctor. They planted his given name far and wide through the desert at points of interest like Darwin Springs, Darwin Falls and Darwin Canyon. They retraced the wandering paths of the Jaywalkers and William Manly by the skeletons, ash heaps and broken wagons that had been left behind. With their telescopes they eyed mountain heights for a suspicious glitter of precious metal. They suffered the tortures of Hades in temperatures that reached into the 120's. They scoured a hundred square miles for the Gun Sight Mine and did not find a suggestion of silver.

The trip was an expensive failure. Its principal contribution was further advertisement of the heat in those infernal regions east of the Sierra, a change in the title of Gun Sight Mine to Lost Gun Sight, and the naming of an oasis some thirty miles west of the Panamints "Darwin," where, ironically enough, a very rich body of lead-silver ore was discovered fifteen years later.

Close on the heels of the French party that summer was another company headed by M. H. Farley of Butte County. That group worked over much of the terrain Dr. French had covered, complained of the heat, too, and then returned to Owens Valley where they ran into luck in the Coso Mountains. Farley hurried back to civilization with the news and a hundred-pound pack of ore.

San Francisco, the city of sensations, had a new one on the morning of July 24, 1860. "The Coso mines may yet prove a formidable rival to Washoe," blared the Bay area's major daily *Alta California* at the top of page 1. And in the quiet journalese of the day the cat was let out of the bag: "Yesterday we had the pleasure of an interview with Mr. M. H. Farley who has just returned from a four months' sojourn in the Coso Mines in the eastern part of Tulare County. He brings with him 100 pounds of gold, silver and copper ore from the vicinity of Owens Lake about 120 miles from Victoria. Those specimens have been assayed and give the most cheering evidence of an exceedingly rich and extensive gold and silver mining locality . . . A single piece of ore contains 1,698 97/100 ozs. of silver at $1.34 per ounce—$2,276.61; and 1 31/100 ozs. of gold at $20.67 per ounce —$27.07 . . . A company, of which Mr. Farley is a member, are the prospectors of ninety leads, all of which promise well."

Formidable rival to Washoe! Whoopee! What more irresistible summons for a stampede to the desert could be sounded?

Dr. French had hardly cooled off from his first battle with the sands when he was on his horse again, charging back for a second look. Another doctor, S. G. George, abandoned his San Francisco practice to join the migration. The New World Mining and Exploration Company of San Francisco sprang into existence overnight, and its president, Colonel H. P. Russ, took to the road. A man without a permanent address, who frankly called himself a "professional adventurer," W. T. Henderson headed a detachment to explore the Panamints and Telescope Peak. That made big news, particularly among the desert outlaws, for Henderson was credited with having put the fatal slug into the notorious bandit Joaquin Murrieta.

At the peak of the excitement the Visalia *Delta* asserted that men were leaving daily for the desert mines, that 200 were already there and 100 more were prospecting south and east of Owens Lake. Farley, who started all the fuss, estimated that 500 were in the Coso region alone. Newspapers pictured migrations of fifty wagons wending their way through the Owens Lake area "loaded with valuable goods and machinery," and roads clogged with "a great many thousand head of cattle, sheep and hogs" on their way to market in desert settlements.

In the rush of rumors the ever-gullible Darwin French picked up a bit of gossip reporting that somewhere in the desert was a tribe of Indians that used gold bullets for ammunition. That was just the lead he needed. He dropped his pick and telescope, and began stalking Indians. For eleven months he and eight companions combed the Mojave and dry stretches to the north, trying to attract golden bullets. The tribesmen held their fire. Frustrated and dejected, he went back to the Coso Range and staked out a series of claims there.

The vicarious gold seekers of San Francisco preferred to remain in the comparative comfort and safety of the metropolis and let henchmen do the digging while they footed the bill. Professional adventurer Henderson sent back from the Panamints two of his most loquacious teammates as stock salesmen. They were an immediate success in the Bay city. Investors swarmed about them ravenously, counting out thousand-dollar wads to finance mining projects in a desert they had never heard of.

The two were never seen again, either by the dupes or Henderson. One made off with $25,000; the other lost his life and his bulging billfold in a gun duel at Mazatlán, Mexico. "Timely end of a miserable humbug!" grumbled Henderson when he heard of the tragedy. Meantime, the adventurer himself had pushed his way into the security of Death Valley where he was working the Christmas Gift Mine, which had been discovered on December 25, 1860.

During the next two decades hundreds upon hundreds of mines big and little—but mostly little—were opened in the vast, broken area between the base of the Sierra and the Nevada border. They had names much prettier than the characters who dug in them: Bonnie Blossom, Chrysopoles, Red Bird, Blue Bird, Pluto's Pet, Perserpine, Calliope, Olympic, Golden Era.

On the other hand, one miner complained that he was employed on the graveyard shift in the Coffin Mine, Tombstone Mountains, Funeral Range, overlooking Death Valley.

A few of the ventures grossed magnificent sums, but the gross gave no indication of the net profits. More were a dead loss from start to finish. None ever quite matched in output the wealth of hyperbole expended on them by press agents. Cheered *Alta California* in 1863, for example: "From Chrysopoles the most flattering accounts and rock full of gold are sent down. The latter company is running three tunnels. In Russ district several companies are at work. Mount St. George appears to be a complete network of leads of the richest mineral. The Eclipse is turning out very rich ore and is of equal extent. If it is not the richest mine in all California, we are mistaken."

The *Alta* correspondent was mistaken. The richest mine of all was somewhere in the Panamint or Funeral mountains. A prospector with the euphonious name of Breyfogle found it— Jacob Breyfogle of Austin, Nevada. Jacob added a new word to Western mining lingo, as well as a legend. Until he stumbled onto the Breyfogle mine, *jackassing* was the accepted term for mineral prospecting in the desert. He changed it to *breyfogling*, and around Death Valley all Argonauts became *breyfoglers*.

At the site of his discovery Jacob picked up ore chunks of fabulous worth—pounds of almost pure gold. He was on his way back through Death Valley to tell the world about it when he was either clouted over the head by an Indian or demented by heat and thirst. He never could clear up that point. But through all his distress he clung to the precious specimens. Days later, when he showed up among sane men, he was bloodied, bruised, barely alive and incurably crazy. Eyes popped when they saw what he carried.

Misanthropes, desperadoes and vixens tenderly tried to nurse him back to health during the following months, though their interest in Jacob was not entirely humanitarian. At last they got him on his feet, and he cheerfully led them to Death Valley, but his befogged mind just would not come into focus. He could not pin down the exact site of his discovery, either for their benefit or for his.

Breyfogle never relocated his mine. Nor did anyone else, though hundreds tried. One breyfogler with a singleness of purpose devoted forty years of his life to the one objective and failed to find a single rock specimen that resembled Jacob's. Like the Lost Gun Sight, the Breyfogle became the Lost Breyfogle. In search of those two elusive mines—one of silver, the other of gold —deposits worth millions of dollars were unearthed. As decoys they served a cunning purpose.

The wealth in the arid hills east of the Sierra was not to be sneezed at. During a period when silver was worth from $1.28 to $1.34 an ounce, the Beaudry furnace at Cerro Gordo reported that for the eleven months between August 1, 1870, and June 28, 1871, 23,680 bars, weighing 2,060,160 pounds were produced. And the operators explained, apologetically, that the record would have been much better if 14 days had not been lost while the boiler was under repair, 14 more for "want of water" and 31 days while the furnace itself was being overhauled. "Size of furnace: 22 inches inside and 8 feet high. Only one furnace." And Cerro Gordo had a great many furnaces.

In fact, the mines at Cerro Gordo, halfway between Owens Lake and the edge of Death Valley, held the undisputed production record for the whole region during the 1860's and 1870's. But nobody kept a reliable tally. Imaginative estimates ran as high as $28,000,000. By 1872 the Beaudry syndicate alone was operating eleven mines, one of which was "sending up" 70 tons of ore a day, and the company was about to increase its furnace capacity to turn out 150 eighty-three pound bars of bullion every twenty-four hours.

Silver was coming out of the hills faster than it could be carted away. Indeed, transportation over the desert roads was a more taxing problem than underground engineering, for the heavy bullion had to be freighted all the way to Los Angeles on huge, clumsy wagons. It took weeks to make the round trip. The Cerro Gordo Freighting Company had 56 of these wagons on the road, each drawn by 16 or 20 mules, and still it could not keep up with the output.

Around Cerro Gordo the backlog of bullion was stacked up in the open like cordwood. In a country where there was more silver than lumber, and always a housing shortage, the bars were even used in building temporary shacks. Greasers lived in slums of silver. Six thousand tons of bullion was the production estimate for 1874—far too much weight for any freighting company to cart away.

But the overhead was enormous. It cost $20 to mine a single ton of ore, and other expenses were commensurate. Everything from bacon and beans to hoists and trap hammers had to be shipped in over impossible highways. The cut taken by the Cerro Gordo Freighting Company amounted to robbery—up to $120 a ton. The only fuel for the insatiable furnaces was wood or charcoal. Pine or oak from the Sierra cost $10 a cord, plus transportation, charcoal 32½¢ a bushel.

A mine or furnace could be shut down for a month at a time while everyone waited for minor parts to arrive from San Francisco. The nearest supply center to the north was the booming village of Aurora, Nevada, and that was 200 miles up the valley, and the coach fare there and back totaled $78.

Water was sometimes worth half its weight in silver. It was piped in, but the pumps ran only sporadically, and when they did the water bill for a single hoist, ran to $120 a day. A train of fifty pack mules plied constantly between Cerro Gordo and Owens River, carrying water. Retail, the lukewarm liquid sold for 10¢ a gallon; wholesale for 8¾¢. There was good reason for the modest dividends paid to investors in Cerro Gordo silver.

They received less for investments in mines high in the Panamint Range on the western rim of Death Valley. Scores of claims were staked out there, but they were so inaccessible that they could be made to pay only after huge sums had been sunk in roads, machinery and transportation facilities.

A roving promoter named E. P. Raines saw where he could make a fortune for himself. He secured bonds on the principal claims, agreed to finance a camp at Panamint, and packed half a ton of carefully selected ore samples to Los Angeles. Displayed in a barroom there, they obviously represented values running into thousands of dollars.

Raines' demonstration became the talk of Los Angeles, but cagily he did not try to do business there. His eye was on San Francisco, so he packed up and moved north. The rave notices of the Angelenos preceded him to the Golden Gate. By the time he had arranged his exhibition, men were queuing up to buy stock. The $1,000 put down in cash by Senator John P. Jones disappeared in a gala celebration the first night.

The Senator was due in Washington and departed before the promoter got wind of it. Raines followed him to Washington and came back with an advance of another $15,000. Jones and a Senatorial colleague, R. B. Stewart, were persuaded to head up the Panamint Mining Company with capital stock of $2,000,000. Eventually the camp at Panamint cost the two Senators just about that amount. But Raines did all right for himself.

A host of fly-by-night Panamint companies gradually merged into the Surprise Valley Mill and Mining Company. When a San Francisco journalist arrived to look over the scene he claimed that the population of Panamint was between 2,000 and 2,500. And what a town!—a mile-long confusion of tents along the bottom of a narrow canyon, interspersed every few yards with ramshackle bars and gambling dens; tents, bars and gambling places occupied by "an assortment of the worst desperadoes on the coast outside the penetentiaries." The sourdoughs settled disagreements their own way, making it necessary to appropriate a plot for a cemetery long before there was even a road to the tent city.

There were rich ores at Panamint, but no yield could balance the cost of mining, milling and transportation. The beneficiaries of that operation were the stockholders of the Cerro Gordo Freighting Company, which extended its services to Panamint and charged five cents a pound for all the tons of bully beef, booze and big machinery they hauled in. Eventually optimists as imaginative as Senators Jones and Stewart had to acknowledge that

Panamint mining was not a paying proposition, and Surprise Valley was evacuated.

The opening of Inyo County as a mining center was an incalculable benevolence to San Francisco, the rough Sierra towns and the rest of California: it cleared the western three-quarters of the state of its worst riffraff, the most obnoxious blackguards and renegades. They found refuge in Inyo. There was plenty of space for their accommodation in this enormous triangular-shaped county, bounded by the Mojave, the Sierra and the deserts of Nevada, an area larger than Massachusetts—larger than Connecticut, Delaware and Rhode Island combined.

Inyo was carved out of adjacent Tulare and Mono counties in 1866, just in time to welcome the flow of refugees, and Independence—a remote village halfway up Owens Valley—became the county seat. Regional law was administered from Independence. Obviously no legal arm was long enough to reach all the way across the arid lands into Death Valley, or the hundred-mile length of Owens Valley. The setup was ideal for any fugitive. And if a sheriff did pick up the scent of his trail, there was easy escape on all three sides: the Mojave to the south, with free access to Mexico; the extraterritorial bounds of Nevada to the east; the fastness of the highest and most rugged mountains of the United States to the west.

If California ranked as the frontier of the lawless West, Inyo County was the front of that frontier. San Francisco was another world, distant three days and nights by stage—and a fare of $60. News from Los Angeles was considered hot if it reached Independence in four days. Trains and telegraphs belonged to a far-off civilization. Even the Indians helped to accent the remoteness. Mobs of them, like the lawless whites, had escaped to the east side of the mountains, and in the sixties they were fighting the kind of last-ditch wars that Eastern tribes had fought a century before.

This was the setting for Gangland, U.S.A., in 1866, and it did not change much during the next fifteen years. Here was a wonderful hide-out where two-fisted, two-gun jail truants could travel in the open, and better than that, a place where a big operator could go to work without having to answer questions. That was the prime provision in the social code of the desert: questions were not asked. It was bad manners—and dangerous.

In Inyo County there were silver, gold, lots of capital, a great many gullible souls, long, lonely stretches of so-called highway for holdups, deputies who understood what was good for them if they wanted to stay alive, and a right smart resident lawyer, Pat Reddy, known to have rescued legitimately at least a hundred killers from inquisitive judges and "a summer at the shore," as San Quentin tenancy was referred to in those parts.

Early one evening in 1871, a shot slammed through the door of Frank Dabeeny's drinking den at Lone Pine, in answer to Sheriff Passmore's order to open up. He knew that Sam Palacio was inside, and Sam had been wanted for a long time—particularly that night, because he had just murdered an Indian in cold blood. A second bullet splintered the door panel.

"Boys, I'm shot," the sheriff confided to his posse, handing his six-shooter to the nearest man. Then he slumped to the porch floor, dead.

That was all it took to get the boys mad. Lead riddled the flimsy wooden building in a fusillade, but the door did not budge. Not a sound from inside. One by one the members of the posse took what shelter they could behind hitching posts and horses, and occasionally sent a bullet through a door or window, just as a reminder that the battle was still on. It looked like an all-night seige. They talked of firing the building or using dynamite, but the wind was too strong to risk setting a fire in the middle of town, and dynamite could get the wrong man. After brief consultation a messenger was dispatched to Independence for re-enforcements. That was eighteen miles away.

The gun bout was still going strong when the re-enforcements arrived toward morning. The outlaws realized now that there was no point in postponing the showdown. Palacio and Dabeeny ran out, blazing away as they came. But they did not get beyond the porch steps. Eighteen bullet punctures were later counted in Palacio's body.

One by one the others were ordered out of the building. They approached quietly, unarmed, with hands up. The upholders of law now assumed the roles of jurors. Most of the survivors were declared guilty of nothing more than keeping bad company. Their guns were restored and the men released. Two, however, were advised to leave town at once and not to return. They left. Next day the two bodies were found in the road to the south. Four dead scapegraces to one dead sheriff was an acceptable rule-of-thumb ratio for the administration of vengeance. No one ever thought to ask who might have put the fatal slug through Passmore's ribs.

So commonplace were incidents of this nature that offhand reports of three or four melees could get into a single issue of the weekly Inyo *Independent*—on page 3.

Killers brought into court to answer for their crimes normally could prove, with the help of Pat Reddy, that the shooting had been in self-defense. And there was a general tendency to accept the fact that any shady character who became the victim of a gun duel deserved what he got. Homicide, as a result, was regarded as a relatively minor infraction, not to be compared, for example, with horse stealing, while an impropriety like seduction was overlooked entirely.

When Leonardo Dalenguela burst into a boardinghouse in Lone Pine and found his girl friend Tule entertaining an old enemy John Stewart, Leo naturally drew a knife on the usurper. John dodged the thrust, popped out of bed and fulfilled his duty by shooting the attacker. John was soon arrested and "examined" by Justice Pearson, but discharged with a clean slate, "no complaint being made against him." Obviously a matter of self-defense.

In a row that started with a lot of stone throwing and name calling, Pedro Rojas finally pulled a gun on Reducinda Clabel and let him have it. As a formality, Pedro was summoned to the sheriff's office for questioning, but "released on his own recognizance." Case closed.

Over at Panamint, where saloons never closed and where gaming continued around the clock seven days a week, there was not much use for a jail. The little graveyard in Sour Dough Canyon offered more secure and more permanent confinement. "We are pained to record," mocked a Panamint correspondent, "that during an unfortunate affair which occurred at the express office previous to the departure of the stage three days ago, one of our esteemed fellow citizens was compelled to resort to violent measures to protect his person. His opponent will be buried tomorrow in Sour Dough."

That was the only obituary that miner Joe McKinley got after his public shooting spree with Jim Bruce, who survived with a crippled arm. The incident was all too inconsequential even to mention the name of the victim.

The well-known desperado Ed White rode into Benton on a stolen horse for the Fourth of July celebration of 1872. He figured on entering the mount in the horse race scheduled for the afternoon. But unfortunately George Mallory, the owner of the horse, happened to be in town, too, for the big event. He quickly spotted the animal and laid claim to it. Ed was not used to having people charge him with crimes more serious than manslaughter, and expressed his resentment.

In the sally that followed, the whole Fourth of July celebration was broken up. What with the flow of liquor and the high spirits, the shooting exchange between the two men turned into a general cannonade. Everyone except White and Mallory forgot the cause of the outbreak, and in the confusion White escaped, minus the horse. But on the edge of town he was captured, outwitted by a doctor whose horse the desperado tried to commandeer.

Charged with three instances of horse stealing, attempted highway robbery, and assault with intent to commit murder, he was conducted to the jail in Bridgeport. Hanging was too good for him, but, commented the Inyo *Independent*, "As he didn't actually murder anybody, his prospects of spending a few summers at the seaside are exceedingly flattering." In other words, he would have escaped punishment altogether if his transgression had been as petty as murder, rather than horse thieving.

The heyday of excitement in Inyo County came with the arrival of Tiburcio Vasquez on the scene. Vasquez had been a lieutenant with the famous Joaquin Murrieta gang and had inherited Joaquin's mantle when the master was felled in 1851. Since then Tiburcio had spent six summers at the seaside, but San Quentin turned him loose in 1863, as banditry was beginning to bloom on the other side of the mountains. Inyo and the desert were just the kind of retreat Vasquez needed.

During the next decade he committed one rapacious killing after another in various parts of California, robbed stores and stagecoaches, and stole some of the best horse flesh in the state. Before he reached the desert the Legislature had expended $15,-000 on futile attempts to recapture him and exterminate his gang.

On his way to Inyo late in 1873, Vasquez and cohorts payed a call on the little village of Kingston, tied up thirty-five men and left with half the wealth of the town. The robbers, as usual, were "hotly pursued," and as usual, scattered and escaped. But a few weeks later the chief rallied his forces in Tejon Canyon and there laid plans for the march eastward.

The curtain raiser came on February 25, 1874, at the stage station in Coyote Holes just after midnight. A salute of fifteen shots through the walls of the station announced the declaration of war. Six persons were inside. They took stock and discovered that their only weapons were an unloaded shotgun and a rifle without cartridges. So they capitulated and filed out. One of the six, known as Tex, appeared informally with the bottle he had been nipping while waiting for the stage. He was all too friendly, unsteady in his gait, and failed to show proper respect to his captors. A bullet through his thigh altered his attitude.

The others showed better judgment, took their places on a bench, as requested, and accepted with resignation Vasquez's polite promise that the first to move from the bench would be shot. He recommended that all make themselves as comfortable as possible because the stage might be late. Thereupon the outlaws moved into the station where the atmosphere was cozier.

The stage was two hours late, and to Vasquez' disappointment, only three passengers stepped down in response to his invitation, but quality made up for the numerical shortage. One was no other than M. W. Belshaw, owner and financier of Cerro Gordo's biggest mines. He contributed liberally to the Vasquez sinking fund and slipped off his handsome new boots to which the gang leader took a fancy. Vasquez also admired a pair of suede gloves worn by another passenger. The owner, however, declined to deliver them. "Two dollars," bid the bandit. The passenger took the money and surrendered the gloves.

While the bargaining over the gloves was going on the coach driver surreptitiously dropped forty dollars from his pocket onto the ground and scuffed sand over them. That was personal property. There was no hiding the Wells, Fargo express boxes. Normally, delivery of the boxes to a highwayman was enough, but Vasquez had plenty of time and requested the driver, as a special favor, to break them open for him The coachman complied. Two wagons from the Cerro Gordo Freighting Company came along about then. The teamsters were relieved of their ready cash and joined the gathering on the benches.

Altogether it was a tidy haul. Six of the horses were then unhitched and the bandits rode off on them. Posses combed the area for a week and found not a trace of the gang. Nothing was seen of Vasquez for a month, when he showed up at the Coso mines and held the company treasurer at bay while the bandit cleaned out the till.

That was a minor grab and a mistake, for suddenly the trail was so hot that Vasquez was obliged to high-tail it for Los Angeles. But he left Chavez, a capable associate, in command of the Inyo field, and Chavez carried on adequately. Posters advertising a reward of $3,000 for his capture, dead or alive, were in circulation in every public building in California, but there were few public buildings in Inyo County. For three years he and his fellow travelers raised havoc in and around the desert. Whole stables of horses disappeared; holdups became so common that no stage on the Mojave Desert or in Inyo County was safe.

One of his victims, Barton McGee, a tough old Indian fighter, once came within a hair of collecting that $3,000. Reluctant to do away with a hero of his qualities, Chavez put the question to him frankly: Would he be willing to forget the affair if he and his partner released him?

"Never!" McGee flung back. "Turn me loose and I'll kill the both of you."

The outlaws tied him up, and made their camp for the night close by. McGee had all but wriggled out of his bonds when one of them discovered their peril. Such an ornery captive they had never encountered. They admired his fortitude. It was refreshing after all the scared rabbits they had dealt with. So they threw him, half dressed, onto a mule and let him go. They galloped off in the opposite direction, one of them on McGee's horse.

McGee prodded the mule back to Coso, and within the hour was on the trail of the robbers, riding a borrowed mount.

He came back grinning two days later, on his own horse, and when someone inquired how Chavez had fared, he gloated, "Well, I got my horse, didn't I?"

McGee got his horse and two of the Chavez gang, but not Chavez. Tiburcio Vasquez was ambushed ten miles outside Los Angeles a few weeks later, tried for murder in San Jose, and hanged on March 19, 1875. Once the kingpin was out of the way his kingdom began to topple, and Chavez fell, too, victim of a wary Monterey marksman. The price on his head had been upped in the meantime, and that Monterey bullet netted a plump purse of $5,000.

The elimination of the southern outlaws paralleled the decline of the silver and gold bonanzas in Inyo County. There was still a vast amount of wealth in those ugly, dry hills, but the exploiting of it was to be left to a new generation of prospectors —one that could look upon the half-forgotten miseries of the Sand Walkers with a degree of detachment. Yet, in all the jack-assing of any generation, the ultimate objective—the be-all and the end-all—was the finding of those two elusive mines, the Lost Gun Sight and the Lost Breyfogle.

IV
POLITICS IS ONE THING, GEOGRAPHY ANOTHER

THE California deserts would have been left largely to the mercies of the mine sharks, the desperadoes and the sidewinders, for the rest of the nineteenth century, if it had not been for the intercession of a good party-playing politician in Washington, D. C.—Aaron V. Brown, Southern Democrat and President Buchanan's Postmaster General.

In the laundering process of historians, postmasters general normally bleach out as rather obscure, easily forgotten figures. But not Aaron Brown. For a few months after his appointment in 1857, he made colorful history, executed some far-reaching manipulations that would have done credit to contemporaries in Tammany Hall, and brought a new day both to the Colorado Desert and the Mojave.

Brown hailed from Memphis, Tennessee. So far as he was concerned, the sun rose and set over Memphis, and all highways and byways of the nation radiated from there.

To one who had served more than faithfully as distinguished leader and policy dictator for the Democratic Party, as long-time Democratic Congressman and Democratic governor of his home state, the appointment as Postmaster General was slim comeuppance. A man of less vision would have spurned such a thankless job, involving incessant quarrels over postal routes and rates, perennial squabbles with Congress over niggardly appropriations, and the certain condemnation of every letter writer in the country who never could understand why it took such an inordinate length of time for a missive to travel between two points.

But the Tennessean grabbed the assignment. He saw it as an

avenue to greatness. The most compelling issue of the hour concerned the "sacred balance" of interests between North and South, between East and an expanding West, and—as he sized up the situation—the Post Office could do more than any three other government departments combined to tip the scales a little in favor of the South.

For instance, there was the looming question of a transcontinental railroad. Everyone was rooting for a rail line to California, and as early as 1853, three possible routes had been surveyed, but Northerners would rather have postponed its construction indefinitely than have it cross the South. The men of Dixie were equally adamant about giving it to the North.

From political experience Brown had picked up one pertinent axiom: the line of least resistance for a railroad is an established stage route. It was within the power of the Postmaster General to establish a mail stage line through the South—where it ought to be—and the railroad would inevitably follow. In fact, Memphis would make the ideal Eastern terminus, and a cut through the southern deserts of the West would be duck soup for engineers, compared to pushing over the rock-strewn, snow-bound Sierra Nevada. Brown was a practical man.

Then, too, he would settle once and for all the question that was everlastingly nagging Congressmen: Should the delivery of mail be a strictly self-supporting business enterprise? For Brown the answer was a resounding NO. Regardless of cost, the Post Office should be an aid to settlement, a trail blazer, a pioneer in the Westward movement. It was absurd to continue adding millions to the Aspinwall and Vanderbilt assets by paying them to ferry the California and Oregon mail, slow freight, down the Atlantic Coast, across the Isthmus of Panama, and up the Pacific Coast. That mail should all go by overland express.

From the previous administration, President Buchanan and Postmaster General Brown inherited the go-ahead on a mail route across the continent. Unable to come to terms on a specific location for it—northern, central or southern—House and Senate had finally compromised by omitting all reference to the location and left the selection of an itinerary to bidders on a line and the Postmaster General. In essence, that meant leaving it entirely in the hands of the Postmaster General, for he could accept or reject bids as he saw fit.

Brown could not have invited a better setup. No sooner had

he taken office than he penciled on a map the ideal route. Naturally it started at Memphis, cut southwest to Little Rock, Arkansas, to Preston, Texas, on to El Paso, across New Mexico and
Arizona to Yuma, through the Colorado Desert and up the San
Joaquin Valley to San Francisco. It would have been difficult to
find a more circuitous way of getting from the population centers of the East to the population centers of the West. It passed
through some of the most desolate, least-inhabited regions of the
country, led "from no place through nothing to nowhere." As for
its benefiting emigrants, an unbroken string of 10,000 wagons
was reported trekking over the Salt Lake route, while a train a
week on the desert was a good average.

To his intimates Brown rationalized carelessly that the purpose of the border route was to open new territory, to link the
series of forts built just north of the Mexican line, to create a
military highway, to serve mining interests of the Southwest.
Generally he avoided mentioning the ticklish question of marking off a future rail right of way. The fact that the border beat
was close to 1,000 miles longer than the northern corridors and
that there was no road at all over sections of it seemed to be immaterial.

On April 20, 1857, the Post Office Department began advertising for bids on the overland mail service. Within two months
nine were submitted. As expected, none proposed a route remotely approximating Brown's roundabout loop. So he rejected
them all and summoned his good friend Jim Birch, the biggest
whip in American coaching business. Jim was a man whom he
could trust to establish a route when and where he wanted it.

As a consultant and expert on staging, Birch was a first-rate
choice. Certainly no one could find fault with his record. In
1850, at the age of twenty-one he had crossed the continent in
an oxcart, and on arrival at Sacramento had hitched his horses
to a mud wagon and opened a stage line to Hangtown. From
that lucrative beginning he gradually extended his services until,
in January 1854, he was ready to create the California Stage Company—an unprecedented giant—the largest stagecoach monopoly in the world, operating 111 coaches over 1,500 miles of indif-
ferent highway in California. The company was such a success
in this stageman's paradise that two years later he was covering
3,000 miles in the state with 195 coaches, and Birch retired to
Massachusetts and let underlings run his business in the West.

But Birch was not taking kindly to retirement, and Aaron Brown knew it. The restless entrepreneur gladly answered the summons to Washington. Would he, asked Brown, take on a route across the wastelands from San Antonio, Texas, to San Diego, California?

Tipped off on Brown's scheme for the long southern route, and assuming that the San Antonio–San Diego run would merely be the start of the Memphis–San Francisco chain, Birch leaped at the bait. It was just the challenge he craved to draw him out of the disagreeable state of retirement. Impetuously he signed a contract on June 22, 1857.

Haste was what counted now, urged Brown—haste before Northerners worked up too much sentiment against the southern itinerary. Already Californians were raising funds for a road over the Sierra; 75,000 of them had signed a petition begging for federal construction of a military highway over that range. If they got too much of a head start on their propaganda, the southern rail line might be doomed. The establishment of the San Antonio–San Diego line should be a dramatic *fait accompli* before the public caught on.

Birch loved that kind of talk. A born organizer, he knew how to assemble an outfit that would meet his demand. Without losing a day, he went to work. He had the drive of a young Napoleon and could accomplish the impossible while others were arguing about the impossibilities.

Incredibly, a complete stage mail line of 1,476 miles was organized in exactly seventeen days. Birch was back in action, happily gripping the whip to which he was devoted. Then with the spadework done, he took a fast ship to California to catch up on his interests there.

On July 9 the first California-bound mail left San Antonio. Trailing behind was an armylike retinue of 400 horses and mules, hauling vanloads of supplies and equipment. There was no time to send them ahead, so the line was to be stocked as they advanced. At intervals of 20 or 30 miles over the entire course of 1,476 miles, complements of animals, personnel and staples, were dropped off at makeshift camps and stations.

West of the Rio Grande a road was still under construction. Swollen rivers had to be forded, Indians fought off, rugged mountain inclines navigated. At one point the Indians attacked a relay of mule teams. Two dozen animals were lost, a muleteer killed, another wounded, and a squad of government troops routed, yet the mail went through unmolested. Over the shifting sands of the Colorado Desert there was no road at all. The coachman set his course by compass and the stars.

And on August 31 the first mail coach rumbled into the pueblo of San Diego to a thunderous welcome. Every noisemaker the Mexican-American populace could assemble became part of the thousand-piece orchestra that lined the street to the post office— drums and guitars, six-shooters and homemade torpedoes, and the racket from all these was drowned out by the surge of cheers. Cannon boomed, mission bells clanged; and, following an old Spanish custom, anvils from the smithies and workshops were dragged to the street and pounded with hammers until the whole town reverberated.

It was a day of triumph for Jim Birch and Aaron Brown. Alas, the dreaded desert had served as a thoroughfare for delivery of the first coast-to-coast mail. It was to be the beginning of an illustrious future for the South and the West. The wheel tracks cut in the sand by Birch's mail coach would surely mark the way for a transcontinental railroad.

"If any proof could be sufficient to satisfy the world of the superior advantages of this route for a railroad to the Pacific, it should be such proof as this," a local spokesman sounded off prematurely. "Without scarcely any previous expenditure in opening a road through a vast and unexplored region, mail coaches are at this moment carrying the mails . . . a distance of 1,475 miles, with actually greater speed than we have on the majority of the short lines within the limits of our own state.

"We therefore assume that the establishment of this line must lead to the speedy and rapid development of the country throughout the entire distance, giving us within a few years a continuous succession of farms, ranches, hotels, military posts, stage offices, etc. from one ocean to the other. There can be no doubt that this is very soon destined to be the great overland interocean thoroughfare of the nation, affording not only safer but a quicker and cheaper passage to and from California . . . The immense amount of travel will soon make a railroad a measure of necessity, the immediate ocean termini of which will be Galveston and San Diego."

In the flurry of excitement the San Diegans were not taking into consideration events beyond their immediate horizon. They did not learn until late in the summer that the very man who had plotted the San Antonio–San Diego border route, the incomparable Jim Birch, still in his twenties, was drowned six weeks after his triumph. He went down along with 400 others and a cargo of California gold, worth more than $2,000,000, in the wreck of the *Central America*—one of the major disasters of the century. The greatest transportation tycoon of the coaching era could no longer be counted on to push the border route.

And Birch died, too, knowing that the run to San Diego was not an unqualified triumph for him or anyone else. A month before his impressive train of animals left San Antonio, another pioneer stage driver, J. B. Crandall, had taken a coach over the Sierra from Sacramento to Carson Valley. To Californians rooting for the shorter road across the continent via Salt Lake City, this was convincing evidence that the circuitous desert route was not the only way of reaching the West Coast on wheels.

Moreover, Birch died knowing that he was the victim of the same kind of Washington politicking that had given him the San Antonio–San Diego franchise. His friendship with Aaron Brown won him that prize, and he had been confident that once his route was on the map he would be granted the longer Memphis–San Francisco monopoly. But Brown's boss, President Buchanan, was not beyond playing favorites either; he too had a friend in the coaching business.

Using his administrative prerogative, the President had snatched away the coveted franchise for the longest single coach line ever created and given it to his crony John Butterfield, who vouched that he could run a stage across the continent in not more than twenty-four days. To Birch it was a flout and a double cross that hurt painfully. He learned of it before he boarded the ill-fated ship, though the Butterfield contract was not signed and sealed until September 15, 1857—three days after the *Central America* tragedy.

But the President's interference could not be taken as bad news in San Diego or anywhere else along the Mexican border. The San Antonio–San Diego Company had a firm contract for four years, and Butterfield's new Overland, duplicating much of the same route, merely re-enforced Southern favoritism. Moreover, John Butterfield had been almost as big a nabob in Eastern coaching as Birch had been in the West.

He had won his laurels as a popular stage driver in New York,

where he gained control of most of the routes in the central part
of the state and consolidated them under efficient management.
Then, foreseeing that railroads would soon bring an end to
coaching, he had ventured into other areas of transportation and
communication, built up a Panama freighting business, pro-
moted telegraph systems, founded lines of lake and river steamers, and become one of the country's leading expressmen, with
large interests in the combine known as the American Express.
There was wisdom in the President's selection of Butterfield for
the Great Overland.

Under his contract, Butterfield was given a full year in which
to get his coaches rolling—a more than generous concession, compared to the seventeen days allowed Birch, but still all too short
a time to construct and fortify 165 way stations, stables and corrals, along a route of almost 3,000 miles.

Springs had to be located in the desert, wells dug, cisterns and
water reservoirs built, tanks and water wagons assembled. Fording sites would have to be selected and graded, bridges, supply
bases, blacksmith and repair shops erected. The gigantic operation called for purchase and distribution of 1,200 horses and
half that number of mules. Thousands of tons of hay and grain
had to be carted to the stations; a hundred coaches and mud
wagons manufactured and delivered; and a staff of some 750
men recruited—drivers, conductors, superintendents, agents,
stationkeepers, blacksmiths, stable hands and hostlers.

"Utterly impossible! It can't be done," cried the press, both
North and South. This was one issue on which there was no sec-
tional disagreement.

A circular ridiculing the whole impossible proposition was
broadcast from Washington. "Four-horse stages cannot be driven
from San Francisco across the seven deserts to Memphis in twenty-five days—nor in forty days—not at all," scoffed the pam-
phleteer. "It never has been done. It never will be done."

"Can water be drawn ten miles to a stage house in sufficient
quantity to supply men and horses, and for cooking purposes—
in fine to keep up a hotel for passengers in a daily line of stages?
If carrying water to supply a hotel and horses ten miles off would
be difficult and expensive, by what means would twelve hotels
and stage stations be supplied over a space of 125 miles in the
Llano Estacado? What an army of horses would be required to
draw water over those burning sands! And yet another army to

convey food for horses and men! So with the Colorado Desert. And so for five other intermediate deserts.

"From whence shall supplies be drawn for the support of hotels and taverns or stations in desolate regions? . . . Will it be pretended that Americans can be induced to go into farming like Mexicans and Chinamen with watering pots? Or that, if they did commence such puttering business, they could maintain a line of stages through those numerous deserts and dreary wastes of drifting sands at prices which people in this part of the country can appreciate?

"The Texas border route, skirting the borders of the torrid zone . . . runs at right angles with the rivers, and instead of bearing direct assumes the shape of a rainbow. San Francisco is in latitude 37½°, Memphis 35°. Upon leaving Memphis, instead of traveling northwest to San Francisco along the banks of fine streams of water, it is gravely proposed to travel off southwest across the streams, and across hideous deserts, five and a half degrees of latitude or about 400 miles south of San Francisco, and then turn and travel towards the place sought.

"The border route will be 2,500 to 2,700 miles long . . . Over it from Memphis to Sacramento human ingenuity cannot devise a plan to draw a four-horse stage load of passengers in twenty-five days and repeat the task twice a week throughout the year. Nor will the digging of a few wells in the sand, nor the occasional discovery of a spring in a mountain cave, cause these scenes of desolation to be peopled."

That outburst was calculated to humble the Postmaster General, the President and John Butterfield in one blow. It troubled none of the three. The late Jim Birch had already proved what could be done—on a somewhat smaller scale. During all the months of political and private haranguing, the coach wheels he had put in motion were continuing to race across those "hideous deserts" with the mails, making deliveries on schedule, and now carrying passengers to boot.

Up north, friends were even being won over, and the drivers who had the grit to whip their teams across the Colorado Desert were getting modest recognition. "The sixth mail that left San Antonio, Texas, on the 23rd of September arrived at San Diego on the evening of the 19th of October," acclaimed San Francisco's usually unsympathetic *Daily Bulletin*. "Time 26½ days. The scheduled time for the trip of this line is thirty days. The company brought through four passengers. The entire road is now stocked with 400 animals, 25 coaches and 75 men, messengers and guards."

It was time for San Francisco to sit up and take notice, for San Diego was horning in on Bay commerce, even making a bid for transcontinental passengers. Normally in transportation circles, coach companies arranged their schedules to meet ship departures; but through connivance of San Antonio–San Diego agents, that practice was reversed and ships were jockeying their schedules to take on passengers for the stage line.

The stage company had brazenly set up an agency in the center of San Francisco where travelers were being urged to book passage to a variety of inland destinations. OFFICE OF THE SAN ANTONIO AND SAN DIEGO MAIL LINE, ran the bold advertisements in Bay newspapers. "This line is now ready to ticket passengers through from San Francisco to New Orleans via San Diego, Fort Yuma, Tucson, Mesilla, Fort Filmore, El Paso and San Antonio, as well as to all Intermediate Stations. Also to Santa Fe and Albuquerque, New Mexico. For rates of passage and further information, apply at the office of the Company on Kearny Street (Opposite the Plaza)."

Then an unexpected gimmick played into the hands of the coach line. The sinking of the *Central America* and a series of other marine accidents were beginning to make home-bound gold diggers jittery about taking passage on any old ship. Perhaps stage travel was the safest way after all. A citizen's committee was appointed to investigate the seaworthiness of the Pacific Mail Steamship Company's vessels.

Cagily the chairman ignored official maritime representatives and went directly to the Association of Ship Carpenters and Ship Caulkers, "presuming them to be greater experts in the art and mystery of shipbuilding than lawyers and underwriter's agents."

At a sober mass meeting of men contemplating early return to the East, the chairman gave his report in November. He went down the list of twenty-two ships currently plying the West Coast, bluntly revealing the truth about the condition of each, as it had been passed on to him by the "experts": the *California*, "worm-eaten three years ago; partially repaired then, not overhauled since"; the *Oregon*, "rotten and unseaworthy"; the *Republic*, "pumps defective and useless"; the *Northerner*, "worn out"; *Frémont*, "little better"; *Sierra Nevada*, "a very weak boat"; the *Commodore*, "had five feet of water in her hold the last time she was in port and left without proper repairs"; the *Goliah*, "might be safe for a voyage across the Bay of San Francisco."

The report was a sensation. And it started a raging controversy between shipowners and the public that could not have delighted anyone more than the advocates of transcontinental coach travel. Not even the Postmaster General could have thought up a more effective advertisement for coach service. To homesick, landlubbing Easterners the stages suddenly looked very safe and attractive, and the agent on Kearney Street had to spend most of his time explaining to disappointed customers that the next coach was booked full, the next and the next.

For more than a year the company Birch created had things its own way along the border. There was no competition, there were no travel comforts, there were more applicants for passage than could possibly be accommodated. Anyone who put down his $200 for the excursion to San Antonio did it at his own risk, without guarantee of any sort from the company. It was a trip to remember—more like setting out on a safari to the heart of Africa than a venture into a civilized country.

Passengers were advised to arm themselves for the journey with a good rifle and a hundred cartridges, a revolver and "two pounds of balls," a sharp bowie knife and enough cash to bail themselves out of trouble. As for attire, they would need thick boots and woolen pants, a half-dozen pairs of heavy woolen socks, six undershirts, three woolen overshirts, two pairs of woolen drawers, "a wide-awake hat," gauntlet gloves, a cheap sack coat and a greatcoat. For winter travel an Indian rubber poncho and two blankets were essential; in summer the poncho and one blanket would do. Even the toiletries were specified: four towels, a sponge, hairbrush, comb and soap, all packed in an oil-silk bag. And a repair kit with miscellaneous pins, needles, thread and shears, for fixing up rents and bullet holes would prove useful.

It was also advisable to take along a private larder of crackers, cheese and sardines to supplement the lean fare that might be served at way stations, and certainly a canteen. Water at desert stations could not always be depended on, and although the company did its best to serve occasional meals en route, no promises were made about the quality of the beef and biscuit.

THE GREAT CALIFORNIA DESERTS

In Washington the 1,476 miles of the San Antonio–San Diego Line were known formally as Mail Route No. 8067, but anywhere in the Southwest it was known quite informally as "The Jackass Line." The Jackass had few of the way-station refinements with which Butterfield planned to equip his route, nor any precision scheduling. Traveling on the Jackass was like taking a camping tour under the auspices of a muleteer.

On the road the general idea was to keep the horses or mules at a gallop as long as they could hold out, without consideration for creature comfort and the kidneys of passengers. They were jounced and joggled unsparingly in the close confinement of the coach, squeezed into place by the luggage and broad bottoms of fellow travelers, whose contours and quirks became despicably familiar—three men on the preferred rear seat, three on the front, facing rearward, and at least two on the backless middle thwart. There was never enough space for all the knees, feet, elbows, firearms and treasured satchels. The monotony of it was all but unendurable.

The pitching and tossing could go on without a break for a stretch of 8 hours. With only 20-minute interruptions for the changing of horses, it could continue for 24 or 48 hours when the driver was trying to make up lost time. Sleep for the passengers was no concern of the management. They dozed off for a few minutes on a stretch of relatively smooth roadbed, and from sheer exhaustion eventually learned to sleep at any hour of the day or night as the stage careened down the worst of grades.

Once a week, perhaps, a driver would halt at a station toward sundown and mercifully announce an overnight reprieve. Around open fires a meal of hard bread, beans, jerked beef and tar-colored coffee would be served, and passengers were then allowed to choose their own campsites. They could roll up in blankets and sleep on the clay floor of smoky mud huts, in shelters of brushwood or in no shelters at all. The roof of the coach was always in demand for a mattress. The driver might share the space under the wagon, and, likely as not, some fastidious soul would creep back into the cab to curl up on the familiar hard seat.

The mail took precedence over all else. When an axle broke in a God-forsaken spot, the post was sent ahead on horseback or by mule train, and the passengers left behind to vegetate for hours or even days until repairs could be made. Over the worst stretches of sand and up the steepest inclines the mail bags rode in state and the passengers walked behind.

Traveling from the east, one had covered more than 1,000 exhausting miles before reaching the worst of the desert—through San Felipe on the banks of the Rio Grande; northward to the headwaters of Devil's River; through the hostile Comanche strongholds, where rifles were kept on the ready; below the Pecos; into the Rockies of Texas; down to the Rio Grande again; on to Birchville, El Paso and La Mesilla; across New Mexico and Arizona, where federal guards acted as convoy through the Apache country; along the Gila; and at last to the Colorado River, Fort Yuma and California. Ahead lay the Colorado Desert and the most awesome sweep of all.

Traveling from the west, that treacherous desert came early in the journey—about the third day out—and caught people unprepared, before they were shaken down to the routine. In summer the crossing was a shocking baptism of flaming sun and scorching sand; in winter, at best, it was a long, wearying, gritty grind. And the unexpected always seemed to happen.

William and George Banning gave the most graphic description of the crossing: "A gila monster, hissing from its purple mouth, pushed back beneath a stone. Hissing, too, was the sand in the spokes of the wheels. The hoofs of the sweating mules plunged into it, ankle deep. It spread out on all sides with its wind-worked ribs; it lay heaped in glistening drifts against the escarpments, half filling the arroyos, half burying the few wretched shrubs which had fastened themselves like leeches upon the naked anatomy of the land.

"Lying fierce and defiant in its torture of heat, it was a desolation whose vastness was terrifying, whose bounding rim of slashed and broken hills seemed to hem in some mysterious menace, something lurking above the silence—heavy and oppressive. There was a desperate urge to hurry, to get along; but the barrier of horizon moved on before the stage. The sand clung.

"The soaked and frothing animals, spangled with its glistening particles, pulled heavily into their collars. The driver touched up his wheelers with the stock of his whip, while his swamper went stumbling along by the leaders, prodding them with a stick, though he could scarcely haul his own feet through the drifts."

Only veteran travelers detected the first signs of a desert storm making up.

"The movements of the conductor were strange. His mood seemed to fluctuate between an utter lethargy and the most acute expectancy. Either he sat with his head buried in his arms, the back of his red, wet undershirt exposed to the burning sky, or he arose suddenly as though someone had tapped him on the shoulder; he began staring about from his bloodshot eyes. Then, mopping himself with a scarlet bandanna, he would grumble something to the driver and wilt forward again.

"Even he was aware of something about to happen; and he left his passengers sweltering in their doubts . . . These ever-dangling menaces were maddening. But they were dangling nearer. The stage wagon had reached a point some fifteen miles beyond the dry well of Alamo Mocho when the hot air grew definitely sulphurous; the low sun became dull and tarnished. A black cloud beneath it arose like smoke from the jagged edge of a crater. It covered the sun and became splotched with fire. Long shreds of it tore themselves from the mountains. A great yellowish shadow spread over the world; and a black one came waving like a blanket across the dunes.

"Windstorms are not a common occurrence on the Colorado Desert; but they are listed no less among the potential furies . . . Warning on this occasion had sufficed for some preparation; and the first hot draft found the animals unhitched, hobbled and tied loosely together by their necks, so that, free of the wagon, they were yet unable to stray and could turn their tails to the first blast of sand.

"When it came it was with a sound like the heavy back-sweep of the sea. It struck upon the vehicle like a burst of it, like the green-frothing body of it, breaker upon breaker. It smashed with a dull impact upon the leather of the high forward seats and glanced from the boots like driving hail. The wagon trembled and rocked, the stanch covering of its after-part bulging with the intermittent concussions that pressed in from both sides.

"The animals, with heads nearly down to their forefeet, the blown hair of their hides sticky with the drying sweat, remained as rigid as though made of wood. The gaunt world had turned to a golden yellow; the heavens deep red and gray, one blending into the other, into a sweeping mass, a whistling chaos.

"Hours passed. Distant screams came down from forms that appeared and vanished through the blizzardlike waves. They were the forms of the bending mesquite, yet they appeared to be moving, to be stalking into the sand-blast. It was a land for all things unearthly. . . .

"Then night. There were stars, and the wind was gone. And a certain water hole called Indian Wells had gone with it. So had the covering of the wagon, so had all vestige of road, all land-marks. Mountains would not be visible until daylight; then the hot sun would take its toll of that which the wind had parched. . . .

"The contents of the canteens had become precious stuff; there was no water at all for the team. The beasts slogged on over the dry and starry wastes, through hills of sand which had never ex-isted before, over patches of gravel that were new, *barankas* that were filled, old banks smothered over, strange ones uncovered along with the skulls and bones of other beasts upon whom the sun had once risen too soon . . . The conductor was visibly wor-ried. He seemed to be staking all on the driver's hunch—' 'Pears like I recollect that star.' "

On the stretch of 179 miles between Fort Yuma and San Diego there were eleven stations or watering places, spaced at an aver-age distance of 17 miles, but there was one long hiatus of 32 miles between Indian Wells and Carrizo Creek. That was the region that tested the metal of the driver, the stamina of his beasts and the nerves of the passengers. If the Indian Wells–Carrizo Creek run could be made without difficulty, the rest of the desert cross-ing was easy—sometimes.

Over this same desert route charged Butterfield's thorough-breds with his first Overland Mail late the following summer. Contrary to the convictions of his detractors, he managed to meet the deadline. The 165 way stations were ready for business; the drivers, the agents and stable hands were hired; the coaches, the hay for 1,800 horses and the hams for the itinerants were ready. The contract had given him until September 15, 1858, for prep-arations, and at one o'clock on the morning of September 15 the first coach pulled out of San Francisco. To pacify Northerners, St. Louis had been designated as a terminus, as well as Memphis. For reasons unexplained, the coach did not make a getaway from St. Louis until 8 A.M. on the 16th, but even at that early hour a mob gathered to see it off in a squall of whoops and yells.

There were still plenty of carpers who maintained that the Overland would never get through to the Coast, without cheat-ing of some kind, in the prescribed twenty-four days, in double that time, and probably not at all. The political pull-hauling behind scenes did not give this enterprise an honest look. But aboard the coach was a passenger on whom everyone was counting for a full and unbiased account of the momentous journey— Waterman L. Ormsby, special correspondent for the New York *Herald,* and the only person booked all the way through to San Francisco.

Like the spectators in St. Louis who saw him off, he regarded this as the first authentic cross-country mail delivery. The many trips made to San Diego could be disregarded. One had to travel all the way to San Francisco to chalk up a transcontinental record. The pueblo at San Diego was far short of the finish line.

Twenty-four days later Ormsby was putting the carpers in their place. "It was just after sunrise," he wrote, with the flair of a competent reporter, "that the city of San Francisco hove in sight over the hills, and never did the night traveler approach a distant light, or the lonely mariner descry a sail with more joy than did I the city of San Francisco on the morning of Sunday, October 10.

"As we neared the city, we met milkmen and pleasure seekers taking their morning rides, looking on with wonderment as we rattled along at a tearing pace. Soon we struck the pavements, and with a whip, crack and bound, shot through the streets to our destination, to the great consternation of everything in the way, and the no little surprise of everybody. Swiftly we swirled up one street and down another, and around the corners, until finally we drew up at the stage office in front of the Plaza, our driver giving a shrill blast of his horn and a flourish of triumph for the arrival of the first overland mail in San Francisco from St. Louis.

"But our work was not yet done. The mails must be delivered, and in a jiffy we were at the Post Office door, blowing the horn, howling and shouting for somebody to come and take the overland mail. I thought nobody was ever going to come—the minutes seemed days—but the delay made even time, and as the man took the bags from the coach, at half-past seven A.M. on Sunday, October 10, it was just twenty-three days, twenty-three hours and a half . . . from St. Louis. And I had the satisfaction of knowing that I had gone through with the first mail, the sole passenger and the only one who had ever made the trip across the Plains in less than fifty days."

Most San Franciscans were still in bed that Sunday morning, never dreaming that history was taking place under their windows. There was no great assembly, no mass welcome, no bell ringing or cannon salutes, no hilarity such as Ormsby had witnessed at St. Louis. Folks at the Golden Gate had not believed that the Overland could possibly get through in twenty-four days, and were caught completely off guard.

Apologized the *Bulletin* next day: "The arrival of the Overland Mail by the Butterfield route in the short time of twenty-three days, twenty-three hours caused an immense amount of excitement in our city yesterday. Had it not been the Sabbath, the extempore and spontaneous outburst of rejoicing would perhaps have even excelled the first announcement of the successful laying of the Atlantic cable."

But the embarrassed citizenry easily made up for the oversight a week later with the arrival of the second coach—even though it was the Sabbath. This time the agent in San Jose telegraphed ahead to make sure that there would be a welcoming audience.

"At a quarter after four o'clock the coach turned from Market into Montgomery street," applauded the *Bulletin*. "The driver blew his horn and cracked his whip, at which the horses almost seemed to partake of his enthusiasm, and dashed ahead at a clattering pace, and the dust flew from the glowing wheels. At the same time a shout was raised that ran with the rapidity of an electric flash along Montgomery street, which throughout its length was crowded with an excited populace. As the coach dashed along through the crowds, the hats of the spectators were whirled in the air and the hurrah was repeated from a thousand throats, responsive to which, the driver, the lion of the occasion, doffed his weather-beaten old slouch, and in uncovered dignity, like the victor of an Olympic race, guided his foaming steeds towards the Post Office."

To celebrating San Franciscans, who considered themselves sufficiently sophisticated not to be accused of provincialism, the principal cause for jubilation was the opening of their city to overland communication. But anyone who had worried his way over the stage route knew that the real subject for celebration was the opening of the wastelands, the conquest of the Colorado Desert by wheels.

The *Herald* reporter was blessed with the finesse to shuffle things into proper perspective. He was appalled by what he had seen in the desert and what it meant to establish a route across it. Just west of Fort Yuma he had viewed the remains of a disaster in which 3,000 sheep, being driven by herders to the valleys of California, had been lost in a single, violent sandstorm, buried alive in the shifting dunes, and the bloated carcasses of 1,500 more were scattered along the road. Herders had started across the desert with a flock of 6,000, and had reached their destination with less than a quarter of that number.

On barren reaches Ormsby had passed scores of abandoned cattle—"almost living skeletons, gradually dying of thirst, yet with water within a few miles, some standing, others lying, and others just gasping in the agonies of death, a sight almost enough to sicken the stoutest heart." He had been puzzled about where the cattle had come from until his coach overtook a great emigrant train with hundreds of emaciated animals, and learned that often as many as two-thirds of a drove of cattle were left on the desert road to die of thirst.

At Pilot Knob, the first station west of Fort Yuma, his coach had picked up a Texas family, the Foremans—father, mother, and two young children, including an eight-months-old infant. They had left Texas wealthy, they thought, with ample funds and a herd of 3,000 cattle. Finding no desert trail that answered for a road, they had struck off in the wrong direction, failed to reach water, and had lost their entire herd. Instead of the wealth with which they expected to start ranching in California, they paid their last dollar to the conductor for a ride to El Monte. Ormsby helped the family off the stage at El Monte where they were met by Foreman's sister. So gaunt and rawboned was Foreman from his ordeal that his own sister did not recognize him.

Ormsby foresaw that a regular stage line across the desert would soon change all this. The road would become unmistakable. New wells would be dug and the distance shortened between stations. Already Butterfield had broken the long gap between Vallecito and Carrizo Creek by locating water and fixing a station at a place called Palm Springs. Around these stations Ormsby knew that little towns would quickly spread out.

"One of the greatest benefits of the establishment of this overland mail route," he predicted, "will be that it will indicate to the emigrant, with his valuable droves of cattle, the safest and surest means of transit across these waterless plains, which are so little traveled that disputes often occur among directors of a train as to which is the right road."

Postmaster Aaron Brown had been right, and even northern Californians were beginning to realize it. In hailing the arrival of the Overland Mail, one San Francisco orator had the prudence to point it out. "To the Postmaster General of the United States," he declared, "the thanks of the people of California are especially due, for the liberal and enlightened views which have dictated a policy so eminently calculated to develop our resources and increase our permanent prosperity. Whilst Congress debates and doubts and hesitates and does nothing toward the railroad, it is at least gratifying to perceive that one department of the government is making an enlightened and persevering effort to increase our communication with the East."

Once the resistance of the debaters and doubters was broken by a demonstration of what the San Antonio–San Diego and Overland lines could do, the country flung itself headlong into scheme after scheme for transporting Easterners to the West and Westerners to the East. Everyone suddenly became very conscious of the fact that the California gold rush had done things to geography that politics could not correct. The nation was settled to the Mississippi and well beyond; it was getting settled on the Pacific Coast; but in between was a vast area that had almost been skipped entirely. Thoroughfares over this uninhabited expanse must be built without further delay.

The horses and the coaches were ready. To the southern border routes and the northern Sierra–Salt Lake run were quickly added a weekly service from St. Joseph, Missouri, via Utah City, to Placerville, California; a monthly stage from Kansas City, over the Mojave Desert, to Stockton, California; and a line across the waist of Mexico. Then came the wonderful Pony Express—and to alter everything that had been accomplished, the Civil War.

At a mass meeting in San Diego on May 8, 1859, the citizens had put on the record a wordy resolution that "the regularity, safety and dispatch with which the U.S. Mails have been transported from San Antonio . . . over the pioneer line across the continent, the only one which has never made a failure of any kind—a line organized when the country to be traversed was almost unexplored and known but partially even to the trapper and the tardy emigrant—have demonstrated in the most conclusive manner the superiority of the El Paso and San Diego route."

Therefore, be it further resolved that: "The people of the City of San Diego, in mass convention assembled, do heartily and cordially agree that the Southern route for a railroad from Memphis via El Paso to San Diego is the only practical and feasible one for the construction of a railroad from the Atlantic to the Pacific."

The guns at Fort Sumter soon drowned out the plaintive appeals of the San Diegans. The creation of the Confederacy killed the Jackass Line. Butterfield had to move his Overland north. And at last the twenty-year-old squabble over the best route for a railroad was resolved in the exigencies of civil war. Military necessity decreed that the rails be laid in the north as a bond of steel to hold the Union together. It was a long time being built, but the construction of the Central Pacific over the Sierra Nevada postponed for two more decades the wistful hope of southern Californians to plant a transcontinental rail terminal in their domain.

However, the pioneer efforts of Aaron Brown, Jim Birch and John Butterfield in opening up the desert were not lost. Roads had been etched across both the Colorado and the Mojave deserts. Towns were springing up. Agricultural experts and engineers were explaining how fertile the desert was and how feasible the irrigation of broad sections of it might be. Government surveyors were settling border disputes and already anticipating arguments over water rights. The desert was losing some of the terror that people had long attached to it.

It was quite a different world that journalist J. Ross Browne discovered when he took an excursion through the Colorado Desert in December 1863. "Here was a glowing and mystic land of sunshine and burning sands," he wrote, almost in admiration. "The face of the country, for the most part, is covered with mesquite trees, sage bushes, greasewood, weeds and cactus. Mountains are in sight all the way across. . . .

"Many indications of the dreadful sufferings of emigrant parties and drovers still mark the road; the wrecks of wagons, half covered with the drifting sands, skeletons of horses and mules, and the skulls and bones of many herd of cattle that perished by thirst on the way or fell victims to the terrible sandstorms that sweep the desert."

Brown was putting all these relics of suffering and death in the past tense, as if the sands were already tamed. He described attractive oases and stage stations, and instead of being driven to distraction by mirages, like those who had witnessed them before him, he was delighted.

"There was a scene on a pleasant morning as we sallied forth on our journey from Indian Wells never to be forgotten," he rhapsodized. "The eye that looks upon it once must see it as long as mortal vision lasts. An isolated mountain in the distance seemed at the first view to rise abruptly out of a lake of silver, the shores of which were alive with water fowl of brilliant and beautiful plumage. As we journeyed toward it, the lake disappeared and the mountain changed to a frowning fortress, symmetrical in all its parts—a perfect model of architectural beauty.

"Still nearing it, the ramparts and embattlements melted into a dreamy haze, out of which emerged a magnificent palace with pillars and cornices and archways and a great dome, from which arose a staff surmounted by a glowing blue ball, encircled by a halo. At the same time another mountain on the right, distant many miles, assumed equally strange and fantastic shapes; and when the ball arose upon our palace, another ball answered the signal from the distant mountain on the right; and then a great railway opened up between them, supported by innumerable piles, stretching many leagues over the desert.

"So perfect was the illusion that we stopped in breathless wonder, almost expecting to see a train of cars whirl along and vanish in the warm glow of the horizon. This strange and beautiful display of the mirage has been witnessed by many travelers on the Colorado Desert, who will attest that, so far from exaggeration, I have but faintly pictured its wonders. Nothing of any kind that I have seen elsewhere can compare with it in the variety and beauty of its illusions."

Beauty had at last been found on the desert—beauty both imagined and real.

It was more than a decade before an actual train of cars was seen on the desert, and then the iron horse came, hardly as the Postmaster General and his confederates had anticipated. They had assumed that the road would be built from east to west, on Eastern capital. Instead, the capital was Californian and the first leg of the line looped down from the Bay area to Los Angeles and on across the sand to Yuma. The Southern Pacific, far from being the first line to connect the poles of a continent, was little more than an extension of the Central Pacific which the Big Four—Leland Stanford, Charles Crocker, Collis P. Huntington and Mark Hopkins—had thrust over the Sierra Nevada and on to Promontory, Utah, between 1863 and 1869, in a dramatic race with the Union Pacific.

When asked years later how the Central Pacific became involved in constructing the Southern Pacific, Stanford had the surly reply: "Well, the necessity of obtaining control of the Southern Pacific Railroad was based really upon the act of Congress providing for its construction. It became apparent that if that last was constructed entirely independent of those who were interested in the Central Pacific, it would become a dangerous rival, not only for the through business from the Atlantic Ocean, but it would enter into active competition for the local business in California. It was of paramount importance that the road should be controlled by the friends of the Central Pacific."

The whole start of a giant railroad monopoly was as simple and matter of fact as that. The Big Four had made millions through a bookkeeping process all their own in pushing the rails over the northern route, and they merely applied the same procedure to the building of the southern adjunct. A confusion of construction firms like the Contract and Finance Company, the Western Development Company and the Pacific Improvement Company, was organized on paper, all controlled by themselves; the companies in turn were made to contract with the Southern Pacific for building specified sections of the line, and required to issue and turn over large quantities of stocks and bonds as compensation for the work done.

As a contemporary explained, "The men out on the road seem to have known little about any of the companies . . . Nor was it easy for them to keep informed. The same construction force moved from place to place. The same men in the same pay-car paid off employees of the Central Pacific, the Southern Pacific and the construction companies indiscriminately. The same general shops furnished track materials. The same equipment was found in all the different lines . . . There was small wonder that even the higher engineering officials were unable to locate accurately the stretches built by each of the principal companies which they served, nor that men under them should have been altogether confused."

But, regardless of the artful tactics of the builders, San Diego

and Los Angeles at long last had their overland exit to the East
—to Yuma in 1877, and across the Mojave Desert to Needles six
years later. And all those miles of construction proved so easy
compared to the herculean task of climbing the Sierra that in
the end the old arguments of Aaron Brown showed much more
sense than political bias. His dream of a southern artery across
the South had come true, and in the process of translating it into
reality a giant step had been made toward overcoming and occupying the great California deserts.

V

REVOLUTION IN THE LAUNDRY

THE Southern Pacific rails were laid across the broad Mojave just in time to aid and abet the first big desert industry; and the Santa Fe, too, soon pushed in from the East, as if the scheduling of all this tie and track laying were in accord with some grand design prearranged to accommodate a new brand of prospector.

Fortunes had been made and lost in trying to wrest silver and gold from the mountains that stretched north like gaunt fingers from the Mojave Desert—the Coso, the Argus and the Slate ranges, the Panamints, the Black and the Funeral mountains. For a time even the more conservative grubstakers of San Francisco had been confident that the desert was going to yield the kind of golden wealth that had come from the Sierra foothills and Washoes, but by 1882 or '83 they were stoically accepting their disillusionment and conceding that the real Eldorado might be in the common white stuff that littered the dry lake floors—sodium tetraborate; tincal, as it was known to the mineralogists; $Na_2B_4O_710H_2O$, as it was known to the chemists; "cottonball crude," as desert dealers referred to it; "baking soda," as it was contemptuously misnamed by laborers who helped gather it; borax, as it was known to the druggists.

Although borate of soda had been sparingly used since ancient times by glassmakers, metal craftsmen and dyers, borax was not yet a household word in the 1880's. It was expensive stuff, sold by some apothecaries for as much as two bits an ounce. And there was good reason for its cost. For a hundred years the principal supply had come from Tibet, packed over the Himalaya passes on the backs of sheep, fifty pounds to an animal, and delivered

106

in Calcutta after traveling 500 miles through some of the sorriest terrain on the globe.

In the eighteenth century deposits had been located nearer civilization in the swamps of Tuscany, 65 miles southeast of Leghorn. More recently, commercial quantities had been found in Turkey, in Chile, in Argentina, near Clear Lake, California, and in the marshes of western Nevada. The industrial demand for it was rising sharply.

Metallurgists had to have the salts for the production of alloys. Borax made nickel-plating a quick, practical process. Pottery and ceramics manufacturers were dependent upon it for the smooth, lustrous finish of their wares. Meat packers used it as a preservative. Soap companies had discovered that borax was an effective water softener and buffer. The leather industry required it as a neutralizer in preparing hides for tanning. It was the best-known rust inhibitor, and with interior plumbing coming into vogue, no bathub, toilet, lavatory or kitchen sink, could be properly surfaced without the vitreous enamel produced from sodium tetraborate.

The discovery of this versatile, indispensable mineral in Death Valley was first made in 1873, but nothing much was done about it until seven years later when a far larger deposit was brought to light dramatically. That 1880 find brought a new kind of prosperity to the desert country. Within three years, borax was rolling out of the parched wastelands in quantities that the industrial world had never dreamed possible, and the price was steadily declining. It came by the vanload in some of the bulkiest vehicles to which draft animals had ever been hitched.

Transportation of borax from a place almost as inaccessible as Tibet was, of course, the major problem. The coming of the railroad had eliminated half the haul to the Coast, but it was still 165 miles from Furnace Creek in Death Valley to the nearest railroad station at Mojave, and at first the very notion of conveying vast quantities of anything out of the valley was looked upon as a proposition more impossible than running a stage line across the continent.

The mileage itself was relatively inconsequential. What created the real problems were the oceans of sand, the heat, the long, waterless stretches, the miry salt marshes, and the high mountain shoulders to be crossed with payloads of thirty tons or more. This transportation was not like the business of stage-coaching, lumbering or even oxcart pioneering. No one had ever tried hauling over such terrain and for such a distance the ponderous weights necessary to make borax mining a profitable enterprise.

The 30 miles down Death Valley from Furnace Creek to the last water at Mesquite Spring were as hard a grind as any teamster could reasonably expect to encounter on the American continent, but at Mesquite Spring the hard part of the journey started. From there to Mojave the distance of 135 miles was broken by only three springs.

In the well-watered East, where draft animals were used for hauling enormous loads, watering troughs spaced at intervals of every 4 or 5 miles were considered a bare minimum. Yet from Mesquite Spring to the next watering place at Lone Willow, near the foot of a peak in the Panamint Range, it was 53 miles, and 40 of them were uphill through Windy Gap or Wingate Pass.

The average grade in Windy Gap was 100 feet to a mile, though there were short, winding stretches where the rise was as much as 400 feet per mile. Moreover, it was impossible to maintain any semblance of road through the pass. It was nothing more than a stream bed, a wash, down which foaming waves 20 feet high had been known to rush after a torrential shower. And the showers came just often enough to keep the pass strewn with boulders, cut by cross gullies, and surfaced with a foot or more of yielding sand. So tortuous was one turn near the crest that the driver of a long team of mules actually lost sight of his leaders around an overhanging cliff.

From Lone Willow it was 26 miles to Granite Spring, near mile-high Pilot Knob, then an easy 7 miles to Blackwater, and finally a long, waterless 50 miles into Mojave. The route was as lonely as it was dry. Over the entire 165 miles there was not a sign of human habitation, no hut, no shade, no shelter of any sort—an endless expanse of wind-blown sand and low shrubs. This was the territory over which the Harmony Borax Company, just north of Furnace Creek, expected to cart hundreds of tons of sodium tetraborate.

The worst traffic obstruction, more formidable than Windy Gap, was in Death Valley itself. The refining works were located above the mouth of Furnace Creek Canyon on the east side of the valley. The springs and the best road surface lay on the west side, so it was necessary to cross the salt marsh which extended for a width of from 8 to 10 miles down the full length of the valley. For most of the distance the marsh was a trap of bottomless slime and ooze, impossible to bridge, impossible to fill.

Here and there the slime was crusted over with salt, but that only added to its treachery, for the thickness of the crust was dependable nowhere. A man might walk on it confidently for a quarter of a mile, then the surface would suddenly give way and there was nothing underneath but that deadly pudding of ooze. To satisfy his curiosity, one investigator had taken a 15-foot pole out on the crust, chipped a hole in it, and with scarcely any pressure, shoved the pole down out of sight. Anyone was entitled to make his own guess on how much deeper than 15 feet the sink was.

But after tedious exploration, one area, a few miles south of Furnace Creek, was finally located where the surface seemed firm all the way across—firm, but so fantastically serrated that it resembled the margins of a northern lake after a stiff March storm had blasted out the winter ice and heaped it helter-skelter on the shore. Nowhere was there footing on these jagged salt crystals. Yet if a road were to be extended to Mojave this barrier had to be crossed. And no machine or horse-drawn contrivance could tackle the job. It had to be done by hand, with sledge hammers. Eight miles of chaos had to be leveled by men working in the merciless white glare and in temperatures of 110° and 120°.

Someone remembered the magnificent performance of Chinese coolies in chiseling a railroad bed over the Sierra Nevada in the snow and ice of midwinter. In an inverse climate and setting, this was the same kind of work. A few of them were put on the job with white men. The Caucasians quit. The coolies, in their broadbrimmed straw hats, kept at it.

Gangs of Chinese—a whole colony of them—were recruited in the valley towns and in San Francisco, and transplanted in Death Valley. Equipped only with sledge hammers, they laboriously chipped a swath through the morass of sandy salt, pounding tirelessly at the jumbled crystals, chattering in a dozen dialects, cheerful beyond all Occidental understanding, begging for tea and more tea as the only solace to keep them going. And the brew had to be hot. Under the broiling sun they drank the potent, steaming beverage until the sweat streaming off their bodies seemed to have the look of tea.

Across Death Valley they left one of the strangest roads in the history of transportation—a smooth thoroughfare of salt and sand hacked out entirely by hand, the only sledge-hammer road in existence, and another California monument to the persistent labor from the Orient. All this for a wage of a dollar and a quarter a day. Without them it is doubtful that a wagonload of borax would ever have left Furnace Creek for Mojave. They removed the last major obstruction on the route, and many of them stayed on to help grub for cottonball borax.

The problem of water supply for draft animals on the road still had to be licked. They would have to go dry during the day and fill up night and morning, or morning and night, if it were too hot for day travel. Sixteen or 17 miles a day was the most that could be expected of any beasts in this climate. The 165 miles divided fairly evenly by 10, so 10 stations were marked off on the route. Again there would be no shelter from sun or wind-blown sand at these stations; the wagons were roof enough. But each station would be furnished with a 500-gallon water tank, and feed bins to hold a few bales of hay and a half-dozen sacks of barley. Cached supplies would be consumed on the way out, and the empty wagons would bring in fresh water and feed en route back.

Meantime the designing of wagons worthy of this unique and perilous highway was entrusted to a veteran teamster of the desert, Ed Stiles, and a mechanic foreman, J. S. W. Perry—Perry to be in charge. The Harmony management specified only that the vehicles must be built to carry at least ten tons, for reasons of transportation economy, and must withstand all the rigors of the desert, known and unknown.

Perry went at the assignment like a scientist. He made a study of the heavy freighters in use on the West Coast and looked up everything he could find on the enormous carts that had been used in the East before the days of railroading. He knew that wagons carrying more than ten tons had once been commonplace in New England, that they had monstrous wheels standing 10 or 12 feet high, with rims as wide as 14 inches. He knew that half the work of maintaining these monsters in hot weather was preventing the wheels from drying out, shrinking and loosening, keeping the tires snug on the fellies, with continuous application of moisture. He knew very well that any of the standard wagons in the East or West would soon collapse on the Death Valley—Mojave road under the strain of ten tons of borax. Even

an ordinary chair or table could dry out, shrink at the joints, and
fall apart in a few months.

Perry had to begin from scratch. Lumber for the wheels and
every other part would have to be weathered and preshrunk—
in the desert. He assembled quantities of hickory, ash and oak
at Mojave, and for two months exposed it to the severest punishment of sun and hot air. Then he summoned a squad of expert
wagon craftsmen and exhibited his blueprints.

The drawings called for rear wheels 7 feet high, front wheels
5 feet, each with steel rims 8 inches wide and an inch thick. Hubs
had to be a 1½ feet in diameter, and the cumbersome oak spokes
tapered from a 5½-inch width at the hubs to 4 inches at the fellies. Everything else was designed to the scale of the wheels. The
body would stand nearly two stories high and be massive enough
to carry half the contents of a Southern Pacific freight car.

All parts were custom constructed and custom forged. No one
outside the elite circle of assembled blacksmiths and wood fitters
was allowed to furnish so much as a bolt, and Perry took pains
to inspect each piece as it went into place. Ten wagons were put
together. Each weighed just over three tons, and Perry's bill for
the ten ran up to an astonishing total of $9,000. But they were
worth every penny of it. The Perry guarantee went with the
product. He swore that they could not be worn out, rusted out
or rotted out. And time proved his oath good. A few of them
still stand in the sun of Death Valley, almost as stout as on the
day they were finished.

It was teamster Ed Stiles who contributed the idea of hitching
one wagon to another, tandem, and hitching more mulepower
out in front to draw two or three vehicles in a train, and undoubtedly he borrowed it from the Southern Pacific. In any case,
the novel idea appealed to the economy-minded Harmony management, and from the first, Death Valley's borax moved toward
Mojave in a train made up of two huge vans, with a water tank
trailing behind like a caboose.

Fourteen, 16, 18 mules, plus 2 horses, supplied the draypower.
The front span of mules were the "leaders"; the 2 horses next
to the wagon, and hitched to the tongue, were the "wheelers."
Twenty was the usual total, and 20 were needed on the steep
incline of Windy Gap, heaving some thirty tons of dead weight,
including the borax, the water cart, the unwieldy wagons themselves, and a vast assortment of tools, food supplies and cooking

equipment attached to the sides. Altogether the outfit, in action, looked like a cross between a circus wagon and a Connecticut peddler's cart. Not since the construction of the Pyramids of Egypt had such an impressive rig crossed a desert.

Stretched out on the road, the leaders were a long 120 feet from the skinner, who rode the nigh wheeler or sat enthroned high on the front of the fore wagon. For such an entourage reins were useless. Instead, the skinner held a stout, cotton jerk line in one hand and a whip with a 6-foot stock and 22-foot lash in the other.

The single line was strung through rings in the harnesses of the twenty nigh mules to the bit of the nigh leader. To make a left turn, the skinner pulled steadily on the line. To make a right turn, the line was given a series of short jerks; the jerks made the leader instinctively throw up his head, which in turn pulled a strap attached to the right side of the bit—a system as simple as it was ingenious. The leader took its cues from the line; the rest followed.

Driving a team was easy on a straightaway or on a road with sweeping curves. The test of a good skinner and his trained beasts came at a hairpin turn, where the leaders might go out of sight around the bend, and, because of the curvature in the road, were pulling at right angles to the load. The wagon would at once begin to veer to the side unless the pull of the front mules was counteracted in some way. The two pairs of mules directly in front of the horses—the pointers—were trained to take care of this exigency, and they were worth a hundred times their weight in borax.

If it was an abrupt turn to right, the pointers on the offside leaped over the taut haul chain and pulled like mad, diagonally to the left, dancing sideways as well as forward, to keep the wagons moving comparatively straight until the point of the turn was reached. Then at exactly the right moment they bounced back over the chain and perhaps repeated the maneuver on the opposite side. To the uninitiated observer it all worked so smoothly and simply that he never guessed the operation represented months of training and experience.

Commanding a twenty-mule borax wagon was something like sailing a full-rigged schooner singlehanded, using an oar for a rudder. In managing the team the line was a help; the whip that could flick a fly from the ear of the fourth off mule without disturbing a hair was a help; the brakes were useful; the swamper riding the trail wagon and working its brake was occasionally credited with giving some assistance; and the boxful of rocks kept on the seat to pelt perverse mules beyond the reach of the whip was indispensable. But all these aids were of minimum value in controlling the team, compared to the effectiveness of the skinner's tongue.

An inspired tongue and flexible vocal organs were what kept the animals on course and pulling together. The teamster's words had all the sting of his whip. That badge of trade was held in reserve as a threat and rarely applied, but from the moment a skinner mounted his seat with a "Git ep, ye God-damned — git ep," the flow of profane eloquence was unreserved. The vocabulary, to be sure, was limited. Mule skinners kept it that way on purpose, so they maintained, in order not to strain the intelligence of the animals or the lean-witted assistant, the swamper.

The profusion of four-, five-, and six-letter words had aim, thrust and cut of unmistakable meaning and nuance. Mules were sensitive beasts, each with a name, and when that name was linked with the bite of the driver's rebuke, ears perked up, a tail wilted, a quiver of terror or embarrassment seemed to pass over the hide, as though a lash had struck.

The yarn about the skinner who was converted overnight by a transient evangelist originated at Mojave. In fact, the gospel bearer was so proud of his proselyte that he accompanied him to the wagon next morning to see him off. With the preacher looking on from below, the skinner swung up to his high seat, sober, constrained, humbled.

There he sat for a long moment, trying to summon the magic words that normally set his team in motion. For the first time in his life he was tongue tied, totally bereft of his powers of persuasion. The evangelist had deprived him of the Biblical vocabulary and all the mortifying vulgarisms his mules understood. When he finally bellowed the command to "Get ep," without a single allusion to the Almighty or the organs of sex, the mules stood transfixed in their tracks, and reportedly all twenty turned their heads in unison to stare in wonderment at the master. The evangelist lost a good convert long before the wagons approached Windy Gap.

No question about it, the borax teamster felt compelled to lean rather heavily on diabolic conjuring. He had to be an unyielding tyrant, a wizard and an artist, in one. Yet despite the

Satanic invocation, accidents did occur on the road to Mojave. Miscalculation of a hairbreadth in rounding one of the turns in Windy Gap, the failure of a leader to respond to a yank of the jerk line at a moment of urgency, or the tripping of a pointer in leaping the haul chain, could bring disaster. Everything depended on everything else, and a minor slip-up could send the whole outfit into a cliff or over the edge of one.

In such a mishap the cargo might be lost, a few mules injured, skinner and swamper placed on the casualty list, but those invulnerable wagons merely had to be righted, hauled back onto the road, and they were in service again.

The grade down the mountain shoulder near Granite Spring was the most hazardous stretch. It was straight; it was steep; it was miles long. Here was no sand to drag at the wheels; the surface was hard packed and the great wheels rolled down it all too easily. The difficulty in maneuvering that grade was in braking the wheels. And many times even the mighty brake blocks were not heavy enough to cope with thirty tons of borax, wagon and water pushing from behind. As the wagons gained momentum the skinner threw his weight on the front brake; the swamper did the same on the trailer. Groaning, screeching and sliding, the cumbrous monsters lumbered on faster and faster.

The race with death began when the brakes no longer held and the wagons were out of control. Then the full dexterity of the skinner was called into play. There was no provision in the harness hitch for holdbacks; the animals simply had to be kept ahead of the load to avoid being run down. Their quickstep became a trot, the trot a kind of canter, the canter a dead run, a lope and a gallop.

All precaution was thrown to the winds. Like a succession of pistol shots, the skinner's whip cracked over the heads of the frantic mules. Bowling behind, the wagons thundered their threat. They groaned under their weight, bounced and careened. Occasionally a terrified swamper, seeing certain perdition ahead, abandoned his perch on the trailer and leaped over the side to just as certain an end. But the skinner stuck to his post, barking his staccato profanity, yelling at the mules individually and collectively, pouring forth the last reserve of obscene curses that he kept in store for such occasions.

Often they made it to the bottom of the grade. Sometimes not. And a wagon would come along two days, four days, a week later, to shovel away the drifts of spilled borax from the tangle of wreckage, put a few mangled animals out of the last of their misery, and bury the dead. There were quite a number of unhallowed graves along the Mojave road.

A heap of stones and a weathered slab of wood tacked at a rakish angle to a mesquite stake marked the resting place of a skinner in Windy Gap. GRAVE OF W. M. SHADLEY was the only citation. But a teamster who had found Shadley and helped bury him remembered the scene vividly. "It was twenty-eight days before we found him," reported the volunteer mortician, "and he was mummified. No odor from his body, and when we stood him up, he almost stood alone. Now he was a good man, and a martyr to Death Valley."

The trouble with the Mojave trek was that it served more as a "route" than a road. In mountain gaps it might be well defined, but elsewhere, depending on what sandstorms and washouts had done, a driver might veer a half mile or more off the course followed by the last team. No teamster in a real predicament could count on being picked up by the next wagon coming through. Usually he was not found until word got around that he was missing, and that could take weeks.

Jimmie Dayton died only nineteen miles from Furnace Creek. He happened to be driving a four-horse team on the day of his demise. It was mid-August of a deadly hot summer, and probably a sunstroke got him. In any case, he at least had a momentary foreboding that the end was near. In that moment his one thought was to save the horses. He drew them to a halt and slashed the reins to give them freedom to wander off to water. But then instinctively, as all drivers of the big teams did in coming to a halt, he set the brake. That was a mistake; he might as well have tethered the horses.

The dead animals and the dead man were found three weeks later. The scene told its own story, and Jim was put away where he had dropped. "It wasn't much of a grave," admitted a friend who helped with the interment. "We could only dig it four feet because we got into water at three feet. Jimmie wasn't fit to be moved. We just rolled him into the tarp with the shovels. I slit his pockets with a knife and found about eighteen dollars in silver and a watch. We lifted his body in the canvas and buried it. That was all. The only things that was said was what I said and it was something like, 'Well, Jimmie, you lived in the heat and you died in the heat, and after what you been through, I guess you ought to be comfortable in hell.' "

Few of the casualties on the borax run, however, could be attributed to such causes as wagon accidents and sunstroke. The most common provocation was human. It took 20 days for a round trip between Furnace Creek and Mojave, 20 days under a blazing sun, 20 days living on beans, bacon, coffee and cans, 20 days of wrestling with the elements and the animals on short supplies and ever-shortening tempers. Skinner and swamper were alone for almost three weeks at a stretch, and that proved to be about 19 days longer than any two independent characters could reasonably be expected to endure each other's company and the conditions under which they had to exist.

Status consciousness was in part responsible for the quick decline in rapport. The skinner was the boss, and he was inclined to make that fact incontestably clear. There was an infinite number of ways in which he could show his authority. Never would he trust the swamper near the driver's seat; that was reserved for him alone. He could load his subordinate with chores like harnessing and unharnessing, feeding and watering the animals, cooking meals and washing dishes, until the poor man did not have a moment he could call his own.

And since he did most of the dirty work, the swamper was the only one to be lambasted when something went wrong; when a buckle came undone on a harness; when a mule broke his tether at night or got the colic; and when the beans burned in the pan. The skinner got $120 a month and he took endless delight in reminding the flunky that he was not worth half the $75 paid him.

On the road familiarity bred contempt. Disagreement over trifles expanded into major clashes. Two men would leave Furnace Creek the best of friends and arrive at Mojave ten days later with homicidal intentions. The heat, the solitude and the suspense brought out the worst in them. Vicious quarrels arose over an accidental voice inflection, the way a man wore his hat, a personal preference for crisp or wilted bacon. Skinner and swamper frequently arrived at one end of the line silent and sullen, without having exchanged an unnecessary word for days. They also arrived with fractured shins, broken noses and battered faces.

One swamper, half demented by desert heat and the arrogance of his skinner, shadowed his prey for a week, waiting for the

right moment to vent his spleen. The moment came one evening at Lone Willow after they had fed and watered the mules and eaten their supper in the usual silence. The skinner unsuspectingly squatted by the mesquite fire, lost in his own thoughts. Behind him, poked into the sand, was the shovel with which the swamper had been digging mesquite to feed the blaze. Casually the outraged subordinate picked up the shovel, raised it, and finished off his enemy with a resounding clout over the back of the head.

No twinge of conscience bothered the assailant as he dug a pit next to the spring, rolled the despised body into it, filled the hole, then lay down on the soft earth of the grave for the only placid night's sleep he had known since leaving Furnace Creek.

Next morning he harnessed the team, climbed into the coveted skinner's seat, and headed for Mojave in triumph. But the swamper soon discovered that he knew less about driving a team of twenty mules than he had fancied. In descending a grade a mule stumbled; everything went wrong at once; mules, wagons, borax and water cart wound up in a frightful tangle, and when the would-be skinner worked his way out from under the wreckage he had a badly broken leg.

Painfully he dragged himself from one animal to another and cut them all loose, except one. He mounted that, and with a dangling leg rode to town, bearing a tale of chivalric purport: the sad death of the skinner from some mysterious natural cause; his own courageous attempt to bring in the team alone; the accident; the saving of the animals and the agonizing ride with a broken leg.

The crippled swamper was at once elevated to the stature of a hero, given the warmest sympathy and the best available medical attention. And he would have gotten away with his story and all the honors, except for one error. It had been a mistake to bury that body so close to the spring.

The next teamsters to go over the route noted the location of the grave and decided, in the interests of sanitation, that the corpse should be moved a little farther from the water supply. In the process of disinterment the bashed skull was discovered and the murderer was soon on the most-wanted list of a lynching party.

The doctors, however, took the trouble to turn their patient over to the authorities rather than to the mob. Neither the coroner nor the district attorney had the spare time to make a long investigative trek into the desert on a case involving purely circumstantial evidence, so the swamper was conducted a safe distance out of town and given the freedom of the West.

Less fortunate was a fellow swamper who pursued his skinner to Daggett, seventy-five miles east of Mojave, cornered him behind a blacksmith shop, and pommeled the archenemy into pulp with a handy wheel spoke. The killer was quickly identified and locked up, and when it became evident that the justice was about to release him for the usual lack of evidence, a masked mob took charge. The prisoner was dragged from the security of the jail; a rope thrown over the crossarm of one of the new Santa Fe telegraph poles did the rest.

Yet despite the difficulty of maintaining peace among mule skinners and swampers, despite road accidents and traffic hazards, borax was being hauled out of the desert in unheard-of quantities. Mining was an enormous enterprise, calling for capital investment even greater than the demands of silver refining. Gigantic pans and vats for processing the crude cottonball borate had to be transported to Death Valley from San Bernardino— 250 miles by wagon, and every mile of it was through the desert, a journey of almost three weeks. From San Bernardino, too, were shipped the water tanks, pumps and pipe in thousand-foot lots, all at a cost of eight cents a pound in freightage alone. And from Mojave came lumber, hardware and food supplies at comparable cost.

Prospectors added materially to the necessary expenditures by demanding exorbitant sums for claims they had staked out in the desert. Aaron and Rosie Winters set the precedent on that when they found the "white gold" near Furnace Creek. They charged a whacking fee of $20,000.

Everybody knew their story and savored it, begrudging them not a penny of the fortune they had made. Aaron and Rosie were an impoverished couple who had tried to grub a living from a harsh little oasis called Ash Meadows, just over the Funeral Mountains from Death Valley. They would have lived on and died in the poverty of their hut, half lean-to and half dugout, if prospector Harry Spiller had not happened to stumble onto their ranch one night in 1880.

It was from Spiller that the Winterses learned about borax, the big demand for it, what it was like, where it was found, what it was used for and the price it commanded. Aaron did not let on to Spiller that the description of the stuff rang a bell. He merely let his guest ramble on and on, and made his questions sound as though he were just trying to keep the conversation going.

No sooner was the visitor out of sight than Aaron and Rosie headed for Furnace Creek to check on what they had once seen there. Sure enough, it answered Spiller's description in every detail. The prospector had even confided that a San Francisco dealer named William T. Coleman was very much interested in borax.

To Aaron Winters, Coleman was little more than a name made famous by his heading a San Francisco vigilance committee which had taken the law into its hands, hung four scoundrels, exiled two dozen more and generally cleaned up the city. He had heard, too, about Coleman's Pick-Handle Brigade which had settled the anti-Chinese riots of 1877.

Everyone, even in the remotest parts of California, knew that much about Coleman. He had made quite a name for himself. Aaron was not aware that William T. Coleman and Company represented one of the wealthiest mercantile establishments in the state, with interests in New York, London, Alaska and the Orient, or that William T. himself cut so much political ice that he was being considered in high places back East as a candidate for the Presidency of the United States.

In blissful ignorance of the eminence of the addressee, Aaron sent off his box of cottonball samples direct to William T. Coleman, and sooner than Winters thought possible, Coleman's agent showed up at the Ash Meadows shanty. The eagerness of the agent gave Aaron his clue for setting an astronomical figure on his find. Twenty thousand dollars or no sale. And he held out for it.

Aaron got the $20,000, gave up the miserable lean-to existence at Ash Meadows, took a trip to Los Angeles to outfit Rosie with a new wardrobe, and moved to a more hospitable ranch at Pahrump.

Furnace Creek was a big deal, even for Coleman, so he enlisted the support of another venturesome investor, Francis Marion Smith, who had been dabbling in borax production at Columbus, Nevada, for a decade. Twenty Mule Team Borax was on its way into the American kitchen.

Coleman and Smith were the men who footed the bill for the caravan of giant wagons, paid the coolies for hammering the road across Death Valley, and put up the money for freighting the great processing pans, boilers, vats, tanks, pipe and pumps across the desert from San Bernardino. "Harmony" was the name they gave to the works just north of Furnace Creek.

Nor did they stop with the Harmony plant. Soon there were the Eagle Works at Bennett's Wells in the heart of Death Valley, and the Amargosa Works a few miles to the east in the Black Mountains, with wagon trains running south to the rail depot at Daggett. Two well-churned wagon routes now led to civilization; industry and organization were coming to Death Valley.

The industrial development of the valley was sorely handicapped by the shortage of water, but there was another shortage almost as serious—fuel. All the crude cottonball that Chinamen gathered in the desert had to be processed in the boiling pans and vats, and their furnaces called for enormous quantities of fuel. Coal was half a continent away, and toting wood from the Sierra Nevada was out of the question. Coleman and Smith had to make do with what the desert offered.

In the quest for fuel they virtually had to promote a subsidiary industry—harvesting "desert hay," the bulkiest, weirdest combustible that ever fired a commercial furnace. Desert hay was not grass. It was mesquite and sagebrush, greasewood and weeds, with rarely a twig thicker than a man's thumb.

Away from the alkali flats the brush was common enough. Great thickets of mesquite grew on the outskirts of Death Valley, and from these thickets came the fuel for the Harmony Works and all the other works. In two-ton loads that looked for all the world like hayracks piled high with timothy, the brush wagons rolled into Furnace Creek faster than the borax wagons moved out. At first there were reasonable quantities of it within easy range, but the consumption was so great that scavengers were soon pitching it onto wagons 7 miles, 8, even 10 miles from the plant.

"The gathering of mesquite for fuel in Death Valley is commonly what Californians would call placer-mining or possibly quarrying," suggested an early tourist with a sense of humor. "They cut mesquite wood in Death Valley with a shovel and a mule. It is simply a great, thorny bush, low and scrubby. Sandstorms bury it out of sight grove after grove. Then comes the

fuel-gatherer with his shovel and his mule. A few jabs in the
sand uncovers a tree trunk or root and then the man takes two
hitches with a chain about the old stub, howls with familiar profanity at the mule, and in an instant out comes a stick of wood
pleasing to behold. Mounds burying from four to six cords are
found there. But the gathering of any kind of desert brush or
fuel eventually becomes a pretty heavy drain on the profits of
the industry, for the reason that the brush, being grubbed by
the roots, does not replace itself."

But while it lasted, the mesquite and greasewood kept the fires
burning merrily under the pans at the Harmony Works. "It is
dumped in great heaps handy to the mouth of the furnace," explained an astonished spectator, more impressed with the fuel
than the product it helped manufacture, "and there pitched under the boilers by the pitchforkful. Light and flashing as the fuel
is, I noticed that the fireman was not obliged to keep constantly
at work, but about half the time was occupied in tending the
furnace and half in leaning on the fork or sitting on a rock and
gazing stolidly at the scenes around him."

Eventually crude petroleum took the place of mesquite and
greasewood in the borax furnaces, but long before that the first
inharmonious note was heard at the Harmony Works. The Coleman empire crumbled in 1886. William T. would not get to be
President, after all. The merchant who had started out as a pat-
ent-medicine salesman and risen until he operated steamships in
most of the oceans of the globe, engaged in wholesale merchan-
dising from Anchorage to Liverpool, controlled the California
fruit-canning industry and the borax industry—with fingers in
a dozen other industrial pies—was bankrupt.

In the liquidation of Coleman's assets his partner in borax,
F. M. Smith, acquired the desert properties, and Smith set out
to become the Borax King. He was ready for the coup. While
Coleman had been expanding his interests into every field of
trade that caught his executive fancy, Smith had been concen-
trating in one. A decade before Aaron and Rosie Winters sent
their famous specimens of cottonball to San Francisco, Smith had
been fascinated by the treeless waste of western Nevada that
looked like acres of spilled flour. In Teel's Marsh near Columbus he had located the purest borate of soda then known, and
started marketing it.

But Smith had his troubles in Nevada—transportation troubles, manufacturing troubles, labor troubles. He was a fighter, and he had fought claim jumpers, rival owners and legitimate competitors. His tenacity and his lawsuits had eventually netted him ownership of the entire Teel's Marsh deposit. The intrusion of Winters and Coleman had merely enlarged his horizon. He had moved into the California desert intent on cornering the market there, as he had in Nevada. The bankruptcy of the San Francisco merchant at last opened the way; the borax crown was within reach.

Smith knew more about sodium tetraborate than any other living man, and with the specialist on the scene the pace of events picked up rapidly after 1886. He began circulating a rumor that the cottonball found in dry, white lake bottoms was not the only form in which the ore occurred. It might be located as readily in the mountains or in the gray Mojave, mixed with other compounds.

Figuring that there could be easier money in staking out borax caches than in silver or gold, many a prospector took the hint, lowered his sights, and went on the prowl for "baking soda." Typical of that clan were the amazing Death Valley Lees, a brotherhood of five, lyrically surnamed Philander, Meander, Salamander, Alexander and Leander, alias Cub. They were all talented, all uninhibited, all slightly mad.

Half Indian themselves, they took up periodic residence with a miscellany of Piute squaws, proved prolific in reproducing their kind, and did more to populate the Death Valley neighborhood than all the legitimate newlyweds east of the Panamints. Along with the urge to procreate they were endowed with an equal urge to liquidate, and had no more compunction about using an innocuous human as a target than shooting a rattler.

Collectively they were jacks-of-all-trades, indulging in any kind of employment that came their way: ranching, teaming, mining, prospecting. The family roots were well established around Furnace Creek, and despite their idiosyncracies, employers were so hard put to recruit employees that even a Lee could usually find a job there.

Like everyone else, they did their share of prospecting on the side, and it was Philander, accompanied by a couple of companions, who discovered the first white hill in the Black Mountains and staked a claim. Promptly Borax Smith bought it—for $4,000.

That Lee discovery started a chain reaction. If a man could

pick up $4,000 for simply pointing out a white hill, prospecting for borax was the business to get into. Shortly, Philander was back again with Leander and a report that they had come across another likely looking mountain on the edge of the Amargosa Desert. The white surface looked almost like quartz, they said— apparently a whole hill of hard, glittering stuff. If it was borax, there was enough of it to upset the whole industry.

Smith's chemists decided, indeed, that it was borax—borate of lime—differing from the cottonball borate of soda principally in the way it would have to be recovered and refined. Smith grabbed it, called the new borate "colemanite" in honor of his former partner, and named the deposit Lila C, in honor of some mystery-shrouded maiden. The mad Lees were altering Smith's life and giving an entirely new complexion to an infant industry. Soon there would be no further need for grubbing cottonball from the desert floor, boiling and crystalizing it. Neither Smith nor anyone else had ever fancied that borate existed in such volume.

He organized the Pacific Coast Borax Company, then decided his pet industry had the makings of an international business. A distinguished British promoter, "Lord" Richard C. Baker, was invited to come to California and look over the prospects. He came, and Borax Consolidated, Ltd. was born, and a huge refining plant was erected at Alameda, ready to supply England and Europe, as well as America.

With the same aggressive fight he had used in taking over Teel's Marsh in Nevada, he went on the road to sell Twenty Mule Team Borax to the world. Two decades earlier this product of Death Valley had been a little-known drug. Smith was making it a cheap commercial necessity, essential to the biggest industries of the world, and he was about to put a box of it—with his Twenty Mule Team label—on a shelf in every kitchen cabinet.

BORAX—Twenty Mule Team Brand! blazoned the early advertisements in full-page display, designed to bring romance to the soap dish and the laundry tub. "Across the alkali desert of the Great West, a distance of 165 miles, through the hot, dry dust, with the temperature at 135° to 150°, comes the great Twenty Mule Team hauling the giant load of crude Borax to the nearest shipping point.

"Borax in the past and present ages has stood as the greatest cleanser, detergent and solvent known to the civilized world.

Many so-called Borax Laundry Soaps or Soap Chips contain little if any BORAX, and they fail in their supposed mission. The TWENTY MULE TEAM BRAND contains a large per cent of Borax and, combined with pure soap, works wonders. This combination washes clean and, on account of its hygienic and sanitary properties, leaves the clothes thoroughly disinfected and produces that soft and fluffy feeling to the linen, so much desired.

"Softens the hardest water, washes colored and white goods alike, and for woolens and flannels it cannot be surpassed. This soap is manufactured on scientific principles and EVERY POUND IS KILN DRIED. A STARTLING REVOLUTION TO THE LAUNDRY TRADE. Economy and Labor Saving for the Housewife. Pacific Coast Borax Company. New York, San Francisco, Chicago."

In 1885 less than 1,000 tons of borax were produced in California; fifteen years later the output had jumped to 25,837 tons. The discovery of a still finer grade of colmanite in the Calico Mountains, 8 miles from a railroad, rather than 165, once more radically altered the business. Death Valley was temporarily abandoned and the mining town of Borate came into existence.

Along with other improvements, attempts were made to substitute steampowered tractors for mules, to haul the crude from mine to rail siding. Skinners and swampers brayed their protest, but the objections were premature. On the level, a tractor could draw a whole train of wagons; on an incline, the wheezing engine came to a halt, bucked like a bronco, and sat there churning a hole with its powerful wheels. The mule teams had to work overtime just keeping the monster out of trouble. It was soon given up as a bad job and the twenty-mule teams went back to work in triumph.

What Smith needed was a railroad, and enough money was made on the colemanite of the Calico Mountains to build one—the Tonopah and Tidewater. Three million dollars went into that line which ran to the gates of Death Valley and on up the Amargosa River. But principally it was laid to tap the inexhaustible supply of borate in the Lila C, brought to light by the Lee brothers.

Macadam highway later replaced the rails, and a richer ore called rasorite—found in the Mojave Desert at Kramer—replaced the colemanite of Lila C. The days of twenty-mule teaming were done, but the famous label stayed put on the package.

And, alas, there was not a room in any household in America that did not display some souvenir from the realm of the Borax King. The touch of $Na_2B_4O_710 H_2O$ was on the walls, on the bathroom fixtures, on any photograph, in glassware, textiles or leather, in cosmetics and in the soap dish, in the magazine rack, on the kitchen pots and pans—even in the garage and the tool shed. One could not escape the stuff. In one disguise or another that symbol of the California desert was so commonplace that it was within sight or contact of almost every civilized man.

VI

WE DON'T PRAY FOR RAIN, WE USE THE TELEPHONE

THE marvel of Furnace Creek, more conspicuous than the Harmony Works and the big borax wagons, was its spot of verdure. Here in the middle of an expanse of glaring white was an incongruous field of green. Newcomers approached it warily, expecting an illusion to dissolve in the shimmering air. But it did not fade; the greenery was no mirage. It was real and it was man made.

In this unlikely place were rows of young palms and lacy tamarisks through which the hot desert winds whistled, and acre upon acre of rank grass and alfalfa. Horses and cattle grazed in the fields as contentedly as in San Joaquin Valley, and wonder of wonders, there were birds—flocks of quail echoing their metallic calls across the tropical silence.

Altogether the idyllic oasis was no larger than twenty-five or thirty acres, but, like everything else in the desert where proportions were optically exaggerated, it appeared far more extensive. It even had a name—Greenland.

Greenland was originally the creation of a quixotic fugitive called Tex Bennett, who set up housekeeping for himself in 1870, the first full-time resident of Death Valley. Tex did not like company and he did not like to have people poke into his past. A double-barreled shotgun was his constant companion, and anyone indiscreet enough to make a chance inquiry into his biography was introduced to the companion. Its leveled nozzles usually hurried such interrogators on their way.

Whom Bennett was escaping, and what, never came to light.

It was assumed that even his name was just another alias. Rumor had it that he was a deserter from the Confederate Army, and other rumors, no less reliable, marked him as an escapee from various vigilance committees. That he was the "baddest of the bad men" no one doubted, nor did anyone doubt that there were very damaging charges against him on the record somewhere.

He was a robustious specimen whose physical power was eclipsed only by his lung power. When in good form his voice carried clear across Death Valley, and he was rarely out of form. In his solitude, people alleged that he talked to himself a great deal, and he never modulated his voice, even then. Most folks kept their distance from him, so undoubtedly the observations were well founded. In any case, he soon lost the Bennett alias and was known in the desert country only as "Bellerin' Teck."

For a few years before the coming of Coleman and Borax Smith, Bellerin' Teck claimed ownership of all Death Valley. The voice, the shotgun and a substantial reserve of good United States currency kept the kingdom inviolate. But he had one weakness, a tender love for all things that grew. Drawing on his backlog of ill-begotten currency and the energy of roving Piutes, he proceeded to convert the center of his domain into a kind of Arabian oasis.

Through Furnace Creek—the place—ran a sparkling brook of the same name, fed by never-failing springs in Furnace Creek Wash. With little diversion ditches leading off from the stream, he irrigated the sand and silt of the flat lands. To his delight the surface turned green. Then he directed the runoff into a hollow and delighted himself more with the sight of a pond.

Satisfied that anything would grow there, he made long, cautious shopping trips to civilization to purchase seed and plants. When he lacked the courage to face humanity himself he hired Indians to go in his stead. In return for his generous handouts of trinkets and trifles the Indians rewarded him with a gardenful of plants, shrubs, palm shoots and captured birds. They brought the quail.

Teck had a rare green thumb. For him everything grew miraculously, defiantly. The fertility of the soil in this chosen spot, surrounded by naked hills, amazed him. Overlooking his little pond, he built himself an adobe house, added a wide veranda, and could sit on it in peace, surveying his tiny green world and the bigger dry one beyond.

But playing God in the wilderness of sand was no good for a man who had to keep out of sight. Inevitably his creation drew attention. Wayfarers were not common in those parts, but a few were a lot too many. One day a somber Mormon named Jackson came along, driving a yoke of oxen. Jackson was an escapist, too, and he proposed a partnership. To Teck the oxen looked better than their owner. They were just what he needed for his growing ranch. The landlord kept his gun out of sight, did some quick thinking, and finally reckoned that he'd let the Mormon stay.

The partnership lasted less than a week. In that time Jackson had exhausted all other subjects of conversation and made the innocent mistake of probing into his host's past. The voice rose a pitch higher than usual, the shotgun came out of hiding, and the Mormon took off for Beatty—without his oxen, glad to save his hide and gladder to get out of earshot of Bellerin' Teck.

Then the Lee brothers, a whole fraternity of escapists, began haunting Furnace Creek more and more often, with their occasional wives, assorted children, flocks and herds. Alone, Teck was no match for Philander, Salamander, Meander, Alexander and Leander, alias Cub. They were too tenacious and trigger happy themselves to be scared off by a shotgun and a long-shot voice. An obnoxious Indian guide named Hungry Bill also made himself at home every now and then on the outskirts of Bennett's preserve, and the owner dared not incur the wrath of Hungry's fellow tribesmen by putting him out of the way.

In 1875 some government men, seven of them, under a Lieutenant Rogers Birnie, spent two months as unwelcome guests while surveying the valley. And the same year a borax prospector, Isadore Daunet, with a party of five, retreating from the abandoned mining town of Panamint, came through. Furnace Creek was getting too populated for Bellerin' Teck's peace of mind. He retired from his lovely acres and disappeared as unobtrusively as he had come.

Greenland lost some of its greenery without a caretaker, but there was enough of it left to look inviting to Borax Smith when he took up residence in 1882. Under the supervision of the Harmony management the irrigation ditches were dug deeper, the fields were plowed again, replanted with barley, alfalfa and vegetables, and kept their verdancy as long as the borax harvesters remained at Furnace Creek.

The oasis that Tex Bennett established in Death Valley was symbolic of scores of similar desert ranches springing up on the periphery of California's dry lands and at the water holes along the thoroughfares crossing the Mojave and Colorado deserts. No sooner was a stage station in operation than someone was planting a tree in the front yard or spading soil and experimenting with seeds in the back yard.

If there was no stream that could be diverted into the garden, tenants followed the example of the Indians or Mexicans and carried the water. Westward-bound emigrants took with them an agricultural urge as irrepressible as their migratory urge. Farming was in their bones; wherever they paused they had to plant. And the desert could be no exception. Few people had any intention of remaining for long in a dry spot unless they could coax to life a plot of grass, a fruit tree or a row of onions.

Bellerin' Teck's desert planting was no innovation. There were green thumbs, even among California's forty-niners, among the Mexicans before them and the Spanish padres before the Mexicans. Vast areas of seasonal or fringe desert east of Los Angeles were converted into productive land through the efforts of the Catholic fathers. San Diego, driest of the missions, as early as 1770 projected an irrigation system that was to serve as a model in other settlements for decades. And on the opposite side of the desert similar experiments were tried near Yuma and at other places along the Colorado.

Following the Mexican take-over and the secularization of the missions in the 1830's, the ranches generally went to ruin, ditches disintegrated and efforts to conquer the desert ceased. But it was a short interim. With the annexation of California the battle against the dry lands was renewed where the padres left off. Thousands of acres in the regions of Anaheim, Pasadena and Riverside were quickly brought back into productivity. Plots of greenery broadened here and there along the Mojave River. Mormon colonists, intent on extending the boundaries of Zion, established oases on the trail from Salt Lake to San Bernardino.

Samuel Blythe staked off a ranch at one of the few spots along the deep canyons of the Colorado where water could be turned into the land by gravity ditches. He started irrigating crops in the Palo Verde Valley and soon had a green settlement worthy of bearing the family name.

Some of the most ambitious plans for reclamation of arid

lands were in Owens Valley, "The Land of Little Rain." Men dreamed of transforming the whole expanse of this marginal desert into verdant fields, and there was plenty of water for the job. In the sixties and seventies an impressive network of irrigation ditches was laid out in the valley.

Forty miles north of Bishop was the little town of Laws. There, private capital and a great deal of volunteer labor went into a modest canal carrying water from Fish Slough to hundreds of fertile acres. In the same area also was the McNally Ditch. Serving tracts between Bishop and the Owens River was the Bishop Creek Ditch. The Owens River and Big Pine Canal watered the lands of Big Pine. Later came still more ambitious projects like the Owens River and the Inyo Canals to irrigate farms as far south as Lone Pine.

In those days Owens Valley was considered one of the most promising regions of the state, predestined soon to vie in productivity with the more thickly populated valleys west of the mountains. Inyo was the county with a future. In 1883 it even got a railroad of sorts, a narrow-gauge line, zigzagging down from the outskirts of Reno, Nevada, through the borax works of Teel's Marsh and Columbus, to Keeler on Owens Lake. "Carson and Colorado" was the high-sounding name conferred upon these toy tracks, and for years the line was to bear the brunt of all the inglorious gibes generally expended on rural railroading.

"The tourist who travels in the car of the Carson and Colorado Railroad is not unlikely to wonder which is the more interesting, the road or the desert region," suggested tongue-in-cheek *Sun* correspondent John R. Spears. "He is not unlikely to wonder, too, what the road was built for. The Carson and Colorado is in one respect unique and in several respects remarkable. It does not start at Carson, neither does it terminate in Colorado nor at the Colorado River.

"Its initial point is an arid mountain side, so arid, indeed, that water for use in the little settlement there has to be imported in big tank cars for the purpose; the road runs thence 300 miles across a desert to terminate at a sal-soda lake in California. The settlement at one end is known as Mound House, Ormsby County, Nevada. That at the other is Keeler on Owens Lake, Inyo County, California.

"A passenger train, a freight train and a milk train run each way every day, but in order to economize, one engine is made to pull all three. The passenger train includes one coach and a combined smoker, mail, milk, baggage and express car. It is a short train. There were five passengers in all on mine, besides a newsboy, whom the conductor called Peanuts. Peanuts carried a bundle of San Francisco newspapers one day old, a basket of red apples and a box of Chinatown cigars. By the time we reached Cleaver, he had sold two newspapers and one apple and smoked one of his own cigars.

"There are very likely other interesting features of this road, but I mention only two. Both are remarkable. The Carson and Colorado has throughout its entire length of 300 miles a population all told of less than six thousand people to draw traffic from; the Carson and Colorado managers are able to pay running expenses."

But if the railroad could not bring prosperity to Owens Valley, irrigation and agriculture would. Everyone in Inyo County had faith in the future. With faith, hope and water all things were possible. And in 1903, when Owens Valley was selected by the new National Reclamation Service as one of the most promising areas in the nation for experimental development, things never looked rosier to the Inyoites.

They welcomed the government engineers with community celebrations; for the greater good of all, agreed to surrender water rights previously held by private organizations; endorsed proposals for storage dams and plans for running "high-line" canals along the foothills on either side of the valley, with laterals for proper distribution.

There was enough water to reclaim practically all the untilled land in the valley, claimed the government experts. Moreover, the cost estimates demonstrated that the Owens Valley project promised "greater results for the necessary investments than any other federal project that had been completed or that was then under study." The Inyo farmers were sitting pretty—or thought they were.

It never crossed their minds that bigwigs in the city of Los Angeles, 240 miles away, were talking greedily about stealing the bountiful Owens River, that the reclamation officials had two irons in the fire, or that the superb system of high-line canals would never be more than pretty designs on paper.

Meantime, a stirring call to action in transforming an even larger desert area into ranch land was being sounded 300 miles to the southeast. In comparison to this, the grand visions of the Inyo rustics were humble indeed. Down on the Mexican border land speculators were considering the possibility of converting millions of worthless acres of the Colorado Desert into a Garden of Eden—an oasis to stop all oases, the biggest desert reclamation ever attempted. In fact, wild-eyed visionaries had been considering it for a long time—rather quietly. To avoid being laughed at they had learned the advantages of not airing their ideas too publicly.

The spark had been set aglow back in 1853 by William P. Blake, a young geologist just out of Yale Scientific School, who discovered the wonders of a huge, dry lake called the Salton Sink. At the time he was accompanying a group of topographic engineers on an expedition to find a practical railroad route to the Pacific Coast. But his interest in railroads was soon superseded by his fascination with the Salton Sink and its surroundings.

It was geologist Blake who first translated into words the autobiography written through the ages by the rambling Colorado River on the rocks, the mountainsides and desert floor of Southern California. He was the first to perceive that the Sink had once been an arm of the Pacific, that the great river formerly emptied into the Sink, and then—in building its delta toward the head of the Gulf of California—had isolated the arm and left it to dry out and turn into a desert almost 300 feet below sea level.

He observed that the silt-laden Colorado, constantly raising its bed and banks with sediment, was now rolling to the Gulf on self-imposed layers of silt, high above the adjacent country. He saw, too, how easy it would be for the river to break through its levees and once more sweep into the lowlands. And carrying the principle further, he realized that it would be relatively easy for man to make a controlled cut in the banks and simply let the water into the desert to bring it to bloom.

The floor of the Sink was not mere sterile sand; it was rich silt brought by the river and its many tributaries from Arizona, Utah, Colorado and Wyoming. "Why," he exclaimed, "the desert could be made to yield crops of almost any kind."

He said it too openly and too often. His theory was soon good for a guffaw anywhere in the West. The crazy young upstart of a scientist thought he could alter the handiwork of the Lord, did he!

Blake had a strong hankering to stay in California and give his critics a chance to retract their cynicism, but at the moment he was committed to the government and railroading, and when the surveys were completed he went on to a distinguished career as explorer and mining engineer in Alaska, Japan and other parts of the world where people laughed less easily at his ideas.

Dr. Oliver M. Wozencraft of San Francisco was one of those who did not laugh at Blake. He was neither a geologist nor an engineer, but he had imagination, money and important friends in both Sacramento and Washington. As a successful forty-niner, he had cast his lot with the rooters for boom-state California, and one of his pilgrimages from the East had taken him across the Colorado Desert. Blake's theories made sense to him. Agricultural miracles could be wrought in the Salton Sink.

To satisfy his own curiosity and to check on Blake, he talked the surveyor for the County of San Diego into looking over the situation and making a detailed report to prove or disprove the feasibility of Blake's scheme.

Not only was it practical, declared the surveyor after a few months of study and field work, it was highly desirable. He went so far as to recommend an exact canal location. The Colorado could be tapped just above the international boundary line at a point of rocks near Pilot Knob. He proposed a canal 25 feet wide and 10 feet deep, dipping down into Mexico for a considerable distance, to circumvent the sand hills on the American side. By actual survey charts he showed that there was a fall of 5 feet per mile along the entire route. There was no question about it, claimed the surveyor, hundreds of thousands of desert acres could be converted into the richest farmland in California.

Wozencraft was satisfied, so satisfied that he boldly took his plan to the Legislature in 1859. The California lawmakers caught his enthusiasm and promptly adopted a memorial to Congress, asking for a cession of 3,000,000 acres of desert in southeastern California for reclamation by irrigation.

In 1859 and '60 Washington had more pressing concerns than wild schemes for salvaging sands 3,000 miles away. When the memorandum was finally brought out of the legislative hopper, it drew a few jocular remarks and was irreverently referred to the Committee on Public Lands. Not until 1862, when the country was head over heels in civil strife, did the committee get around to taking action. It recommended that the request be granted. But the House felt otherwise. A few days after receiving the recommendation, it was rejected summarily.

Wozencraft did not give up. To everyone else, watering the Salton Sink was a lost cause after the Congressional rebuff, but not to Wozencraft. He kept talking and talking. With the devotion of a fanatic, he talked about little else for forty years, until the Salton Sink was accepted as the subject for a good jest in California as well as in the East.

Journalist J. Ross Browne drove across the desert, after listening to the doctor, and joined in the jesting. "Doctor O. M. Wozencraft has spent many years in advancing this great measure," he slyly remarked. "The plan of irrigation proposed by him is generally ridiculed as impracticable, and the doctor enjoys rather a visionary reputation based upon his Grand Colorado Scheme, which has been compared by unthinking people with the Great South Sea Bubble.

"I don't intend to establish a farm there myself until the canal is completed, but still I see no great obstacle to success except the porous nature of the sand. By removing the sand from the desert, success would be assured at once."

But on sober second thought Browne admitted that "Extensive belts of rich soil, which irrigation would render productive, occupy a large portion of the country. In these are seen the evidences of sudden and extraordinary vegetable growth in seasons of abundant rain or when the Colorado River overflows its banks. Proofs are not wanting that Montezumas and early Spaniards redeemed extensive ranges of country that would otherwise have remained valueless."

With his persistent preachment Wozencraft helped to defeat his own cause, principally by inspiring crackpot opponents to argue against him. "There has been a great deal of talk the last few years about turning water upon the desert and cutting it up in forty-acre ranches." summarized a typical antagonist. "It should not be done. There is no doubt but that the preternatural productiveness of California is due to the warm air of its surrounding deserts. They furnish health to the human being and strength to the plant. *The desert should not be reclaimed.* The sink or depression in Death Valley is probably the greatest heat generator in the world. It has a great influence in producing dry air. To turn this desert into an agricultural district would increase humidity that would practically nullify the finest air on the continent. Good air and climate are as essential to the human body as proper nutriment."

Famed naturalist John C. Van Dyke joined the dissenters. He was dead set against any kind of tampering with the desert. He wanted it left just as was. "The simplest in form and the finest in color is by all odds the most beautiful." He sighed. "It is owing to just these features that this Bowl of desert is a thing of beauty instead of a dreary hollow in the hills. It might be thought that this forsaken pot-hole in the ground would never come under the dominion of man, that its very worthlessness would be its safeguard against civilization, that none would want it, and everyone from necessity would let it alone.

"But not even the spot deserted by reptiles shall escape the industry and avarice of man. It is said a million acres of desert will be made arable, fitted for homesteads, ready for the settler who never remains settled.

"A laudable enterprise, people will say. Yes; commercially no one can find fault with it. Money made from sand is likely to be clean money, at any rate. And economically these acres may produce large supplies of food. And yet the food produced may prove expensive to people other than the producers. This old sea-bed is for this area probably the greatest dry-heat generator in the world, because of its depression and its barren sandy surface. It is a furnace that whirls heat up and out of the Bowl, over the peaks of the Coast Range into Southern California."

Then, as evidence that there was a common source of anti-irrigation literature somewhere, Van Dyke topped off his attack with the familiar refrain: "To turn the desert into an agricultural tract would be to increase humidity, and that would be to nullify the finest air on the continent. How is the water supply, from an economic and hygienic standpoint, any more important than the air supply? The deserts are not worthless wastes. You cannot crop all creation with wheat and alfalfa. The deserts should never be reclaimed. They are the breathing-spaces of the West and should be preserved forever."

Aligned against the desert dilettantes who bitterly opposed any human rearrangement of the sands was still another group of insurgents who despised the place and wanted to do away with it altogether—drown it out of existence. Their chief spokesman was a retired army surgeon, Dr. J. D. Widney. He managed to sell the editors of *Overland* on his exciting dogma.

Widney spearheaded a back-to-primeval-nature movement. Here in the Salton Sink, he pointed out, was a parched area, 180 miles long and thirty or more wide, that had been covered by a beautiful body of water. Let's flip back the pages of the geologic calendar and restore the lake, said he. The restoration would cure all the climatic ills of the southlands.

The evaporation from the lake, according to his computations, would be sufficient to supply twelve inches of rain annually to 86,400 square miles—an area more than double the size of the state of Ohio. Moreover, the rain and the lake would lower appreciably the temperature of the adjacent territory, which in turn would add to the general rainfall of the West by "increasing the condensation of vapor."

The drop in temperature and the "augmented dampness of the atmosphere" could work miracles on the relief map of California. No telling, the Mojave Desert could turn green, forests would sprout on treeless mountains, the new upland woods would give birth to tumbling brooks and rivers. It would be like Genesis all over again.

"Can the Colorado Desert be filled with water?" he asked rhetorically.

"Yes," he answered with expansive reassurance, "simply by turning the Colorado River into the Salton Sink." The irrigation plan did not go far enough. He would divert the whole river into the desert and let nature do the rest.

Dr. Widney made his first proposals in January 1873. He gathered under his banner a great many noisy disciples, and in the background an equal number of hooting critics. Undismayed by all the commotion, year after year he and his followers kept pouring out their persiflage—as persistently as Wozencraft and Van Dyke poured theirs.

Thirty-three years later, in June 1906, it looked as though Dr. Widney was going to win the argument—not through superior oratory or article writing, but through a slight engineering miscalculation down on the border. Nature and the Colorado River seemed suddenly to have taken sides and chosen J. D. Widney as their partisan. The dream of a sweeping oasis in the Colorado Desert was fading fast that spring, and bookmakers rated the odds about twenty to one in favor of a Salton Sea rather than a green Salton Sink.

The Colorado was on a wild rampage, and in the judgment of almost anyone except the clique of Dr. Widney, the greatest natural disaster in the history of the Southwest was in the making. The entire flow of the river—100,000 cubic feet a second, 8½ billion cubic feet every twenty-four hours—was surging over a break in the banks and rushing into the desert.

A week earlier the crevasse had been only a few hundred feet wide, now it was more than half a mile. The water cascaded down, spread out over an area of 8 or 10 square miles, then collected into separate streams as it ran down the slope of the historic basin.

Under water were thousands of acres of cultivated land in newly created Imperial Valley, and thousands more were so eroded and corrugated by the torrential streams that they would never again be cultivated. At every bend in the runaway river's course a curling brown current flung itself against high banks of silt and sand, dissolving them as if the soil was sugar, undermining the surface and toppling globs of earth as big as barns into the raging flood.

The works of New Liverpool Salt Company were under 60 feet of water. Miles of the Southern Pacific tracks had been carried away or were deeply submerged. The Salton Sink was rapidly becoming the Salton Sea, rising at a rate of seven inches a day over an area of 400 square miles.

The flood tended to veer into two main channels, the former dry streambeds or barrancas of the so-called New and Alamo rivers. Both discharged into the Salton Sink. And the channels in these old beds posed the worst threat of all. The water was gouging deeper and deeper. A cataract had formed at the mouth of the New River on the edge of the Salton Sea, and through the cutting action of the flood the brink of a twenty-foot waterfall was steadily moving upstream toward the border towns and farm settlements, widening massively as it went. If it ever reached the bed of the Colorado itself, all hope of stopping the madcap river would be gone.

As the waterfall approached Calexico and Mexicali its height increased to 30 and 40 feet—an astonishing phenomenon. The banks were being undercut and the channel widened by the hour. It looked as though both towns were doomed. Native families were fleeing the onslaught. Stunned spectators watched in fascination and horror as monumental hunks of earth broke away and

plummeted into the river, throwing up clouds of dust and spume.

In Mexicali they saw house after house tremble, teeter and then crash down the embankment, to be caught up in the swirl and carried out of sight in a flash. Larger buildings crumpled section by section. They stood on the banks with bared bedrooms and kitchens one minute, and the next were rumbling out of sight into the maelstrom below.

"What the devil are you doing to stop this?" demanded a furious railroad superintendent as he stepped off a train to see his chief engineer lounging in the shade of the Southern Pacific station at Calexico.

"Not a God-damned thing," replied the engineer testily. He had seen enough of the power of the Colorado that morning to realize that he might as well surrender to the inevitable. "Got any suggestions?" he asked, after surveying the scene with his superior.

The superintendent looked over the edge of the embankment and decided he had none. A few minutes later the two stood back to watch the station collapse and slide over the bank. A brick hotel soon followed the station.

Dynamite was the only weapon with which the mighty stream was being fought there. If the cataract could be deepened to lower the level of the floodwaters, its spread might be lessened. Guided by lines from either bank, rafts loaded with dynamite and long-spitting fuses were launched and the charges exploded over the lip of the waterfall. Under the shock, monstrous blocks of riverbed peeled away and spectacular showers of water and debris were catapulted high into the air. The maneuver worked; the flood was dropping into a fifty-foot chasm when the falls finally crept past Mexicali and Calexico. The generous use of dynamite saved all the streets back from the river's edge.

Up near El Centro the torrent broke through the levee of the main canal, putting the streets of Imperial under a foot of water, drowning nearby farmland, and threatening much wider devastation. But the population there fought back fiercely. Slogging through the water, they gathered all the gunny sacks that could be found in stores, sheds and pantries, filled them with sand, and toted them to the breach. Working around the clock, crews of men packed sandbags and brush matting into the sides of the rift, laboriously narrowing it—while their women frantically sewed more bags out of old petticoats and tenting cloth. On the third day they finally plugged the break and saved most of the outlying farms.

West of Imperial there was a different kind of trouble. Wooden flumes which carried irrigation water over the New River barranca had been swept into the Salton Sea, leaving 30,000 acres of cultivated land high and dry. No water was almost as bad as too much.

From as far away as Volcano Lake, deep in the delta country of Mexico, word came that the lake was overflowing, swiftly spilling northward to the border and driving homeless Mexican families before it.

But the most alarming menace continued to be the cutting back of those cataracts, sometimes almost halting, sometimes moving at a rate of 4,000 feet a day. If they reached an irrigation main, the whole river might be directed into Imperial Valley and in days it could be enveloped, eroded and utterly destroyed.

The Southern Pacific engineer had sized up the situation about right: locally a few protective measures might be taken, but as long as the river was in full flood there was not a thing they could do to stop it. Heavy flooding usually lasted through June and July. It might be another month before the engineers could launch an effective attack. Meantime, the river was rolling into Salton Sink, and the prehistoric Salton Sea that Dr. Widney doted on so effusively was in the process of being recreated.

A crowd of events had set the stage for this magnificent drama. Wrangling over the destiny of the desert tapered off in the early 1890's. The notion of taking over the Salton Sink as a state irrigation project was dropped, so a group of promoters took advantage of the lull and went to work under the corporate title of California Irrigation Company. As technical assistant they hired a young giant of an engineer with broad shoulders, a long stride and a bulldog appearance—Charles R. Rockwood—and sent him to Yuma to make actual surveys for a ditch running from the Colorado to the Sink.

Rockwood plunged into the job and in a few weeks convinced himself that, if anything, his employers were underestimating the worth of their project. He marked off a canal route almost 50 miles long, following closely the tentative course set by the San Diego surveyor years before, except that he went 12 miles farther upstream for an intake at Potholes.

Rockwood, too, wanted to avoid the line of sand hills in the southeast corner of California, so he blueprinted a long, sweeping curve across the border into Mexico, paralleled the course of the Colorado until the ancient overflow channel of the Alamo River was reached. That channel formed a natural ditch all the way to the Sink; it would merely have to be re-excavated here and there, realigned and re-enforced with a few levees. The whole plan was feasible, and taking into consideration the million acres the ditch would reclaim, it was bound to be a paying proposition for the company. They could create a great oasis, the like of which had never been attempted anywhere in the world.

But no sooner had Rockwood submitted his plans than he learned how poor his employers were. They could not begin to back their enthusiasm with the necessary funds; they could not even pay his engineering fees. The California Irrigation Company went into bankruptcy two years after it was incorporated, and, in lieu of salary for services rendered, the bulldog engineer was paid off with the surveys, records and data he had compiled.

Disgusted with his patrons, but still sold on the prospect of reclaiming a million or more acres of silt and sand, Rockwood took off for New York to start a fund-raising campaign of his own. For five years he plugged for the potential wonders of the Salton Sink—the new subtropical garden.

But Wall Street was not interested. How on earth, scoffed the capitalists, could anything be made to grow in an arid, alkali desert where there were only two inches of rainfall in a year and where the thermometer in the summer commonly registered 120°? No sane farmer could be induced to work in such a climate. Even if the land was watered, cultivated and planted, the alkali would come up and kill the crops.

Disregarding both the derision and the apathy, Rockwood proceeded to incorporate the California Development Company in 1896—not in New York or California, but in New Jersey. Two years later his bait was snapped at. For a few weeks it appeared that his canal project was assured. He needed only a few signatures to back up golden promises. But, three days before the checks and the contracts were to be signed, the *Maine* was blown up in Havana Harbor. The United States was at war; the deal was off.

The stubborn promoter was ready to forget about the Salton Sink and the Colorado when support suddenly came from an unexpected quarter. The world-famous land reclamationist, George Chaffey—now an old man, but crowned with honors for plotting enormously successful irrigation projects in the West and as far away as Australia—was interested in the California desert. "Let me do one more big thing before I die," he pleaded to those who tried to steer him away from such a wildcat venture.

Rockwood rushed back to California and threw the reins to Chaffey. Events began to tick off with phenomenal speed. Chaffey accepted the presidency of the California Development Company and readily poured his own funds into the project. He eliminated twelve miles from the length of the canal by proposing that the cut into the banks of the Colorado be made at Pilot Knob, nearly opposite Yuma, instead of farther north. Aside from that, Rockwood's plans were virtually undisturbed.

In addition to heading the company, he agreed to serve as chief engineer, and on April 3, 1900, signed a contract binding himself to construct the main canal and some 400 miles of side ditches for $150,000. It was a bargain. Labor and equipment were quickly assembled and they went to work.

"Half our trouble," fretted Chaffey, when the job was well along, "is the picture people have of a sandy inferno, alkali flats, a salt-layered sink and barren, ugly desert. Let's forget 'Salton Sink' and give the place a pleasant name. Call it a valley. Something like—ah! *Imperial Valley.*"

And from that day on, Imperial Valley it was.

The development company was organized to supply water only. Needed immediately was an organization to tell the world about Imperial Valley and its impending blessings, to excite Easterners and Westerners alike into a new land rush—an advertising and sales agency. With a closely interlocking directorate, the Imperial Land Company sprang into existence, and while the dredges and mule-drawn scoops were hard at work on the canal channel Chaffey and his corps of salesmen were just as busy hawking their stock.

STOP! THINK! ACT! cried the fliers and full-page newspaper advertisements across the country. "There are thousands of people who have money to invest and who are looking for investments. There are thousands of others who would be glad to put a little money where it would do the most good. The attention of both is called to the rapid development now in progress in the settlement of 500,000 acres of land under the Imperial Canal

System in the eastern part of San Diego County, California.

"This settlement is no boom proposition. It is founded on the largest and most fertile tract of irrigable land to be found in arid America. The Imperial Canal System is what its name indicates—the most abundant supply of water that can be used for irrigation purposes in America.

"Not only is the water abundant, but it is cheap. Experience shows that 500,000 acres of such land, when under irrigation, will support a population of 150,000 upwards. Such a population must support and maintain at least one city of metropolitan proportions and several cities of less magnitude—from 5,000 to 10,000 people each.

"THIS IS NO DREAM. Look over Southern California and see what it has done. What has been done must be done again under similar conditions. The Imperial Land Company has plotted three town sites: Imperial, Paringo and Calexico. One of these towns will become a large city. All will become cities. A judicious investment in any one of them will return manifold profits.

"The policy of the Imperial Land Company is to give early investors a chance to make *Big Money*. We want to interest thousands of people financially in the Imperial settlements, because the more are interested, the better it is for the investors as well as for the prospectors of the water system and the town sites.

"For further particulars apply to Imperial Land Company, A. H. Heber, General Manager, Stowell Block, Los Angeles, California."

To people as far away as Portland, Oregon; Elgin, Illinois; Concord, Massachusetts; Toronto, Canada; Portsmouth, New Hampshire; and Montpelier, Vermont, the advertisements sounded wonderful. They answered in throngs and came to dry Imperial Valley in throngs, bought stock, bought land.

A year almost to the day after the ditchdigging started, headgates at Pilot Knob were raised and water from the Colorado rolled down the 40-mile jugular vein into the arteries that carried life to 100,000 desert acres. In days the dry land turned green. The oasis was a magnificent success. Plowmen were already in the fields. Tent cities blossomed at Imperial, Calexico, Brawley, Holtville and El Centro, and as fast as mule teams could bring in lumber and mortar, the canvas shelters were replaced with frame and adobe homes.

Not since forty-nine and the gold rush had anyone seen the

like. In 1900 there was not a single civilized resident in Imperial Valley; by December 1901, 1,500 were living there. The population jumped to 2,000 in 1902; 7,000 in 1903; 10,000 in 1904. That was the year when the Southern Pacific realized that Imperial Valley was no fly-by-night promotion scheme and built a spur into the heart of the booming area. It was also the year when another 200 miles of ditch had to be dug to take care of all the demands. More than 300,000 acres were under cultivation.

Vineyards were producing superior harvests. Melons, lettuce, beets, carrots and tomatoes matured months ahead of the northern crops and commanded premium prices. Alfalfa could be cut five or six times a year. The finest quality of Egyptian cotton yielded more than a 500-pound bale to an acre. And early experiments showed that the soil was well adapted to the cultivation of grapefruit, oranges, lemons, olives, figs, dates, pomegranates, apricots, peaches and pears.

But statistics did not tell the whole story. The California Development Company could not hide the fact that it was faced with formidable troubles which were mounting month by month. Chaffey had withdrawn in 1902, as soon as he had done "one more big thing" to his complete satisfaction; and bulldog Rockwood was back in the saddle as chief engineer. Most of the difficulties were referred to him for solution.

At first the most exasperating enemy seemed to be the United States Government. In 1902 the Bureau of Soils had sent in a team of experts to analyze the soil. After making careful studies, the scientists pontifically declared the land was so deeply impregnated with alkali that it was absolutely impossible to grow anything but a few crops like sorghum, sugar beets and perhaps date palms, "if the climate will permit." They implied that thousands of investors had been swindled and recommended that the worthless lands be abandoned at once.

The farmers on the spot could laugh at the experts. The very fruits and vegetables which the Department of Agriculture claimed could not be produced in Imperial Valley were growing rankly and yielding highly profitable crops. But the report did not sit well with investors in Toronto, Concord, Massachusetts, or Montpelier, Vermont, who could not see what was actually taking place in the valley. Eventually the Bureau of Soils was compelled to retract the report, but it was too late to repair all the damage it had done.

Next, authorities in Washington discovered that the original federal survey of the area was inaccurate and defective. The homestead entries which settlers had made in good faith were declared invalid until the Salton Sink could be resurveyed and boundaries redefined. That could take years, and meantime the farmers held no legal titles to the land for purposes of mortgage or sale.

Then the Reclamation Service stepped in to inform the development company that it was taking water illegally from the Colorado River. The rights to all that water were under the sole jurisdiction of the federal government, and Uncle Sam could not spare any of it for irrigating Imperial Valley. That was too much to take. The company all but literally thumbed its corporate nose at Uncle Sam and went to Mexico City for permission to tap the same water on the Mexican side of the border.

Foreign bureaucrats were less hostile than Washington bureaucrats, but they were also slower. The application was made in September 1904; official authorization was not received until December 1905. Meantime, the company was told unofficially that no objections would be raised if the Colorado was tapped.

Rockwood went ahead, and soon regretted it. He ordered the cut made four miles south of the border. In the middle of the river at that point was an island, half a mile long and a quarter wide, which he thought might prove useful in controlling the swift currents. It proved otherwise.

Digging the opening and making connections with the original canal was a simple proposition. A bank intake sixty feet wide was adequate, and the distance to the existing irrigation canal was only a little over half a mile, all through material that could be dredged easily. The whole job took less than three weeks.

He thought twice about breaking into the bank without first erecting a heading that could be closed in case of a severe flood, but he had before him the twenty-seven-year history of the river, as recorded at Yuma, and in the light of that record, construction of a protective gate was unnecessary. If worst came to worst, the break could be blocked readily in flood season, with brush mats and sandbags.

The new intake actually served a double purpose. Besides getting the company out of a jam with the federal government for stealing American water, it eliminated the necessity of dredging the four miles of canal below the original intake at Pilot

Knob. In three years of operation that section had become so clogged with silt that it did not carry enough water to the system in dry seasons, and the company had been sued time and again for failure to deliver guaranteed footage. The Mexican cut was completed late in September 1904. It solved the most pressing problems that confronted Rockwood—for almost five months.

Early the following February the first big flood of 1905 came rolling out of the Gila and down the Colorado, with its usual cargo of logs and debris. It swept past the new intake and left it undisturbed, except for lodging at the mouth a tangle of flotsam that had to be dug away.

Hardly had the water from that flood receded when it was followed by another, and then a third. In the twenty-seven-year records of the river nothing like this had ever been known in the winter. In March, Rockwood decided they had better close the new gap as a precautionary measure and use the abandoned upper intake.

A dam of piles, brush and sandbags was hastily thrown up, and Rockwood felt easier—until a fourth flood came raging down the river and washed out sandbags, brush and piles as if they were so much papier-mâché. Moreover, it appreciably widened the intake. In the respite of a few weeks that followed the dam was solidly replaced and all was secure once more.

But spring floods from the Colorado proper came early that year. The roaring tide started in May—a fifth flood of unprecedented volume. Its first onslaught carried away the new dam, changed the contour of the island in the middle of the river, and clogged the channel on its left side so that the flow of the stream was deflected toward Rockwood's cut.

In a few hours the width of the intake was enlarged from 60 to 160 feet, and suddenly a good portion of the raging Colorado was spilling over the banks and following the lines of least resistance to the lowest point in the Salton Sink.

Here was real cause for alarm. The annual spring floods were just starting; they usually lasted for two months, and nothing could be done to stop the flow until they receded. Every second, 90,000 cubic feet of muddy water was being voided into the desert.

Not until the middle of June did the settlers in Imperial Valley begin to realize fully the seriousness of their plight. Then all at once it occurred to them that the river was really out of control; if the breach could not be stopped, the Salton Sea—as it was already being called—would rise steadily until it reached sea level, and their whole oasis would be submerged.

Officials of the development company were in a desperate predicament. They had started all this and they had neither the financial means nor the physical equipment to stop it. The one big man of finance who had major interests in the desert was Edward H. Harriman, president of the Southern Pacific Railroad. Frantically they appealed to him for help and a loan of $200,000, figuring that as much as $20,000 might be required for stopping the river and the rest used for cleaning up and a few improvements.

To the surprise of the petitioners, Harriman responded immediately and sympathetically, and as further evidence of his good will dispatched one of the railroad's most talented engineers, Epes Randolph, to look over the situation.

Randolph took one look and wired his boss that a mere $200,000 would never halt this catastrophe. No one could guess what the cost would be. It might run to at least three-quarters of a million.

ARE YOU CERTAIN YOU CAN PUT THE RIVER BACK IN THE OLD CHANNEL? the rail magnate wired back.

I AM CERTAIN IT CAN BE DONE, replied Randolph.

GO AHEAD AND DO IT, ordered Harriman.

Randolph and the Southern Pacific virtually took over the management of the California Development Company, and with it took over the generalship of the battle to turn back the runaway river.

For a full year it was a losing battle. Attempt after attempt was made to dam the overflow; to push jetties out into the current; to install barriers of piling; to lay brush mats; to build up silt drifts that might deflect the flood back into the old channel; to construct head gates for a by-pass. All failed; all where torn out by a series of merciless new floods.

On November 29 and 30, 1905, the worst deluge yet roared down the Gila and into the Colorado, sweeping masses of driftwood and debris ahead of it. At Yuma the water rose a foot an hour for ten consecutive hours. The discharge over the banks where Rockwood had made his bumbling cut increased from 12,000 cubic feet a second to 115,000. Everything that had been done to conquer the surge was swept away. The river was pour-

ing over a crevasse 600 feet wide, and nearly the entire flow of
the Colorado was emptying into the Salton Sea.

The situation grew worse during the early months of 1906,
and then a crisis even more devastating occurred up north. On
April 18, San Francisco was wracked and set ablaze by the worst
earthquake in the history of the United States. The shudder was
hardly felt in the Imperial Valley, but Western headquarters for
the Southern Pacific, on which the salvation of the Valley depended at the moment, was crippled.

Harriman hurried from New York to the West Coast. Epes
Randolph met him there, and in the midst of all the turmoil
gained his ear long enough to brief him on the other calamity on
the border. The rail president promptly gave him carte blanche
and another advance of $250,000 to stop the Colorado.

Randolph returned to find the river more defiant than ever
and steadily rising. The crevasse had widened to a quarter-mile
and four billion cubic feet of water were gushing into the Salton
Sea daily. Bulldog Rockwood had given up the battle and re-
signed. That was the state of affairs as forces gathered for an all-
out, desperate stand late in the spring of 1906. And as the weeks
went on into summer and fall there was little cause for optimism.
The people of Imperial, Brawley and El Centro seemed almost
ready to concede that it was only a matter of time before their
great oasis would be swallowed up.

The time had come for a showdown. Flood season or not,
there could be no delay in launching an attack. It was now or
never. Randolph summoned his Southern Pacific assistant,
Harry T. Cory, a crack construction engineer and ex-college
professor. He did not ask him, he told him, that he was in charge.

"What about expense?" asked Cory. "What's the limit?"

"Damn the expense," bellowed Randolph. "There is no limit.
Just stop that river."

It took him more than six months, but Cory stopped the river,
and in the process scooped another $2,000,000 dollars out of
Harriman's open purse.

His most confusing problem at first was contending with all
the eminent engineers who swarmed to the site with free counsel.
Like a plague of fire chasers, they descended upon Yuma—as
many as fifty at a time. Here was an engineering stumper unprecedented in history. One of the great rivers of the world had lost
its bearings and was running uncontrolled, menacing 2,000

square miles of potentially fertile land with inundation, threatening to compress into a few weeks the kind of earth sculpting that usually took centuries. Geologic and geographic history was being made, and the scientists wanted to witness it.

Nobody had ever tried to hold back a river that was discharging some 360,000,000 cubic feet of water every hour, vomiting it down a 300-foot slope into a basin big enough to hold Long Island Sound. The most ominous prospect was that the whole lower Colorado River bed might be gouged out and made into a deep gorge from which water could never be taken for irrigation.

The beginning of the process was happening before the eyes of the engineering celebrities as they watched the magnificent cataract eat its way upstream. They agreed that once it reached the river channel itself it would keep on working northward. Even the Laguna Dam, then under construction twelve miles north of Yuma, would be destroyed; the topography of a broad section of the Southwest, as well as the upper corner of Mexico, could be utterly transfigured.

The challenge Cory faced was without engineering parallel. Among the distinguished spectators were men who had worked on flooded rivers like the Nile, the Yangtze and the Mississippi. They granted that their experience could not be applied here. Most of the notables shook their heads and admitted among themselves that Cory was wasting his time; the closure of the river was a physical impossibility.

Brush matting, rocks and piling—the usual materials for stanching such a flood—were all discounted, as far as the volunteer advisers were concerned. But contrary to their counsel, it was exactly the combination Cory was going to use. The piles would have to be stouter and longer; there would be rocks and more rocks; and quantities of clay and gravel for packing. Spurning the wisdom of the most eminent engineers in the land, Cory drafted his campaign plans as though setting out to conquer an invincible foe.

He built a nine-mile spur of the Southern Pacific, merely to bring in materials and supplies to the crevasse. He constructed a camp to house an army of 2,000 laborers, and when his call for white workmen brought little response he recruited hundreds of Indians from a half-dozen tribes of the Southwest: Pimas, Papagoes, Maricopas and Yumas from Arizona; Cocopahs and

Diegu+eños from Mexico. Gangs of drifters and Calamity Johns trooped in from every part of the country. He hired them, too, just to get them out of the way.

To boss the army, he assembled ranking engineers from the staff of the Southern Pacific—men he knew he could depend on, and with them came superintendents, mechanics and skilled workmen.

Lines of mules, straggling to the scene, stretched out for miles, and then the Imperial Valley farmers got together and offered a battalion of 500 horses and drivers.

Still more impressive was the gathering of rail and steamboat forces. Three hundred "battleships"—monstrous side-dump cars with a capacity of sixty tons each—were borrowed from the Union Pacific. Ten work trains and 1,000 flatcars were gradually assembled at sidings in California and Arizona. Up the river came three stern-wheel steamers and a flotilla of barges, loaded with steam shovels, giant pile drivers and other heavy equipment.

Los Angeles was constructing a new harbor at San Pedro. So much material and equipment was commandeered from that job that it slowed to a halt. Cory needed vast numbers of the longest, heaviest piles obtainable. Eleven thousand of them—all 90-footers—arrived from Los Angeles, along with the message: "We have exhausted all available supply of piles in San Diego and Southern California."

Carload after carload of heavy timbers—19,000 feet of them—arrived for trestle construction, and it was not ordinary lumber. Every piece was sound pine, 8 by 17 inches. There were items like 100 tons of dynamite, 40 miles of steel cable, 2,000 cords of brush, 3,000 carloads of rock and fill.

A quarry was especially opened at Pilot Knob, but it could not begin to supply the quantity of rock that was needed. Hundreds of carloads were shuttled from Tacna, Arizona, 60 miles to the east; from Colton, California, 200 miles to the west; and over two mountain passes from Patagonia, Arizona, a distance of 485 miles. "I suppose we handled rock faster than it was ever handled before," Cory acknowledged. "We brought in about three thousand flat cars loaded with rock from those immense distances, and we put in altogether about eighty thousand cubic yards of rock in fifteen days."

For weeks two divisions of the Southern Pacific, 1,200 miles of main line, were tied up. During the height of the emergency both freight and passenger services were disrupted and shunted into sidings, while Cory ruled as dictator over the Southwest. It was a dictatorship in more ways than one. Under arrangements with the Mexican Government the whole region was under martial law, with a Mexican commandant and his *rurales* policing the scene.

Cory's attack was bold and simple. Against odds of frightening dimensions, rail trestles were constructed over the great crevasse, and from their heights rock was dumped into the break faster than it could be carried away. Thousands of rail cars converged on one small spot over a period of a month—night and day—with just four minutes' headway between the long trains.

Three times during that month, as dams were nearing completion, they were swept away, and in a single flood of twenty-four hours, all the work of months—representing an investment of $1,500,000—was wiped out. In an attempt to create a temporary by-pass for the river, a 200-foot head gate—the largest of its kind ever designed—was erected at a cost of $122,000. A morning flood lifted it out of the banks like a plaything, flung it into a trestle, carried that away and sent the wreckage helter-skelter into the Salton Sea.

But through it all the pile drivers kept pounding; the trains continued to roll; Cory refused to accept defeat. Again and again he ordered a new attack. For months his men worked around the clock in relays, fumbling at night in the dim illumination of strings of kerosene lanterns hung over the crevasse.

On the morning of November 4, 1906, resounding cheers echoed over the battleground. The frustrated waters were swirling down the ancient river channel for the first time in eighteen months. Newspapers across the country heralded the event: THE CHANNEL TO THE SALTON SEA IS CLOSED. THE COLORADO RIVER HAS BEEN TURNED BACK INTO THE GULF OF MEXICO. But the jubilation was premature. Exactly a month later another cloudburst swamped the Gila and a new raging flood came down the Colorado with pent-up fury. Before nightfall on December 5, there were three breaks in the levee just south of Cory's dam. The brown monster had eaten its way through the banks and was out of control before the menace was discovered.

The river had to be conquered all over again with the same expensive procedure. Before Cory could claim complete victory, he had constructed and re-enforced more than twenty miles of rock dams. Not until the night of February 10, 1907, was the final leak plugged and a captive river at last flowing to the Gulf in the old channel the mapmakers had assigned it.

In the hour of victory there were two outstanding heroes—engineer Harry T. Cory and financier Edward H. Harriman—and strangely enough, in all the flag waving the financier was all but forgotten. He had paid out over $3,000,000 to save Imperial Valley, and unquestionably, without that support, California and America would have lost its Colorado Desert under a vast Salton Sea—just as Widney wanted it.

Congress at the time could not have cared less, and even the great conservationist in the White House, Teddy Roosevelt, was not particularly disturbed. Once he had been a close friend of Harriman, but the President had turned on him in a monumental antitrust suit, and not even the threat of losing a few million American acres could budge him to lend a hand. Let Harriman do it, was the attitude in Washington. Although at the height of the crisis Harriman was given ample reason to believe that Congress would reimburse him, never in his lifetime was a federal dollar forthcoming, or even an official thank you.

Due ultimately to Harriman and Cory, dates and carrots would continue to grow in Imperial Valley. They had averted a national disaster. Along the Colorado banks were miles and miles of deep, ugly gorges, some of them bordered by sheer walls as high as eighty feet. Later someone estimated that the scourings from the overflow amounted to four times all the rock and dirt that was excavated in the construction of the Panama Canal, but that was scarcely a hint of what would have happened without the philanthropy of Harriman and the courage of Cory.

California had a modest-sized Salton Sea rather than a Salton Sink, and it also had—for all time—a wonderful, sprawling oasis that was the envy of every arid country in the world. "We don't pray for rain here any more," bragged the Imperial Valley ranchers, "when we need water, we just telephone the company."

VII
PRETTY GOOD ROCK,
BUT TOO FAR FROM COMSTOCK

THE quest for California gold and silver never actually ceased; it was just a matter of fluctuating fervor. Desert sophists compiled quite a catalogue of alibis for the slackening of the rush in the eastern extremities of the state during the late seventies. They claimed that the diggings were dug out—which was not true. They blamed it on the 1875 crash of the Bank of California, on the panic that followed, on tax and mortgage laws, on the heavy toll taken by highjackers, on scandalously high freight rates—any of which might have been in part responsible for the decline.

Too long and too close an alliance with the forces of Mammon was the reason aired from the pulpit and accentuated by pietists with a hangover of New England conscience. Soothsayers possessing the cosmic outlook convinced a great many people that griefs in the gold fields were a by-product of certain conjunctions of stars, and pointed out that in 1874 the earth had passed through the tail of a comet. Against such odds, what could be expected in a gambler's world?

And there was another very good cause for the slump. Mine after mine was all but washed out of existence during the last days of July in 1874. A series of ominous, freak storms lashed the canyon country and brought on floods almost comparable to the Colorado River rampage. The tempests struck locally, but the targets were widespread, extending for a thousand miles down the length of the Great Basin. Skipping here, there and yon, the downpours inflicted catastrophic damage all the way from Winnemucca in northern Nevada to Yuma on the Mexican border. Reports, following the eerie onslaughts, came in piecemeal. For example, passengers on the Central Pacific's Overland Express, after pulling out of Mirage Station near Winnemucca on the afternoon of July 24, were thrilled with the sight of a spectacular mirage—a sparkling lake stretching halfway to the horizon. Making up for lost time, the train plunged directly into it. Before and behind, the tracks were seemingly engulfed.

Then suddenly, as the cars sped westward, the mirage faded, the sky turned night black, and the cars rushed into the heart of a cloudburst in which everything was blotted from sight. A bewildered engineer reached for the clutch that controlled his steam brakes, but it was too late.

On a dip in the tracks the locomotive literally dove into a river seven feet deep—at a spot where running water had never been known before. The engine shuddered off the tracks and came to a jolting halt, half submerged, with the river gushing through the cab. In a cloud of steam the fires went dead. Engineer and fireman felt their way onto the canted coal car and from there climbed down to the cars to survey the damage. They found terrified, hysterical passengers, but fortunately no casualties. Almost immediately the skies brightened; in ten minutes the deluge was over, the sun came out, and—as if the mighty river had been a thing imagined—it quickly settled and left a dry channel.

The train was delayed for half a day while wrecking crews repaired the roadbed and eased the locomotive back onto the tracks. And, oddly enough, the rescuers brought word of an almost identical accident near the Utah line where another train was derailed by a flash flood. But in that wreck five lives had been lost.

From Wells came a report that thirty feet of Central Pacific track had been washed out; from Carlin that two longer sections had been destroyed by a waterspout. And from Austin a more alarming flash: "A thunderstorm, accompanied by rain, burst upon this place this afternoon. The storm exceeded in violence anything of the kind ever witnessed here before. The thunder rolled continuously, and in point of deafening noise could only be compared to the near firing of heavy batteries of siege artillery. Lightning flashed incessantly, the rain poured down in torrents, making a scene beyond conception. Such was the violence of the rainfall that two minutes from its commencement a torrent upward of a foot in depth swept through the streets."

Hardest hit of all places in Nevada was Eureka, a sizable town pressed into a narrow canyon below the mouths of four smaller canyons, ordinarily dry. Showers of "unprecedented violence" had passed over the town during the morning; at noon villagers noted that a cloudburst struck the top of the mountains, high above the canyons; then three hours later came still another downpour, "such as is seldom seen in our country." Three horsemen galloped down the streets to spread the alarm, but close on their heels came the flood.

"And such a torrent!" exclaimed a scared Eurekan. "Over the entire ridge extending from Pinto to Ruby Hill the massive clouds had broken—literally broken. Toward the summits there was no rain—but a deluge, and down Railroad, Eureka, New York and Goodwin canyons flowed the water at an almost inconceivable rate of speed, gathering strength and fierceness in the descent.

"Where the canyons unite and our valley approaches a quarter of a mile in width, the ground was covered by a terrible seething mass of waters at least three feet in height, bearing heavy timbers, the wrecks of cabins, and even masses of rock in its angry, headlong career. As the valley narrows toward the center of town, the current increased in fierceness and power.

"Within ten minutes each street and gullyway was converted into a river. But still the inhabitants thought themselves safe in their houses. They reckoned amiss; for suddenly there came thundering down the canyons from two directions a torrent which carried everything floatable before it. So great was the speed and volume that it fairly tore up the ground and mingled the dust of the earth with the spray of foaming waters.

"One house after another toppled and fell, and the angry billows beat upon the wreck and dashed it to pieces, many with families inside. The sight was magnificent in its terror. Those who remained in their premises were now hemmed in beyond the possibility of escape. Every moment houses were moved from their foundations and came down the torrent. The women and children, thank heaven, were with few exceptions saved. It was in the act of saving them that men in most instances lost their lives."

The heart of Eureka was destroyed in twenty minutes and fifteen citizens were lost.

All the way down the Great Basin occurred similar torrential showers and floods. "Heavy rains have fallen all over this section of the country," summarized a Yuma correspondent on July 28. "The roads are almost impassable. The Gila and Colorado rivers have risen two feet."

From Prescott, Arizona, issued a typical item: "The California buckboard arrived this morning twenty-four hours late, detained by a cloudburst in San Diego County desert near French Station. The driver had a narrow escape with the lives of himself and horses. The wagon and mail were swept a quarter of a mile from the road; one sack of mail, the way bill, etc. were lost."

Up north, above Owens Valley at Benton, a rainspout descended upon a mule team, swept it for yards along the road, killed four animals and severely injured the muleteer. Roads, crops, mines and homes all through Inyo County were damaged by thunderstorms and waterspouts, following a crazy course over the desert.

Notorious horse thief Billy Killingly happened to be camping that night at the mouth of Furnace Creek Wash in Death Valley. Clouds burst over both the Black Mountains and Funerals; water gushed down the sides, converged at the mouth, and charged toward Billy's camp. The roar awakened him just in time. Abandoning his gear, he dashed for higher ground. The flood was washing his ankles before he had gone a hundred yards; it was hip deep before he reached a rocky slope and safety.

"Last week Sylvania, Panamint, Swansea, Lida and several other places in this region were visited by waterspouts, some of them of extraordinary force and volume," reported a roving Inyo *Independent* correspondent. "The furnace at Swansea and a good portion of the town was flooded several feet deep with water, sand, wood and charcoal. A thousand cords of wood and many tons of charcoal were washed out of the canyon and scattered over the plain. The Panamint toll road was swept from end to end and is impassable."

The report on Panamint was understatement. Just twenty-two days before, in a fusillade of firearms and a flow of firewater, Panamint had celebrated the opening of that toll road up Surprise Canyon. It vanished in fifteen minutes on July 24, and along with it went most of Panamint in the same kind of watery wave that cleaned out Eureka.

Black clouds dumped their cargo on the heights of the mountains. A dozen dry gullies, etched long before into the three-sided bowl above the town, gathered up the brown water. The gullies became rivers and the rivers rolled into one before the flood reached Panamint. It was like a tidal wave when it struck.

Tents were snatched away like handkerchiefs. Shacks, dugouts, saloons, bawdyhouses and gambling hells were gobbled up in the maelstrom. Whinnying horses and braying jacks were cast into the churning porridge of liquor barrels, chuck-a-luck tables, roulette wheels, pianos, beds, wagons, chairs, lumber and schools of bottles. Most of the miners heard the roar in time to climb a cliff or scramble out of the way, but no one knew on a given day what the population might be, so a casualty count was never taken.

The center of the town was flushed clean. The waters rumbled into Panamint Valley, thousands of feet below, and dumped the residue of the settlement halfway across the valley toward the Argus Mountains. Great was the fall of the roughshod community that did not mind being called "the toughest, rawest, most hard-boiled little hell-hole that ever passed for a civilized town."

Panamint made a quick comeback. The road was patched up and regraded, men went back to their diggings, another tent city replaced the old one as Senators Jones and Stewart poured good money into the place. But it did not pay off. Panamint soon turned into a ghost town.

Those storms of 1874 were evil harbingers. The washout at Panamint was representative of the fall of scores of other mines and mining communities. For two decades the Sierra had been pockmarked with deserted villages that were once rousing, rich and gold mad, and the same blight was moving to the dry uplands on the Nevada side of the big range. The cloudbursts, the bank crash, the panic, changing times, the playing out of surface deposits, all contributed to the slack period in the gold fields.

Since the rough-and-tumble heyday of Poker Flat, Hangtown and Jackass Hill, mining methods had altered materially. The pioneers were placer miners. The pick, shovel, pan, rocker, sluice and long tom were their tools; gulches, ravines, riverbeds and bars were their chief sources of wealth. Little capital was required for that kind of mining. But after the surface areas were worked out the nomad operator was done for.

Individual prospectors were as busy as ever, and a few of them hacked and dynamited holes in the hills, but not many of them got rich on the endeavor. The new findings in the desert called for deep shafts, tunnels and drifts, heavy machinery, reservoirs, mills, pumps, hoists, expensive transportation—capital and a corporation. Prospecting could still be a good business, but Argonauts did not work on the finders-keepers principle any more. They established ownership to a claim, then sold it or leased it on shares to a capitalist.

The biggest money in the West had been made on Nevada's Comstock Lode, and after 1875 all the serious prospectors were ranging the deserts south of Virginia City, believing implicitly in the theory that the Comstock Lode had to show on the surface somewhere—anywhere between the Washoes and the Mexican border. The wild popular scramble for gold and silver had petered out, but no one could convince a devoted prospector that he could not start another rush, once he found the other end of the Comstock.

It was this search that took one-blanket, one-burro prospectors John McBride, Larry Silvia and Charley Mecham into the foothills north of Barstow in the spring of 1881—grubstaked by the sheriff of San Bernardino, John C. King. Their picks hit pay dirt, whether or not it was true Comstock, and the sound was heard across the land. A place that had never before had a name was dubbed Calico.

Wagon trains moved in. Saloons opened up. The usual tent city blossomed. Big Eastern operators came running with big money. By summer, main street was swarming with a population of 3,500 and lined with establishments like Lil's Saloon, Lane's Mercantile Store, Wells, Fargo & Company, the Hyena House and Hank's Hotel. In the next fifteen years $86,000,000 in high-grade silver was brought to the surface at Calico.

Permanent was a relative word in the West. Californians always talked about building *permanent* towns at the site of their major strikes, and Calico rose from the desert with *permanency* in the minds of the builders. The word differentiated between a camp that might last for a few weeks and one that might survive for a year or longer. Calico was very permanent. It burned to the ground two or three times and was quickly rebuilt. Conflagrations and reconstruction merely added to the aura of age. Fifteen years was a long time for a gold or silver settlement to stay permanent. Calico was an ancient town when it was abandoned in 1896.

But to impress the world with the fact that gold digging was not dead in California, before Calico was abandoned another town of its kind was being built in the heat of Mojave Desert some forty miles to the northwest.

In 1894 a feature writer for a Brooklyn, New York, newspaper, F. M. Mooers, wangled an assignment on dying mining camps of California. He was as callow a greenhorn as ever ventured West, but it did not take him long to catch on. Before his assignment was written he had contracted gold fever. He threw down his pad and pencil, substituted a hammer and shovel, and started on the search for that elusive outcropping of the Comstock Lode.

With another amateur rock hunter, C. A. Burcham, whom he had encountered on his beat, he crisscrossed the desert for weeks, avoiding the tracks of other prospectors. It was hard going, so they purchased a couple of mules and a lumber wagon and set out in earnest. For months, dawn to dark, they stalked gold phantoms in the Mojave.

One night in October 1895, the two camped in a dry canyon twenty-five or thirty miles north of Kramer, just off the old twenty-mule-team road between Death Valley and Mojave. It was Burcham's turn to scout for greasewood roots for the campfire. He had dug an armful when his eye was caught by a protruding rock. He dropped the greasewood and his shovel and ran back to the wagon for a hammer, calling to Mooers on the way.

They returned to the protruding rock and knocked off a chunk. "We could hardly believe our eyes," Mooers confessed later. "The gold was sticking out in pinhead particles. We knocked another chunk off the butte and examined it with a magnifying glass.

"Burch, we've struck it," cried Mooers. "There's no need to look farther. All we've got to do is shovel that whole mountain into a stamp mill and barrel up our gold."

A chunk of rock, the size of a cabbage, was taken to Los Angeles for assay. They were offered $950 for it.

Mooers and Burcham gathered up a wealth of supplies and quietly headed back to the desert, making sure that they were not followed. They were determined to keep their find a secret until they could fully explore the area; and—miraculously—

they did keep it undercover for almost a year while they carefully went over the ground, studied mining procedures, and
cagily investigated financial backing. Yard by yard they surveyed
the canyons, examining every likely spot until they had located
eight mines. Finally they called in an old quartz miner, paid him
liberally for his promise to keep mum and to give his opinions.

He expressed the opinion that his employers were millionaires, but he failed in the rest of the bargain. Hardly had the
lucky prospectors staked and firmed their eight claims before the
secret was out and a mob was descending upon the quiet canyon.
Randsburg, named for Africa's famous Rand gold fields, came
to life.

"Of all the stampedes of men and youths to new mining camps
there have been in California and the Southwest Territories in
the past twenty-five years, none has quite equaled in spontaneity,
intensity and permanence the rush to Randsburg this season,"
wrote a *Harper's Weekly* journalist who entrained West four
months later to get a story on the fellow journalist that deserted
his calling.

"The stampede began last October and has grown each week.
Old miners, who have been to every mining camp on the Pacific
Coast during the last generation and have joined in a score or
more of stampedes of excited men to new diggings, say that
Randsburg is now where Virgina City, Nevada, was in 1868, just
before the Bonanza ledges were found and the $178,000,000
therefrom was yet to be dug.

"In this land of boom and mushroom towns people say that
no town has ever grown so fast. Lawyers, ranchmen, orchardists,
merchants, prospectors, college teachers, Mexicans, Yankees and
people of all nationalities, except Chinese and Indians, have
joined in the stampede.

"The Southern Pacific and Santa Fe railroads run within
thirty miles of Randsburg, and passengers for the mines leave
the railroads at Mojave and Kramer stations. Hundreds of
miners and others have been so poor and at the same time so
eager to get to the diggings, lest Fortune shall have distributed
her favors ere they arrive, that they have started pell-mell on foot
across the desert from Mojave or Kramer to Randsburg with
their blankets and camp kettles, pans and simple tools suspended
from their necks and across their backs.

"One year ago the site of Randsburg was as desolate, barren

and forbidding a locality as one can imagine anywhere in the Union. None but men hungry for gold ever would go there. The locality of the mines is among dead, bald and scarred foothills along the western hem of the Mojave Desert. A remorseless waste of yellow sand stretches away as far as the eye can reach to the south and east. Fifty miles farther, beyond hazy purple mountains, lies Death Valley.

"The community began to grow last September. Two miners had produced $24,000 in ten days and shipped the ore to San Francisco in sacks. No one knows how the information got out. The news passed from one miner to another in Los Angeles. Twelve hundred men were in Randsburg by the middle of October, 2,500 by November, though the heat then was 110° to 118° in the shade and the only food obtainable was canned meat, vegetables, stale breadstuffs, pork and beans. A few died of hunger and privation, but by January 1st the population was 3,000, by early spring 5,000."

Every reporter from the East who ever witnessed the sprouting of a Western mining town was so astonished that he used the same superlatives, the same terms of exaggeration, and the same round figure of 5,000 to describe a booming, transient population in which no census could be taken.

But there was good reason for the application of superlatives for Randsburg. Colonel George Ellison, one of the nation's most famed mining engineers, with experience in Alaska, Colorado and California, and just back from Rand in the Transvaal, looked over the prospects in the Mojave gulches and announced: "This is the richest gold camp 'on top' I ever knew. If the ledges now being developed extend a thousand feet into the ground, it will be the greatest mining town the world has ever seen, notwithstanding the fierce summer heat. I've seen this week chunks from four mines here that have assayed at the rate of even three thousand, eight hundred dollars a ton."

The wild scramble for claims started in October of 1896. In less than a month 800 were posted; by the following February 4,300. Every canyon within 100 miles of the Rand ledges had been searched, and claims reached out over an area of 15 square miles.

In three months Randsburg grew from a desert waste to what the *Harper's Weekly* analyst called "as lively a mining town as there is in the world." Scattered over the adjacent hillsides was

an encampment of close to 1,000 tents. In the town proper were four buildings of light wooden sheathing labeled "hotels," where men queued up at night hoping to register for a room—which meant getting a hard mattress on one of the four-tiered bunks squeezed into dormitories as jam-packed as a furniture warehouse.

The bed cost a dollar. The views of the desert through the cracks in the siding were gratuitous. There was no plumbing—inside or out. Public toilets were out in the sagebrush. Nor did the hotels supply free water. Randsburg had no water. It all had to be trucked in twelve miles from Garlock and was sold—to those who used it—for twenty-five cents a gallon.

Packed to the rafters, the hotels at best could accommodate 100, though there were few nights in the early weeks of the town when 500 bunks would not have been filled if they existed. Instead of taking a room, more fastidious transients preferred to rent a blanket for fifty cents and go off to a hillside where they could sleep in privacy.

Meals were served around the clock in five restaurants, all of which were built within thirty days, but there was no room in them for such luxuries as tables. The beans and corned beef were served on chin-high counters of bare redwood plank, running the length of the building, with just room enough between them for two back-to-back bodies. A poor dinner cost as much as a bed. Water was extra.

But eating was a perfunctory habit. Most of Randsburg was on a liquid diet. And in the spring of 1897 there were twenty-four saloons to supply it—with more going up as fast as lumber could be shipped in.

The largest structure in town, of course, was the dance hall, an ark of a building with a showy false front and a veranda. The men called it "stately," "handsome," "elegant," but the adjectives were perhaps a strained reference to the feminine occupants, rather than to the building itself. Some enterprising trafficker had recruited from Los Angeles and San Francisco a whole constellation of painted damsels, who glittered indeed in a man's drab desert.

Aside from its gold, Randsburg existed for the night life. "The saloons, dance house, gambling places are filled to overflowing with a continuously changing crowd," observed an apologist with warm sympathy for the habitués. "Not many are there to gamble, or drink, or dance, but most simply to pass the time in talk where it is comfortably warm and light. It is quite the thing to make the rounds of these places each evening—to go from the Elite to the White Fawn and thence to the Oriole. This is supposing you have not had the honor to be made a member of the Steam Beer Club, the most exclusive social organization of the camp. The hotel lobbies are just as well filled—so dense as hardly to allow sufficient room for the movement of the elbow.

"A church is building at Randsburg—and if it will allow a suggestion, there is no way in which it can serve the cause it stands for so well as by keeping its main hall open every night, warmed, lighted, supplied with papers, magazines and books, and occasionally with light entertainments of music and amusing speaking." But even church vaudeville would have been too tame to draw much of an audience.

Six months after the world had horned in on Mooers' and Burcham's secret, eighteen big companies were sinking shafts into the rocks at Randsburg, and to followers of the stock market the names of the Mojave mines were as familiar as old friends: Olympus, Yellow Aster, Gold Coin, Minnehaha, Yucca Tree, Monkey Wrench, King Solomon, Wedge, St. Elmo, One-Two-Three. Mooer and Burcham had the satisfaction of turning down an offer of $400,000 for a half interest in their holdings.

The population of the town was never stable. Early losers moved out; new optimists moved in. Dan Kelsey, one of the alumni of the old Death Valley–Mojave borax run, hauled a single load of lumber into Randsburg, saw what was going on, and quit freighting on the spot.

"Dan was used to the drought of the blistering desert and dared much where other men would be timid," attested one of his admirers. "He spent two weeks following 'float' from a ledge up Yucca Canyon. He hammered and picked his way for six miles, and one Sunday he chopped off a piece of quartz that made his eyes swim. That piece of rock is now exhibited in a bank in Los Angeles and it led to Dan's getting a partner to invest $20,000. The mine, known as the Blue Daisy, was sold for $170,000, with which Daniel Kelsey and family have now gone on a tour of Europe."

Cyrus Drouillard was eking out a bare existence as constable for Kern County when he was sent to Randsburg to serve some legal papers. An hour's exposure to all the excitement was more temptation than he could resist. He turned in his badge and adopted a more remunerative vocation. Weeks later, while munching a lonesome supper of corned beef and crackers six miles east of Randsburg—and wishing he had been less hasty about throwing over the secure constable's job, he noticed a mass of "live" rock at his elbow. Next morning he set off a stick of dynamite in it, and when the dust had cleared he let out a whoop. He had located St. Elmo. Repeatedly he declined offers of $300,000 for it.

The Randsburg rock seams did not quite come up to Colonel Ellison's estimate, but nobody complained. One of the Mooer-Burcham claims, the Yellow Aster, paid and paid; it was still going strong twenty years later and it was reported to have yielded $10,000,000. Randsburg, at least, was not destined to become a ghost town. It had durable permanency.

Laymen and official chroniclers alike generally conceded that the California gold bubble burst in the 1870's and that there was little doing in the mines during the next two decades. But there was plenty of scattered activity. In terms of the '49 gold rush and the Comstock follow-up, there was a lull and a letdown. The boom lost its momentum. But places like Randsburg and Calico never let the excitement die down entirely. And the intermission ended abruptly in 1900.

To folks of the desert country east of the Sierra, May 19, 1900, is as memorable a date as January 24, 1848, when Marshall set the country on edge with the discovery of gold in Sutter's Creek. Another Jim, James L. Butler, made history on that May 19. He carelessly knocked a hunk of rich ore off a boulder at a place the Indians called Tonopah and triggered the starting gun for another gold marathon that made Randsburg look like a preliminary runoff.

Butler's signal was sounded on cue, just at the moment when the West needed a dramatic incident to perk up its economy and bring back the spirit of the frontier days. The Mojave spectacle had lost its thrill, and Nevada had lost a third of its population as production in the Comstock Lode slumped from the peak of the $47,000,000 it had known two decades before to a mere $3,000,000. The West sorely needed some publicity in 1900, and some new gold plating. Jim Butler provided it.

Tonopah, of course, was across the state line in Nevada. But the border had little geographical significance at that time. Prospectors crossed and recrossed it without giving a thought to which state they were in, and, until a few years before, even government surveyors had been confused about the exact location of the line. The whole region was oriented to California, as well as to Las Vegas, Virginia City and Reno. People were inclined to associate the Amargosa Desert and places like Tonopah with California's famed Death Valley. If their misconception of Western geography was corrected, they would shrug it off: Who cared? What did it matter?

Butler shared this rather careless sense of whereabouts. Although he owned a ranch in Nevada and was district attorney for Nye County, he considered himself more or less a dual citizen. He had been born and brought up at Logtown, El Dorado, California, in the thick of the gold rush—"born not with a gold spoon in his mouth," as one of his biographers put it, "but with placer tailings in his blood." At heart he was a Californian, and he had crossed the line only because his parents had moved to Nevada in their pursuit of richer placer diggings.

Among his accomplices Butler was known as Big Jim; among less sympathetic colleagues he was known as Lazy Jim. Both had supported his candidacy for the office of district attorney—for the simple reason that no one else could be persuaded to take the thankless job. Nye County was about twice the size of Massachusetts and had a population of approximately one citizen to each 6,000 acres. It was such a law-abiding county that the position of district attorney was as inconsequential as that of pound-keeper in a dogless town.

Besides, the post paid only $50 a month in script—$35 in real money. Since Jim had no education, legal or liberal, he could not have argued a very strong case for the state even if he had been called upon to take his place in court. It was the sort of employment that appealed to both Big Jim and Lazy Jim, and at county expense it gave him ample freedom to spend most of his time on his principal occupation—prospecting.

He was prospecting just within the county limits on the day of his big find. The simplified version of Jim's story leaked from the pen of Sam P. Davis, chairman of the Publicity and Industrial Commission of Nevada in the early 1900's. According to Davis, Jim was having trouble with his burro on the day of the great event: "He picked up a slab of rock and threw it at the refractory mule in a fit of anger, and the stone, after bounding from the flank of the animal, fell at his feet. He picked it up to throw again and, its weight attracting his attention, concluded he had hit the mule enough and placed the piece of rock in his pocket for future reference.

"A week later he asked an assayer to determine its value, and added that he lacked the dollar and a half to pay for the assay. The assayer replied that as soon as he found anything of value in the rock he would let him know, and pitched it out of the window as soon as Butler was out of sight. It lay there eight months, when another miner picked it up and, attracted by its appearance, had it assayed by the same man who had previously thrown it away.

"This discarded piece of mineral showed an assay value of eight thousand dollars to the ton. Think of it, if you can think of it calmly, of the pranks which chance plays with the mining industry! Had Jim missed that mule, or had that rock, after hitting the animal, not bounded back just as it did, neither Tonopah, Goldfield, Bullfrog, Rhyolite, nor a dozen other prosperous camps of southern Nevada might ever have been discovered. Over a hundred million dollars staked on a single throw!"

That was the Davis version. Others have added embroidery until neither Jim Butler nor his mule could possibly stagger across the desert under the weight of the legend, but regardless of the bonus in disputed fact and fiction, Jim invariably came off as the uncontested hero of the date of his find—May 19, 1900. He and the benefactor who forfeited the dollar and a half for the assay went into partnership, located over a hundred claims, and leased them out on a royalty basis of 25 percent until midnight December 31, 1901.

The very first shipment of ore, a mere forty-eight tons, netted a check for $574,958.39. Tonopah was made. A few of the claims barely paid expenses; some brought fortunes. As the days of 1901 ticked off and the "leasers" faced the December 31 deadline, the frantic pace in the mines steadily increased. Operators were determined to strip from the hills every glob of gold within reach while the agreement with Butler remained in effect.

Many a leaser pleaded for the privilege of extending the time limit. They offered as much as $1,000 a day for an extension of the franchise. Butler cheerfully declined all offers. He knew what he was doing, and with exasperating regularity reminded the capitalists that all deals would be off at midnight of New Year's Eve—at the stroke of the clock in his cabin.

Excitement mounted as that fateful hour approached. "By preconcerted arrangement," a leaser recalled, "as the clock struck, Butler discharged a six-shooter in the air, and the busy hundreds of miners, working like fiends to get every pound of the precious metal possible, dropped their tools at the sound of Butler's shot, as if they were striken with paralysis.

"Out of hundreds of men, some of whom were taking eight thousand dollars' worth of gold per day from their leases, not one of them ventured to touch another ounce of the precious metal after the sound of Butler's weapon signaled the stroke of midnight. Such was a miner's word and a miner's honor."

Fantastic sums had been made in that year. Jim was now Mr. James L. Butler and on his way toward being a millionaire. He had accumulated his pile and was ready to sell out while the market was good. With his ore samples and a stack of financial statements, he took off for San Francisco to find a buyer.

Bay investors were impressed with the specimens and they were impressed with the record, but the take was not quite up to Virginia City standards, and no one could guess when the veins would run out. "Pretty good rock," they told him indulgently, "but too far from Comstock." No sale.

But Easterners who had been left out of the Comstock bonanza were more than eager to take a flight with this new venture. Agents were already swarming into Tonopah. Philadelphia capital was as good as San Francisco's. Butler let the Philadelphians have his eight original mines for $336,000. He went back to prospecting.

From that beginning sprang the great new gold rush of the West. Tonopah, the tent city, took on the *permanent* look of a lusty industrial town, with the usual hardware stores, livery stables, blacksmith shops, restaurants, hotels, gambling joints, dance halls and saloons. Ole Elliott opened a saloon; Harry Ramsey opened a saloon; Jim Butler opened a saloon; Wyatt Earp opened a saloon; Tom Kendall and Jack Carey opened the Tonopah Club, the rip-roaringest saloon of them all.

Transportation of Tonopah ore, of course, was the major problem. So exorbitant were freighting charges that it did not pay to send out anything that assayed under $50 a ton. The ore had to be sacked at the mines and loaded on mule teams which carried it a two days' journey to Candeleria and Sodaville. There it was transferred to a narrow-gauge railroad which took it to the Central Pacific line, where it was again unloaded and reloaded for broad-gauge shipment to the smelters. A hundred head of horses and mules, with five wagons and trailers, did most of the freighting the first year. After that there were 1,000 animals on the road. They were not relieved until the railroad reached Tonopah in 1904.

But long before then Tonopah had become a city of "5,000." In the meantime more Easterners arrived at the boom town, ready to put down cash for mines. They were given the brush-off. All the good claims had been taken up. In a huff they moved the respectable distance of twenty-five miles to the south, and more or less at random began sinking expensive shafts in the crater of an extinct volcano, far outside what was accepted as the "mineral zone"; far off course for outcropping of the Comstock Lode.

Old-timers chuckled and guffawed at the stupidity. "Case of quick parting of fools and their money!" they joshed. "Greenhorns! idiots! buffoons!" From Tonopah to Truckee, from Sacramento to San Diego, the story of these simpletons drilling into a volcano for gold brought roars of amusement. They were the laughingstock of the West.

But the fools who knew nothing about mining struck gold— blundered onto a deposit of "jewelry ore," ridiculously valuable, and mines of it far more extensive than those at Tonopah. In 1904 all that marked the site of affluent Goldfield was a cluster of dirty tents. Three years later the city was populated, not with the elastic "5,000," but with 20,000. Any superlatives one cared to invent in describing the wealth of Goldfield were inadequate. With the laugh turned on Tonopah, the first lucrative mine was labeled Grand-pa.

Eleven earlycomers got together and each put up $10 to survey a townsite and mark off lots. In a few months those lots were caught up in the greatest real estate boom America had ever known; some of the bites of land were selling for $145,000 apiece. Rich mines like Combination and Jumbo were added to Grand-pa. Ordinary mine town excitement developed into hysteria. Eastern investors arrived in droves to outbid the throng of Westerners.

Recruiting labor often presented serious difficulties in establishing a mining community, but there was no such trouble at Goldfield. The highest wages in the country—up to $5 a day—were advertised, and the pay lured thousands of applicants. White-collar workers stripped off their starched shirts and neck-ties, donned blue denim, and posed in the employment lines. But it was not the $5 compensation in which they were inter-ested. Men fought for the opportunity merely to get into the mines where they could surreptitiously pocket a few $100 nug-gets of the "jewelry ore" on a single shift.

"High-grading" they called it. Strikes and violence threatened Goldfield when the mine owners finally clamped down and in-stituted change rooms where work clothes and pilfered ore had to be left. I.W.W. stepped in to help organize indignation meet-ings; after all, high-grading was one of the traditional fringe benefits to which a hard-working miner was entitled.

Management won the tussle, but compulsory disrobement could not stop this form of grand larceny. Miners at Goldfield lived like the sons of Croesus and squandered their wealth like prodigals on twenty-dollar-a-day hotel rooms, at the gambling tables, on women, on liquor—particularly liquor.

A prudish Easterner, who set out on the twenty-five mile jour-ney from Tonopah to Goldfield in 1905, was mildly dismayed to see the first signs of the bibulous outpost before relatively sober Tonopah was out of sight. "A few hundred yards from the limits of the town we saw an empty bottle, lying near the highway," she complained. "A rod beyond it lay another. After that the trail was more than abundantly blazed with these signs of pene-trating civilization. A blind man could have smelled his way un-erringly by those bottles."

But that was only an introduction to what she was to see later in Goldfield proper. "One man had builded his shack entirely of mud and bottles. There were thousands of bottles, tons of bottles, pyramids of bottles—all of them empty, at the rear of every saloon in the place."

Merely getting to Goldfield in the early days of the rush was an achievement. Explained an experienced globe girdler who succeeded: "It is all a desert country—waterless, treeless, for-bidding. For months a gold-fevered people have been sacrificing anything and everything to get to the vast arena. A little gold has a wonderful way of illuminating miles of desolation. A railroad to Tonopah, recently completed across unpeopled territory,

penetrates the region to a point some thirty miles from the field
of gold. From there the way is made, theoretically, by stage or
private conveyance. Many hurried persons walk. On the railroad, over two hundred carloads of freight were blocked the day
I arrived, so inadequate were all the means of transportation
and so unrelenting was the torrent of supplies, machinery, hay,
tools and material being hurled toward the center every hour.

"The railroad town or terminus was thronged with people, all
excitedly endeavoring to hasten onward. The streets were filled
with bell-jangling mule teams, merchandise, outfits and human
beings. Three stages a day were whipping across the desert,
loaded to the breaking point; and four days ahead the seats were
sold. Ten hours before our arrival the last private rig had been
engaged to make the drive. Not even so much as a saddle horse
remained for hire.

"From twenty sources came the tale of no beds to be had, for
love nor money, in the new camp whither we were heading. But
the traffic in, and bribing for, means of transportation increased
as the morning advanced. The price of a stage seat had risen a
dollar in the night. It was now four dollars, and cheap enough.
Men, however, were offering eight dollars, ten dollars, fifteen
dollars for a ride on any conveyance which would start at once.
This was the ordinary spirit of extravagance and panic."

By tramping alongside an overloaded four-horse van and persistently imploring the driver to take on one more passenger, the
itinerant was finally rewarded with the invitation, "Oh, hell!
Come on."

Like a mountaineer, he struggled up the side of the freight
van, finding footholds on the stoves, chairs, bicycles, beds, dynamite kegs, trunks and tents with which the wagon was burdened,
and squeezed himself in among seven other passengers on a summit of mattresses. His nearest traveling companion turned out
to be a woman who identified herself as a "trained nurse." The
intruder looked her over and concluded uncharitably, "Parrots
frequently undergo similar training, usually at the hands of ingenious sailors.

"Up every hill our horses barely dragged the load," continued
the tourist, "down every declivity they trotted madly, the wagon
swaying and creaking like an overburdened ship. The road became two roads and spaced along on either one were clouds of
dust, one after another, marking the teams ahead of ourselves,

all of them straining toward one far-distant goal. There were
teams, teams, teams, wherever the sight could follow the way of
the road. Many were coming toward us, laden with golden cargoes—sacks of ore as ugly as so many heaps of rags, and as rich
as butter with the bullion concealed in the rock.

"Our 'fast freight' was driven around a typical desert caravan
—a train of twenty raw-boned, sweating, dusty mules, straining
at two large wagons and a smaller conveyance trailer, containing
feed and the teamster's bed, coupled on behind another. The
cargo was, as ever, the mixture of things incongruous—beds,
engines, food, lumber, shingles, drinkables, clothing and imple-
ments of mining, gambling and cooking.

"The teamster, driving with a jerk line, was a hero. No man
save a hero, cast in some manner of mould, could face that constantly roving desert gale that sweeps up the dust from four
times twenty beating hoofs and drives it upon him all day long.
He was gray with the desolation's essence. There were two small
clean spots left on the man's exterior—his eyes. Bright and sharp
and clean were those two brown eyes in all that nimbus of float-
ing grime. The inside lining of his mouth was likewise free from
dust, but he had to keep up a 'divvle of swallowing.'

"Two desert stations were on the route. At both of these the
price of watering a horse is twenty-five cents. The proprietors
are getting rich so fast they are dazed. Each station has a large
backyard where stands a multicolored pyramid of bottles; each
has an eating house and a bar. The woman on our load had a cup
of coffee for which no charge was made. Said the landlady, 'Oh,
I couldn't ask any pay for that. I guess we make enough money
on the water.'

"The fast-freight barely crawled by afternoon, for the ruts of
the road were twenty inches deep and the sand was ceaselessly
following the wheel spokes upward out of the ruts only to trickle
and flow and fall to its bed again and lie in wait for the next
wagon. And the 'dead soldiers' strewn along the road on either
side were yet a little closer together. The land was so barren that,
as the teamster said, 'The chipmunks have to bring their lunches
along when they come to the place.' "

Newcomers did not expect to find an orderly community at
Goldfield, but the disorder they found was shocking, even to the
hardest customers. The terminal for coaches and wagons alike
was an enormous corral—the town depot. Night and day it was

a hive of activity, cluttered with hundreds of mules, horses, cattle, men, dust-shrouded wagons, trying to find a path among the
heaps of baggage, lumber crates, bedrolls, gaunt iron boilers,
stacks of furniture and domestic oddities.

And Goldfield itself exhibited the same kind of confusion.
"Mules and horses, merchandise and wagons blocked the thoroughfares," remonstrated a dazed maverick. "Men in khaki and
corduroy were everywhere—merchants, assayers, brokers, bankers, lawyers, doctors, dentists—these and innumerable others
were more than represented. A thousand men were lined up before the post office, hoping for mail. A score were lazily hounding
a worried-looking man who had recently made a new strike and
fetched a rock of fabulous value. For three days and nights he
had been attempting to escape his self-appointed guard, whose
one intent was to follow him back to his rich discovery. There
was no peace for him; there was no peace for anyone in such a
camp.

"Aside from the one straight street on which the business
houses fronted, there had been but little attempt at providing
for regularity of highways. The living places were planted almost
anywhere among the scattered rocks. There were dwellings in
every stage of construction and of every conceivable type. A few
ambitious builders were cracking up boulders of which to make
cabins; by far the greater number were using adobe. New tents
were going up in every direction. Thin frame houses and dwellings were scattered here and there on the scene.

"There were dugouts conveniently hid in natural banks of
earth and stone; there were houses built of packing cases labeled
'soap,' 'dynamite,' 'tobacco,' 'Boston Baked Beans.' Someone had
fetched a hundred factory-made doors to camp and sold them,
ready to build a house around. Many of these were gorgeous
with redwood panels and stained-glass radiance. They had sold
like the proverbial hotcakes, and there they were, set into mere
shanties of mud or bottles or patchwork, of packing-case lumber.
Anything more incongruous is hard to imagine.

"More than half the raw structures were roofless. The famine
of lumber and shingles had not yet abated. Mud houses, stone
houses, wood houses—all were gaping open at the top. Here,
there, everywhere the first essential was haste. And with lumber
and tools at a premium, nothing was safe. A carpenter put down
his saw to go for a hammer. When he turned about the saw was

gone. A plank, a beam, a board, neglected for a moment, disappears. The appropriator, if caught, is willing to pay, but have that board he must, and never again will its owner behold its shape and color."

Countless mules and horses, milling about the streets, in the depot and everywhere else, created a minor problem of sanitation in the disposal of manure. No one thought seriously of the accumulation as a health hazard, but it was an inconvenience to pedestrians. The problem was quickly solved. Noting the acute shortage of construction material, an imaginative miner, who was not doing well in the pits, went into the manure-and-housing business—supplying building bricks made of this superfluous by-product of the drayman's trade.

His dumpcarts and shovelers regularly policed the thoroughfares and conveyed the manure to his plant on the edge of town where it was mixed with mud and water, shoveled into 4-by-9-by-15-inch molds, and allowed to dry for a week. The manure bricks, guaranteed to last for half a century in the walls of a pleasant cottage, sold at $75 a thousand, and a thousand were just about enough for a small residence. The manufacturer could not begin to fill the demand. "Manure has become the building material for an empire," cracked a prospective householder.

The hectic confusion on which the town thrived spread over the adjacent slopes. A visitor climbed to a hilltop near the center of the district and described "a thousand holes where the human ants have burrowed after gold."

"The holes are like the tunnels made by worms that eat into the stumps of fallen trees," he suggested. "But for one who finds the precious metal there are always a hundred who fail. Mining ordinarily is not a business; it is merely a gamble. Industry, perseverance, economy, sobriety—none of the well-known business virtues will insure success. The most deserving lose, along with the wise, the skillful and the prudent, while the shiftless, the ignorant—anyone, in a word—may come upon the streaks of gold and shame poor Aladdin in the night."

He told of a group who laboriously sank a shaft by hand for 150 feet and then drifted from the bottom, discovered nothing, and having exhausted their combined capital, abandoned the mine and went to work for wages. "Day after day they had flung their coats across a monster dorsal fin of dark, volcanic rock, outjutting from the hill nearby, and given it never a thought. That ledge was fabulously rich. The leasers who followed found it shot full of gold. They channeled it out as men might channel a ditch and recovered over fifty sacks of ore worth $400 a sack."

He observed the toils of two partners who feverishly drove a hole in the ground, shoveling their way through gold worth a million dollars, all of which was cast aside as waste. A couple of harpies, who knew ore when they saw it, patiently watched the operation for months until the amateurs had spent their last dollar and quit.

"Three months of toil and hardship and denial were required to break the eager spirits, to beat them—to clean them out!" he moaned sympathetically. "Three months the vultures waited and made no sign; and their moment finally came." They grabbed the claim and shoveled up stuff so precious it was not trusted to sacks. They packed it into empty oilcans and soldered them before shipping. A single ton of ore yielded them $250,000.

A miner who staked five early claims was so penniless that he had to sell two of them to get enough capital to go to work. The two he sold brought a fortune; the three retained produced nothing. And a lucky devil, who bought a fifth interest in two claims for $40, netted almost $250,000 in less than six months.

The drudgery was all in the daytime; sorrows could be drowned after dark. Like Virginia City, like Calico, like Tonopah or any mining town of the forty-niners, Goldfield did not really come to life until nightfall. Then it was bedlam. One writer purposely picked a rainy night to describe Goldfield, assuming that the rain would dampen the spirits of the revelers sufficiently to make his account more plausible.

"The street was ablaze with lights from a score of saloons and gambling halls," he summed up. "Music arose from these thronged abodes of carelessness. It swept in interrupted gushes above the storm, laughing out its frivolity against the stern, deep roar of thunder from the hills. To me it was threat and portent, fearful and majestic, that the gods were sounding. But two thousand men had fled to the shelter of the gay saloons, and a Negro here and a woman there were beating, *sans* peace, on loudstringed pianos and piercing the storm with ragtime song.

"All night there was gambling in every direction. Every saloon was wide open for games of chance. Roulette, Klondike, faro, poker and stud poker, craps, twenty-one—anything that anyone could wish was frankly spread before the crowds. The way to make money in a mining camp is to let the other fellow dig it out of the ground—then take his money away from him as quickly as possible, and leave him good-natured.

"Coin—more golden coin, more twenty-dollar gold pieces were displayed in the banks of the games than a man would see in a mint. Chinamen, Mexicans, Yankees, college graduates, Portuguese, Dutchmen, Italians, Russians, Canadians, Japs, Indians, all were there, large and small, tough and tender, young and old, rich and poor, hopeful and hopeless—a heterogeneous, ill-assorted, rough-clad lot, drawn there like so many living atoms by the undiscriminating magnet—the gold all about them in the rocks.

"A few were drunk; a thousand were drinking. A few women drank here and there with the men. A month before, the camp had experienced a famine of food for men and of hay and grain for the beasts. But there had never been and never will be a famine of drink. Whisky is the one known liquid that will flow up every hill.

"A thousand dollars strewn upon the hills in dust of gold outshines a hundred thousand worth of bread or a million's worth of hay or common potatoes. Gold the blinding, gold the crazing, gold the relentless—how shall its victims be counted—how shall its new-made favorites voice the might of delirious joy?"

Goldfield was an offspring of Tonopah, and Goldfield was soon giving birth to progeny that reflected the parental character —Bullfrog, Rhyolite, Fairview, Greenwater, Searchlight, Mizpah, Diamondfield, Lee, Echo, Schwab, Harrisburg, Skidoo, and they in turn supported subsidiary diggings with names like Golden Slipper, Cyclone, Hailstone, Keystone, Ida, Climax, Hot Onion. Each mining town had its cluster of heroes, patriarchs and patron saints; each developed its individual traits, its wild saga and its own folklore, but they all borrowed from Goldfield. Goldfield outdid them all.

That phenomenal city sprang out of a desolate crater. It had a fast, raucous youth and matured into an adult and prosperous metropolis as quickly as it passed from birth to puberty. And then it set a new precedent for all the mining towns of the West. It became civilized.

Goldfield continued to live in high gear, but it took on an element of refinement that had never before been known among either Nevada or California gold communities. Goldfielders continued to spend lavishly, but they also spent elegantly; they continued to drink, but they drank decorously; they gambled, but they gambled in style.

The tent encampments, the dugouts and the disorder, disappeared. By 1906 Goldfield had class—and, some thought, culture. The railroad came the following year, and the first locomotive hauled in that symbol of luxury and comfort, a Pullman car. Its passengers were met by fashionable cabs and a plush omnibus which dashed them off to palatial hotels built with wainscoted lobbies, private baths and Turkish baths. On Main Street were brick and stone buildings designed by San Francisco's foremost architects, banks with millions in ready capital, and a new $50,000 Montezuma Club was going up.

"Nestled in the volcano's crater, people lead a volcanic existence," a visitor observed respectfully in 1907. "The place is a very turmoil of speculation. Last winter in the midst of the stock excitement brokers sold stocks to people in the street from the third-story windows of their offices. One New Yorker made $250,000 in twenty-four hours, and some of the boldest plungers are women. Ladies' Night in the old Montezuma Club would astonish a New Yorker. He would pause in wonderment at the beauty and fashion in evidence. Many of the cleverest people of the country have been drawn to this vortex of money-making.

"Stopping at a stand to get my boots blacked, I found one man working where there were two chairs. 'Where's your partner?' I asked, as I took my seat. 'Oh, he's just run down the street to buy a mine;' replied the bootblack, 'he'll be back in a minute.' The janitor of the Montezuma Club, a venerable old darky, has managed to accumulate over a hundred thousand dollars by listening to conversations in the Club and governing his investments accordingly.

"Gold seeking has thrown together a decidedly mixed population from all over the world. The keenest brains are there— lawyers, students, orators, men of letters who talk Greek and Latin, adventurers, soldiers of fortune, gamblers and sharpers, all mingled in the same swirling vortex. Nearly every man who has been successful owns an auto and these greyhounds of the desert have been a tremendous factor in the development of the country.

"In the old days, to inspect a mine meant a long and tedious ride over the hot sands on jaded horses, with lack of water and many other discomforts. Now an investor has but to drop into the waiting automobile, and a few hour's speeding over the waste lands him at the scene of a new discovery one hundred miles away, and if he is pressed, he can return the same day.

"A new pattern of automobile, built especially for desert travel, is being manufactured at Goldfield. It is long and low, designed for high speed. These cars seldom break down, and crossing a twenty-five-mile stretch of sand on a moonlight night in one of these machines, where the going is as level as a billiard table and nearly as hard, is a most exhilarating experience."

Motorists riding across Death Valley by moonlight, top-hatted millionaires coming in by Pullman, ladies fancied up in furs and feathers at the fashionable Montezuma Club—these indeed represented a new kind of desert rat. Hardy old prospectors like Jim Butler, John McBride, Dan Kelsey and Shorty Harris looked upon them with mixed pity and disdain, and were not unhappy when the panic of 1907 came along and put an end to the show.

Many, many more millions were to be dug out of the desert, but after 1907 the digging was a calculated business enterprise, instead of a big, noisy, hysterical gamble. The last American gold rush was over, and a long line of ghosts stood by, ready to ride their brooms into the towns and cities that had shown such an uncanny capacity to come to life, bloom, boom and die in a day.

VIII
THEM HOBOS DUG THAT BLOOMIN' DITCH

THE big gilded balloon of the West did not burst after the Panic of 1907; it deflated—wilted in a slow, lubberly, tawdry spectacle. Communities like Goldfield, Rhyolite and Skidoo died hard.

The capitalists and the social royalty were the first to pull out. Tradesmen, landlords and faithful servants hung on for years, living off their earnings of the fat years, half expecting that another Philadelphia Midas would come along to give the balloon a magician's puff. But there was no magic inflation this time.

The quietus was taken most philosophically by the miners. They always traveled lightly, and they liked the pitch of the rumors that kept drifting in from Mojave where jobs were said to be going begging. It seemed that they were actually wanted over there. Of course, no $5-a-day compensation such as they had known in the gold mines, and certainly no gratuities from high-grading, but steady work that paid $3 a day, plus good camps, good food, good company.

To speculative gold diggers it all sounded too attractive to be true and a little daffy, but if there was any honesty in the gossip, Los Angeles had run out of water and was fixing to plant a pipe line from Owens Valley at the foot of Mount Whitney, clear across the desert and through the mountains to San Fernando Valley and the Coast, some 250 miles. They were going to spend $23,000,000 on the thing—a bonanza worth getting in on.

Some said the proposition was bigger than the ditch New York City was digging from the Catskills, more mountain boring than the Swiss were doing in the Alps, five times the length of that trench Teddy Roosevelt wanted to cut across the Isthmus of Panama.

Well-seasoned itinerants in the mine towns liked to think of it in terms of where they had come from—the geography they knew best. Why, digging a ditch from Owens River to Los Angeles was like running one from the St. Lawrence River to Boston, from Lake Ontario to New York, from Lake Erie to Louisville, from Lake Michigan to St. Louis, from Mount Shasta to San Francisco, from the Rhine at Frankfort to Berlin, from Lake Geneva to Paris! And a starry-eyed Irishman confided that a ditch that long could slice his homeland in half.

The distances were about the same, but none of those proposed itineraries could quite stand comparison with the route across California's desert. They were all through civilized country. The Los Angeles aqueduct had to cross one of the most desolate, dry regions of the world, miles from anywhere in particular, scores of miles from essential supplies and equipment. The only rail stop anywhere near the proposed location of the line was Mojave, and Mojave was generally considered the outpost of a desert hinterland. A mere mention of the town could bring a laugh, even among those most frequently lured to its barrel houses.

In fifty years Mojave had actually become a rather famed oasis. The stages had changed horses there. It had been a home base for twenty-mule-team borax wagons. Gold prospectors and mining outfits counted on pausing there overnight. It was a major railroad watering stop. But no one seemed to think much of Mojave. "Nothing but a drinking trough," a more sophisticated through traveler sniffed. The town had a dumpy depot, some railroad sidings, blacksmith shops, a fairly wide choice of disrespectable saloons, and not much else of note—except a perpetual wind, hot in summer, cold in winter, and dust laden in any season.

"It's always blowin' in Moharvey," testified a forthright citizen to artist-author E. Roscoe Shrader, who stopped there in the early 1900's to ask questions and daub some water colors. And Shrader appreciated the truth of the testimony as his drawing papers fluttered in the wind and attracted a plaster of grit.

"There's nothing to stop the wind," he concluded. "Mojave squats low and alone in a vast plain of sand which rears only a useless growth of greasewood, cactus and sage. The town boasts a couple of cement-block buildings, but, for the most part, frame structures and tents anchored to stout poles line its streets. A scarce half-dozen in number, these, after the short space of a couple of 'blocks,' discouraged-like, blur themselves in the scorched surrounding barrier of nothingness. The municipal board of Mojave needs to go to no expense for street-sweepers, for the ever-present wind keeps its thoroughfares clear and clean."

Shrader discovered that there was not much to paint in Mojave proper except saloons, and facetiously credited the bibulous population with absorbing a good share of the wind-blown sand: "From the active patronage of the thirst-quenching establishments, of hospitable title and multicolored design, I should judge that much of the spare sand lodges in the throats of the inhabitants."

"Mojave, for nearly a half-century," he digressed in an effort to be fair with his appraisal, "has been an important port of the Great American Desert. It has outfitted numberless Jasons who have fared forth from its shelter to search for golden treasure. It has received the wagon trains of ore rumbling down from mines in the barren northern mountains, and more recently it has received prospectors of a new order. From Los Angeles, a rapidly growing community across the Coast Range to the southward, they have come in search of water, much more precious to that community than silver or gold.

"The prospecting engineers made their way across the desert, past Death Valley, and up among the noble Sierra Nevadas to the base of Mount Whitney, our highest land. On the sides of this great watershed they found the solution of their difficulty— an abundance of pure water. But they have a real tussle of a job to bring a ditch through the Mojave Desert. Thus it was that the dusty little town in the midst of the desert awoke one day to find itself important. It was as if an army of conquest had made it its headquarters."

Shrader did not exaggerate the new prominence that came to Mojave in 1907. Through no effort of its own, except merely being there, the "port" was suddenly selected as capital for a great $23,000,000 venture. At its dingy station tons of freight and machinery were accumulating. Every train brought detachments of engineers in corduroy, khaki and high boots. Groups of laborers, 50 or 100 at a time, poured off the work coaches, looked around bewildered, and moved off in a body to the nearest saloon for orientation.

More workmen—miners, ex-prospectors, tramps and transients—straggled in on foot from the gold cities of Nevada, walking the rails. They joined the milling saloon crowd. Others bummed in on the endless procession of mule teams converging on Mojave from south, east and west. In the streets, at the blacksmith shops, in the saloons, at the railroad station, knots of men mustered before a foreman or recruiter for a briefing and nose count, and shortly gathered up their duffle bags or shabby traveling kits, climbed aboard mule carts, and headed down one of the new wagon trails that led off into the desert.

Despite the deposits of big machinery, the stacks of pipe and supplies, there was nothing in Mojave yet that hinted specifically of the nature of the mighty aqueduct that the city of Los Angeles was preparing to build. But there was no longer any question that it was going to be built. In half a decade much had happened in Los Angeles, in Owens Valley and at points in between.

Less than three years before, the farmers of Owens Valley had still been confident that the United States Reclamation Service was going to promote a wonderful network of irrigation canals down the 150-mile length of the valley—a project that would have turned thousands of semiarid acres into superb apple orchards and alfalfa fields. Joseph B. Lippincott, chief engineer for the service in the Southwest, had given them every reason to believe that the undertaking had high priority among the reclamation plans of the federal government.

Lippincott had played with grand ideas for the future of Owens Valley. But then he had been bothered with second thoughts. Los Angeles needed water too. With him it was an honest question of distributing the limited supply of California water where it would do the most good, benefit the largest number of people, bring the greatest economic return.

In essence it boiled down to a choice between oranges and alfalfa—orange groves in San Fernando Valley or alfalfa fields in Owens Valley. His statisticians had figured out that for the same amount of water it took to grow a $40 crop of fodder along Owens River, a $3,000 crop of oranges could be grown on the outskirts of Los Angeles.

"The only certain security for retention of a water right in the West lies in its beneficial use," he asserted over and over again. With him the statement was axiomatic. As far as potential benefit was concerned, the two regions could hardly be compared. Against a scattering of a few thousand farmers in Owens Valley, Los Angeles had a population of 200,000 in 1905, with the expectation of doubling that figure in twenty years. And wild optimists were mentioning an eventual concentration of 2,000,000. The area between Lone Pine and Bishop could never attract more than a small fraction of that number.

After years of squabbling over stream rights, Californians were pretty generally accepting the principle that their scarcest commodity would have to be parceled out where it was most needed. Certainly, reasoned Lippincott, no better example of the principle could be cited. Without Owens River water, the growth of Los Angeles would soon be stunted. Moreover, he pointed out, most of that river was going to waste anyway. It flowed into Owens Lake, which had no outlet, covered a hundred square miles, and had "an annual evaporation loss of seven feet in depth."

Lippincott was never to be pardoned by the occupants of Owens Valley, but his arguments won out. Los Angeles moved in, bought up the valley, and won the support of even the highest officials in Washington. "The opposition of a few settlers in Owens Valley . . ." summarized Theodore Roosevelt from the White House in June 1906 after he had been called on to arbitrate a magnificent quarrel, "must unfortunately be disregarded in view of the infinitely greater interest to be served by putting the water in Los Angeles."

In one of the most bitter regional battles ever fought on United States soil—without general recourse to arms and open warfare—the big city won the day, won from Congress a right of way across the Mojave, and won at the same time an obligation to construct a 250-mile aqueduct from the foot of Mount Whitney to the Coast—"the most Titanic struggle ever undertaken by a municipality."

Not through ordinary rolling sand desert would the aqueduct have to be engineered; rather, most of the distance was across dry mountains and dry canyons, a jumbled desolation shunned even by jack rabbits and coyotes. To satisfy a sporting curiosity, an amateur legman set out to follow the row of markers staked by the first survey crews. He gave up after a few days, appalled by what the engineers were attempting. He, too, had shared the popular misconception of western wastelands until he could judge the topography for himself.

"Burning sand and ragged growth is the desert which is most familiar to the uninitiated," he cautioned. "Only those who have traveled within its borders can know how much more of death and desolation is expressed by its mountains. They have a character all their own. Theirs is not the grandeur of the Rockies, whose pinnacles rise mightily into the blue from out a mane of forest growth. Theirs is not the possession of luxurious beauty laden with the scent of pine and spruce and redwood, such as is given the lofty Sierras.

"They are tumbled together in tawny, maze-like confusion, ugly, sullen, repellent. The desert herbage straggles over their surrounding sides and upward for a space, and then, faint-heartedly, dies out. Their summits, rounded and stunted by erosion, are crumbling slowly, inevitably to the level of the plain. Here and there, in bold, rugged outcrop, the rocky framework of their interior is bared against the brazen sky. Down in the canyons the blighting heat of the sun is conserved and multiplied to almost furnace-like intensity . . . In many places the engineers' footsteps were the first to echo among the baked walls."

That was the terrain over which the engineers hoped to dig, blast and bore a waterway for almost 250 miles. The surveyed route started at an intake from the Owens River 35 miles north of Owens Lake. It was necessary to go that far above the lake to avoid the alkaline sink. In effect, the course of the river was being changed. The flow would merely be redirected into a canal which would run for 60 miles along the range of foothills high above the old riverbed and the lake, intercepting and gathering in other mountain streams as it headed south.

Two hundred feet higher than Owens Lake an entirely new body of water would appear—Haiwee Reservoir, covering 15 square miles and bottling up over 20,000,000,000 gallons of water —enough to satisfy the thirst of Los Angeles for three years without adding another quart, if the intake were stopped.

From Haiwee to the floor of the Mojave Desert was the worst stretch, a distance of 75 miles where the water would have to be carried successively in huge, concrete-covered troughs, through giant inverted siphons, flumes and tunnels.

Across Mojave Desert to the western end of Antelope Valley

was another 70 miles, mostly of concrete conduit. There it would empty into Fairmont Reservoir, a "control" lake to regulate delivery of water through a pressure tunnel that had to be cut for 5 miles under the Coast Range. From the tunnel on the south slope of the mountains, the water would drop 800 feet down San Francisquito Canyon into the turbines of two giant hydroelectric plants; then it would pass on by conduit for 7 miles to another drop of 700 feet to generate more power; and a final run of 16 miles to a third power plant and the San Fernando reservoir. Conduits would carry the water the remaining 20 miles to Los Angeles and the towns and orchards of San Fernando Valley.

The dimensions of the aqueduct would vary according to the grade and pressure. At the intake the canal would be 50 feet wide and 10 deep; some of the circular siphons, down which the water would plunge at enormous velocity, would be not more than 10 feet in diameter. But a width of 12 feet and a height of 10 was a general average.

Through the aqueduct 260,000,000 gallons of water could be rushed daily from the Sierra foothills to that thirsty city on the edge of the Pacific. But the building would take an estimated five years.

From the start the aqueduct was engineer William Mulholland's baby. An Irish immigrant, he had been brought up on the water problems of Los Angeles, and—in one of those story-book examples of democracy on the march—had actually risen from ditch cleaner to superintendent of the city water department and chief engineer.

His ascendancy started one day in 1879 when he was industriously shoveling muck and refuse from the open canal that coursed alongside Los Angeles streets. A particularly nasty shovelful of the muck landed at the feet of a sedate gentleman who happened to be passing on the street. Naturally the gentleman objected, shouted remonstrance to the ditch cleaner, and inquired what he was doing down there anyway.

"None of your damned business," Bill yelled back, without so much as pausing in his labors.

"You just told off the president of the water company," a boss shortly informed Bill. "Might as well go get your time before you're fired."

Mulholland climbed out of the ditch and followed the suggestion, but the president had reached the office before him. Instead

of being fired he was commended for his Irish fervor and pro-
moted to ditch-gang foreman. Bill Mulholland was on his way
to the top.

Encouraged by the president, he started studying at night—
a self-imposed curriculum of geometry, drafting, surveying and
civil engineering. Within five years he knew more about hydrol-
ogy and the Los Angeles water system than the directors of the
city water works. When a municipal water department was organized in 1902, Mulholland was named chief engineer, as well
as superintendent, and as soon as the way was cleared for construction of an aqueduct from Owens Valley, the title of chief
engineer for that project was added to his panel of honorifics. He
did not know much about Owens Valley, so he chose as assistant
chief the one man who did, Joseph B. Lippincott of the Federal
Reclamation Service. They were a good team.

"Whoever brings water will bring the people," Mulholland
had philosophized back in the days when he was a ditch-cleaner.
He clung to that conviction. The chief was intent on populating
the County of Los Angeles, and to hurry along the immigration
movement, supplying plenty of water for bathtubs, lawns and
orange groves.

But for five years after 1906, Mulholland was seldom seen in
his adopted city. He was at Mojave, conferring with surveyors
and engineers; in Washington, settling arguments with the federal government; in New York, talking finance or ironing out
transportation problems with Southern Pacific officials; in New
Jersey or Pennsylvania, discussing specifications for penstock; in
Tehachapi, setting up a cement factory; and between times he
was somewhere along the line of the aqueduct.

He had promised Los Angeles all the water it wanted by 1913,
at a total cost of not more than $23,000,000, and a board of con-
sulting engineers—after looking over the plans and the grounds
—had validated his estimate. But Mulholland knew better than
anyone else that it was going to be a race against time, and there
was small margin for error in his budget.

To cut costs they would have to rely on home talent and home
industry from start to finish. The steel for the giant tubes would
have to come from Eastern mills, but the chief's figures took for
granted that just about everything else of consequence would
have to be produced under city-owned enterprises. He could not
afford to waste money on subcontracting and the usual distribu-

tion of gravy that went with it. It was a unique operation plan that only a man as practical and parsimonious as Bill Mulholland could have dreamed up.

It meant that Los Angeles would have to go into business as no American city had gone before. Besides purchasing tens of thousands of acres of real estate far outside the municipal limits, the city would have to construct 500 miles of highway in Inyo and Kern counties; set up a telephone system along the aqueduct right of way for 240 miles; erect housing for some 4,000 laborers and stables for about as many mules and horses—a grand total of 2,300 buildings; it would build and operate, for instance, its own factories to turn out 1,000,000 barrels of cement, its own hydroelectric plants, repair shops and mechanical plants; lay a pipe line of 270 miles—longer than the aqueduct itself—to supply water for work camps and construction facilities; and before crews could be set to work on the big ditch, a 100-mile, city-owned railroad would have to be built from Mojave to the terminal of the old narrow-gauge Carson and Colorado at Keeler on Owens Lake. Mulholland was courageous enough to take on all this. The preparations alone rivaled the excavation job.

Consulting engineers could not be brought around to agreement on all the details the chief carried in his head, but on one point there was no dissenting voice: the completion date of the aqueduct would be controlled entirely by the time it took to drive a tunnel through the five-mile crest of the Coast Range. This was Elizabeth Tunnel—ornery Elizabeth. She could be attacked from two headings only, and a mile a year was considered a maximum rate of progress.

Building the railroad and the access roads, setting up work camps, stringing the phone lines, assembling a work force and hauling in supplies, would take a full year, they reckoned. But Mulholland's timetable of five years for putting water in the taps of Los Angeles householders did not permit the wasting of that year in getting started on ornery Elizabeth. That could not wait.

Despite the fact that the headings were twenty miles from the nearest railroad base, the first drills were hammering into the flanks of the Coast Range early in the fall of 1907—less than four months after the Angelenos, on June 12, had voted a go-ahead in a city referendum. The location at least had the advantage of being west of Mojave's sands, and since only a few score of men

could be employed anyway in the limited space at the headings, recruitment of labor presented no problem.

But the energetic Mulholland was not satisfied with merely an early start. He was determined to get speed, spirit and efficiency from his men, and he had learned from watching baseball that the best way to urge Americans on was to give them a stake in the outcome, to get them competing, to make a game out of it. So he announced his "bonus plan." Eight feet of excavation a day for 3 crews of 16 men would be the standard rate of required progress, and the base wage for miners and timbermen would be $3 a day. For all extra feet of excavation, over the standard 8, every man would get a bonus of 40¢.

The bonus was all the incentive that was needed. One crew competed against the next. Crews at one end of the tunnel fought like fiends to outdo those at the other. Later on, the crews at Elizabeth challenged crews in other tunnels, and everyone was racing. Company officials stirred up further enthusiasm by reporting the results in newspapers, and for a time Southwesterners were more interested in the scores being chalked up on the aqueduct than in the batting averages of big-league baseball players.

"The men in a bonus crew themselves eliminated the drones," asserted a tunnel superintendent, "and did not tolerate loafing. They became interested in the success of the work. The duties of the foremen and superintendent were almost entirely confined to getting the necessary supplies and equipment. As the bonus profits materialized, the miners not only remained longer on the work, but sent for other workmen whom they knew and who would do their share in increasing the speed."

The bonus idea was such an impressive success that progress for one period jumped 72 percent, and practically all of the tunnel crews were earning substantial amounts in extra pay—as much as $1.95 a day. In fact it proved almost too successful. Before Elizabeth Tunnel was half drilled the city auditor, alarmed at the steadily increasing pay rolls, demanded a full-scale investigation to justify any bonus at all. The demand was carried out, and the report was so favorable that it silenced the most vociferous critic.

Meanwhile, preparations for excavating the main line of the ditch were proceeding at a less frantic pace. The different parts were so far flung that not even Mulholland and Lippincott could get any real conception of how much was being accomplished.

Mojave was the nerve center. The town was growing by leaps and bounds until it looked like the headquarters for a major military campaign. But everything depended on getting that indispensable rail line built from Mojave north, and it was the slowest project of all. Unfortunately the chief could not boast of any experience in laying track. He had tried to get help from the Southern Pacific, and the company had turned him down. But then, in the spring of 1908, just when the work looked most discouraging, S.P. officials, as if taking pity on the amateurs, changed their minds, offered to build the whole thing and run a permanent branch line into Keeler.

Though Mulholland had set his mind on making the aqueduct and all its ramifications a civic enterprise, he gladly relinquished this department and contracted to pay freight charges on some 320,000 tons of materials, instead of involving Los Angeles in the railroad business.

But even the Southern Pacific engineers took much longer than a year to lay that hundred miles of track. It was put into use, section by section, as fast as it was completed, but the first freight did not roll into Keeler until October 1910.

Californians capitalized on every opportunity to complain about these delays and the slow progress in general, but when an impartial observer from the East rode out from Mojave to look over the scene soon after the branch was in operation, he had nothing but praise for what he saw.

"This work of establishment was painfully slow," he commiserated. "Wagon roads had to be built through a trackless country; camps to live in this land of little moisture must have water found and brought to them; power must be developed before the drills and dredges could be operated.

"The work of preparation, however, has been well done, and the great ditch is now pushing through the earth at a record-breaking pace . . . There is still much teaming to be done, for the line of work lies well up in the mountains, several miles distant from the railroad. Although these mountains from a distance appear to be old piles of rotting, disintegrating sand, they present to the workmen a core of the hardest rock. Instances have been met where every inch of a road had to be shot out with dynamite. It is slow going and expensive road building, this.

"With the exception of a point near Tehachapi, it was necessary to go nearly as far north as the intake for water for power and camp use. Four water systems were established, and mains soon made their way along the course of the ditch. With the major issue before them, these men are not for long concerned with the laying of a paltry sixty miles of three- or four-inch pipe. It looks in places as if they had dragged it after them as though it were a hose. It will span lightly an arroyo to climb straight up the sheer wall of the cliff beyond, and then descend as precipitously the other side. In such a place it must be anchored every little distance to keep it from breaking apart of its own weight.

"Three hydroelectric power plants have been established in places of sufficient water supply to operate the dredges at work on an open canal at the intake, some of the power shovels, the machine shops and air drills. Power will also come from them for lights and to maintain the complete telephone system which binds all the camps together.

"The engineers with their young, vigorous assistants in the field are making good. What is it that brings a young engineer chap out here to these lone places? Though not so many miles separate him from the busy world, he is as effectively removed as his fellow in Panama; he suffers as inhospitable a climate. He represents a new impulse in the world—the impulse to make useful useless places, to loose the powers lying long latent in our great natural resources. The open life makes him most democratic. He cannot move with too much nicety among his men. He must have them with him. You most always find him at the general mess.

"He has a complex army of men under his control—clerks and draughtsmen, mechanics and miners, and the rank and file—the hobos. 'Stakers,' as these well-known gentlemen are termed on the ditch, make up the general mass of laborers. They come in from somewhere and work awhile at a camp, then, leaving with their roll of blankets and a bottle of water, foot it to the camp below, and so on out to the comforts of civilization. It is said the aqueduct is being built by hobo labor."

But this hobo labor, constantly funneling into the desert through Mojave—and departing almost as fast—had little to grumble about as far as living quarters were concerned. Itinerants who had knocked around mining camps, lumber camps, construction camps and ranch camps all their lives, found a hospitality in Mulholland's desert villages that they had never been exposed to elsewhere. Instead of the usual bunkhouses and squalid dormitories, here they were shown into neat frame housing units where a man had only one roommate and could live in comparative privacy and luxury.

The units were designed especially for the climate, to be reasonably comfortable when the thermometer soared to 110° in summer, and still comfortable when it dropped to zero in winter. Roofs were adequately insulated with boards, but in place of tar paper which gave most work camps a drab, unsightly appearance, white tent canvas was substituted. And whether or not it was planned for effect, that one construction feature gave the villages an air. The white roofs belonged to the desert and seemed to make a settlement look civilized.

Village life was on the rude side, but it was not rowdy like Panamint or Calico. There were no saloons, no gambling places, no dance dives. The mess hall was the common meeting place, but it could hardly be considered a social center. "The polite, conversational meal of civilization is banished here," chaffed a visitor who cadged a meal there. "This is the place to eat—the talk can come outside. A big pan of meat starts at the head of the table, and stays not in its going until it reaches the foot, its contents vanished. Cook's boys struggle back and forth with mountains of bread and huge pots of coffee.

"Their fate is to catch all the boisterous joking. But from their vantage point between the rows of bending backs revenge is swift and easy. Here an eater dodges from a rap on the head with a ladle, there a roar resounds among the rafters when another is punched over into his plate. The pie is downed and, with little lingering, the men get out, each one with a fresh puncture in his meal ticket by the steward on guard at the door."

But after supper, instead of a raucous evening around the bottles, there were baseball games or horseshoe pitching, exchanges of rough wit on the office piazza, and even cacophonous renditions of "Sweet and Low," "Clementine," and "Old Black Joe," as inspired by the banjo of some young engineer fresh out of college.

However, the conduct in the work villages tended to give a false impression of the total character of the hobo labor. The men had to have their letdowns, and they got them on payday or on long weekends. At the least provocation, gangs took off on foot for a "rag camp"—one of the tent saloons that sprang up along the railroad branch or just beyond the territorial jurisdiction of

Chief Mulholland. Better still, they tramped to Mojave, the real Mecca of sin and entertainment.

On paydays Mojave roared from noon to nightfall and on to midnight and morning. The clanging of player pianos and the trumpeting of phonographs never ceased. Everybody whooped it up in the saloons, the gambling rooms and the dance places. A foreman complained that because of Mojave he regularly had one crew drunk, one crew sobering up, and one crew working. Yet a Mojave bartender, who could be counted on to defend his customers, countered spiritedly, "Yeah, but what would you do without 'em? Them hobos are diggin' your bloomin' ditch."

Years later, when there was time for a proper assessment, it was agreed that the bartender was right, but it was also discovered that the average period of continuous employment among the transient laborers was just two weeks.

The labor villages were transient too. Many a hobo returned from his bender, red eyed and fuzzy headed, not quite able to take in the fact that his former residence had vanished, that the entire encampment with its living quarters, shops, hospital, stables, store and warehouses was gone. It was a here-today-gone-tomorrow existence. The site of a town sheltering 1,000 men early in November might have been given back to the wilderness before Thanksgiving, and nothing left to mark the spot except foundation posts, refuse heaps and abandoned streets.

Practically every building was made portable, so that it could be jacked up, slid onto a flat-bed mule truck, and hauled down the aqueduct line as the work progressed. Everything went, and the hobo returning from a two weeks' bout with Barleycorn might have to look for his camp twenty miles south in another arroyo.

For such monumental moving jobs, as well as for hauling heavy equipment, Mulholland was persuaded to try out a new transportation invention then being developed in California—the caterpillar tractor. It was a revolutionary vehicle, described for the benefit of a horse-minded age as "an engine which has a broad continuous track, running over sprocket wheels in such a manner as to give a wide bearing surface and great traction power."

Three of the contrivances roared into Jawbone Canyon on a test run in 1909. For two months the monsters were the hit of the aqueduct show. Engineers took time off from work 100 miles away to see them at work, and "stakers" gave up their Sabbath trip to Mojave to tramp in 15 miles just for a look at the curiosities.

Under the chauffership of expert mechanics loaned by the manufacturers, the tractors put on a marvelous performance, charging up and down mountainsides, heaving loads that fifty mules could not budge. In service as well as showmanship they were a tremendous success. Careful comparisons between the cost of mule transportation and tractor transportation were figured. The caterpillars won out. Meticulous comparisons in speed of delivery and weightloads were made. Again the superiority of the caterpillars was clearly evident.

Mulholland was satisfied. The monsters were turned over to regular aqueduct mechanics and twenty-five more like them were ordered for immediate delivery. It looked as though the caterpillars could trim weeks and months off the construction timetable.

Somewhat prematurely, an advocate of the new machine age made his appearance at Jawbone Canyon and went into rhapsodies over the innovation. "Transportation by mule team was seen to be expensive and ineffectual," he conjectured. "A larger, more powerful means had to be secured. It is up to the engineer to get around his difficulty as best he can. So the caterpillar traction engine was pressed into service of the ditch, to navigate the sea of sage and sand.

"It has proved a most efficient and economical means of transportation. Great weight of machinery that it is, its pace surely links it with its diminutive namesake. But give it time, and it gets there with enormous burdens. The type used on the aqueduct is driven by gasolene motor. You look for a pair of big driving wheels, but do not find them. In their place a chain of broad links of steel, corrugated to grip the sand, revolves about small wheels. This is its own road which it carries and lays as it goes.

"A single broad wheel in front serves to steer its course. Perched in the rear, up under a flapping canvas canopy, sits the helmsman of this new 'ship of the desert.' A caterpillar, slowly topping a rolling wave of the desert floor, with broad-tired freighters grinding heavily in tow, joins itself in your mind at first thought to all traditional forms of desert travel. But when you see its burden, equal to that of a dozen caravans; that a great piece of machinery, which makes the load of one entire wagon, could not be gotten by a dozen mule teams up the canyon grade where it must go; and when the horrible racket of its unmuffled motor beats in your ears, you finally confess: 'This belongs to today. It is different; it is new.' "

But this machine-age marvel did not last long. For almost a year the caterpillars puffed and wheezed across the desert and into the canyons. Then, one by one, they began to break down. Every part of the mechanism appeared to be vulnerable. The tractors spent more time in repair shops than on the road. Bills for spare parts mounted steadily and transportation costs skyrocketed. From the manufacturers Mulholland wangled dies and patterns for practically every part of the engine. A special machine shop was set up at Mojave, and all castings for spare parts were made there at cost.

Despite this, the expense of maintaining the noisy "desert ships" was prohibitive. They simply could not be kept in operation. Eventually every one of the twenty-eight monsters was condemned. Like the borax miners before them, aqueduct engineers conceded defeat and welcomed back the old reliable mule team.

"The caterpillars were the only type of equipment that was purchased in the building of the aqueduct that was unsatisfactory," Mulholland sadly acknowledged. "While the engine could be operated at as low a cost per ton-mile as the team, the cost of repairs was as great per ton-mile as the operating cost."

The chief was constantly harassed with troubles like the tractor breakdowns and his transient labor, but real progress was being made by 1911. Dredges and steam shovels were inching their way down from the mountains and into the Mojave Desert. More than 100 miles of ditch were completed. Altogether there were to be 142 tunnels of varying length. One by one they were checked off, and work on ornery Elizabeth was well ahead of schedule. At Mojave, flatcars loaded with giant steel pipe crammed the sidings.

This was the pipe for the massive, inverted siphons that would drop down a sheer mountain, bridge a canyon and climb the next mountain. The blueprints called for 23 of them, totaling over 11 miles in length, and a single section of the pipe could weigh 20 tons. With the tractors abandoned, mule teams had to be depended upon entirely for freighting it—some 3,000 separate trips to different destinations. To convey one length weighing 26 tons, 52 mules were lined up ahead of a specially constructed wagon and driven to almost inaccessible Jawbone Canyon.

Midway in the construction drive, nothing was more impressive than the work on these siphons. Delivery of the pipe to a canyon was a herculean task; getting it into place on a sheer mountainside was a far tougher one. A variety of hoists was used; aerial cableways and derricks were tried for lighter pipe on lesser inclines; but in the largest canyons like Jawbone, Pine and Soledad, it was necessary to construct inclined tramways parallel to the pipe line.

Surveying the labor at Jawbone Canyon, one spectator ruminated: "Here is a place where the engineer sat down, and with knitted brows, turned his imagination loose. To span the gap would require an enormous structure five hundred feet high, a mile or more wide. The aqueduct's cost would go sailing into the impossible. To carry it to the head of the canyon and back again down the other side was, for the same reason, not to be considered. There was nothing to do but go straight to the bottom and climb again to grade on the opposing wall.

"So he traced on his plans a letter V and throughout the aqueduct's course these gigantic initials are being set up. A number are built of steel to withstand the terrible force of water falling from great heights. Some will approach two miles in length. The difficulties in every phase of the work show with what effectiveness old Mojave opposes invasion. I don't believe there is a place in the world where the problems of transportation are more varied and difficult."

Adventuresome Angelenos, who made the trip out to the desert to see how their water supply was coming along, found plenty of entertainment as well as excitement. They hitched rides on the mule teams, climbed into the jaws of idle steam shovels to have their pictures snapped, delighted in feeling their way into the black tunnels, screamed down the precipitous tramways with an off-duty crew. But the greatest thrill came to the daredevil with the courage to board a flatcar of an aerial cableway. That was something to remember. Legs dangling over the side, he calmly took his seat alongside nonchalant, nerveless workmen who rode the car to work every day. Someone shouted a signal, the mechanic released a lever, and out swung the car as though it were a magic carpet.

Warehouses below took on the proportions of chicken coops, men became ants, and the siphon stretching halfway up the far hillside looked like a pencil scratch. With a squealing of pulleys, the magic carpet rose higher and higher until not even the most intrepid passenger dared look over the side.

All too frequently there was a faint jerk on the traction cable and a corresponding chill ran up and down the spine of the daredevil, while workmen behind cooly gossiped over the runaway load that had smashed to smithereens the week before. There was a moment of giddy swinging as the car approached the upper landing, and another moment of temptation to leap to the security of the nearest terra firma, and then—as lightly as a bird—the car let down on the terrace of the upper landing.

A less audacious gawker from the city was sufficiently entertained merely sitting and watching the convulsions of a power shovel. "A steam shovel is no uncommon sight today," he acknowledged, "but the effect produced by one of the big mechanical monsters, high perched against the glare of the desert's dead mountainside, comes differently. It seems almost as though you have been transported to some ancient period, and that the black thing up there, with hoarse snorts and dipping, swaying beak, was one of the prehistoric animals making a gritty meal.

"The steel-tusked shovel leans into the ditch, and with a few stertorous puffs from the engine, noses about for a mouthful. Into the rock it plunges with rattle of chains and screeching grit of steel on rock. A rapid series of puffs and it rears swiftly into the air, dust clouds streaming in its wake. Swaying out over the rim of the ditch, with a grin in its gaping jaws, it drops its load. A few stones, finding no lodgement on the side, go on down to the valley in great skips and bounds, but before the clatter has ceased the shovel is again in the ditch.

"This time it rises with a huge rock in its clutches, and swings over to a bunch of attendants on the bank, who jump forward with crowbars and perform a monstrous dental operation. The rock it is bringing up from the ditch is placed on the outer side, thus strengthening that side and laying the foundation for a road for patrol when the work is completed.

"Perched out on the great beam at his levers and trip rope, like an East Indian mahout astride the neck of his elephant, sits the master of the metal brute. At will, he can make it dig or lift, push, pull or bump."

If there was any one characteristic that marked the labor from one end of the aqueduct to the other, it was teamwork. The steam-shovel operator was backed up by gangs of drillers, dynamite loaders and muckers—working as a team. Surveyors, hoist operators, pipe fitters and riveters, all had highly specialized jobs, but one had to depend on another. They worked together in a common effort, as though the end result was what mattered. Carpenters building forms for lined ditches labored as a team for the masons and cement-mix operators who followed. Everyone seemed to be in a hurry.

Nowhere was the teamwork more evident than in the tunnels. This was particularly dangerous work, a mile, two miles and more from an underground exit. Besides the danger from explosives was the ever-present danger of noxious gases, falling rock, tension wires and the shuttling of heavy electric trains in and out of the tunnels. Safety rules came first, but an almost feverish haste was an easy second. Drilling, blasting and mucking were so closely coordinated and systematized that there was a casual air of routine in the tunnels.

Men worked in eight-hour shifts around the clock. The train that carried one shift off duty carried the next shift back to the heading, while mechanical blowers were clearing the passageway of fumes from the last explosion. Each new shift first cleaned up the loose rock from the previous firing, then drilled, loaded and fired a full round of holes during the period of eight hours.

Blasting out four or five feet of new tunnel was the objective of each crew. Exactly thirteen "cut holes" were so strategically drilled into the heading that when they were fired from carefully timed fuses a center wedge was first blown out, followed immediately by explosions from the top, the sides and finally the bottom "lifters."

While one shift was retreating from the blast, the next was assembling at the tunnel portal, ready to move in. No minutes were wasted. Drive, drive, drive was the word. They were all working for the Mulholland bonus, determined at the same time to beat the excavation scores at Tunnel 17M in the Jawbone Division, the scores at Elizabeth Tunnel, at Little Lake, Red Rock, the Gunnison Tunnel being built in Colorado, the Croton in New York, and even the Loetchberg in Switzerland.

Tunnel excavation had suddenly become a national and an international sport, with crews in California officially racing

THE GREAT CALIFORNIA DESERTS

crews in other states and in Europe. The Californians won all the laurels, including "the World's Record." The honors were duly acknowledged by the press, and appropriate achievement plaques mounted above the respective tunnel portals.

Stirred by the stories of this underground sport, eager essayist Roscoe Shrader put on knee boots and talked a portal guard into letting him get a firsthand view of the contest.

"The way into the tunnel is rough, over a narrow-gauge track and lengths of snaky air tubes," he reported. "The tunnel's air is cooler and begins to take on a clinging dampness. A faint purr falls on the ear from the blackness ahead. It rises louder, a clatter, a racket, and then, as the obscurity resolves itself into mysterious moving forms, becomes a dreadful din, the clamor of a whole battery of Gatlings in swift discharge.

"This is the drill shift. Two machines are raised on a platform, attacking the upper part of the rock, a man, grime streaked, at each. Braced mute against the vibrating drills, their eyes strain forward as though they can see the mysterious line which the transit men have pointed them through the mountain.

"They work amid the eternal furor of battle. Nothing can be heard until the drills are changed. All orders must be given by signs. There is a unity in this effort against the rock which shows well-developed teamwork among the men. Like football players, they press forward together against the opposition. The work has, in truth, been made a great game for the men by the aqueduct builders."

But Mulholland did not succeed in turning the ditch and tunnel excavation entirely into a game. His teams made amazing progress, yet every week seemed to bring new, tormenting problems—transportation delays, defective equipment, labor shortages, inconsiderate union demands from the Western Federation of Miners and the radical Industrial Workers of the World, food spoilage in camp kitchens that lacked any kind of refrigeration, resulting mess riots, political attacks in Los Angeles, public accusations of slow work and faulty construction, a summer layoff of more than half the forces, due to a temporary shortage of funds, and a Wall Street flurry on the other side of the continent.

"We are giving the city a magnificent heritage," he confided one day, in the midst of his troubles. "If it were not for looking ahead to the time of reward, a reward of approbation that will

surely come to us five or six years from now, I could not go on
with the work, for I am worn out."

He took the strain and the setbacks in stride. By the end of
1912 there was no longer any question about completing the
aqueduct on time. The tunnels were nearly completed. The
trench across Mojave Desert was lined and covered. The last
of the siphons were being installed. Dams were built to hold back
the water in half-a-dozen reservoirs.

Los Angeles citizens were clamoring for word on how soon the
water would be turned on. After consultations with his corps of
engineers, he announced that water from the Sierra would be
flowing from Los Angeles faucets early in July 1913.

On February 13 of that year an informal group, with Mulholland and Lippincott in the lead, casually sauntered to the concrete landing of the intake on Owens River. The bottle of champagne they carried was not for consumption. The wife of one of
the engineers smashed it against the head gate in a perfunctory
christening ceremony, and then, with trembling hands, Mulholland helped turn the wheels that opened the four controlling
gates. In a thunderous surge, 200 cubic feet of water per second
gushed into the aqueduct canal.

Even at that rate of flow, it took almost three months to fill
Haiwee Reservoir. Meantime the finishing touches were being
put on the rest of the line. Neither Elizabeth Tunnel nor any of
the other tunnels, after all, were to determine the completion
date of the aqueduct. It was the siphon construction. The last
coupling was wrapped around Jawbone siphon early in May, and
the gates of Haiwee were opened to let the first rush of water into
the long tubes across the desert.

For two days and nights Mulholland tirelessly toured the line
to check his masterwork. He lifted manholes to observe the flow
in the conduits; with satisfaction watched the sweat form on the
huge airtight siphons, keeping an eye out for possible "springs";
followed the cement-topped ditch across the desert; ascended to
the reservoir above Elizabeth Tunnel and beamed with pleasure
to see a swirling pond forming there.

He was sure that his ditch was a success. More exhausted than
he would admit, he went off for his first night of untroubled sleep
in five years. No one told him that catastrophe was in the making
in Sand Canyon, ten miles south of Little Lake.

Sand Canyon had given the engineers a lot of trouble. To shave costs, they had decided to build an inclined tunnel down the slopes of both sides of the canyon and connect the two tunnels with a pipe at the bottom. The rock was hard granite, "as hard as any in the entire fifty-three miles of tunnels," claimed a competent geologist.

To make sure that there would be no possibility of leakage in it, the inside was lined with concrete a foot thick after excavation. Though small springs had been noted in tests, the construction appeared to be as impregnable as any part of the aqueduct.

But while Mulholland was recovering from his two-day inspection tour, a bad leak developed. Attempts were made to repair it with steel pipe and concrete. The water kept oozing. Mulholland was summoned. Water was turned off and the tunnel inspected on the inside. A series of cracks in the concrete indicated definitely that the siphon was weak and that there must be seams and breaks in the granite beneath.

The 250 miles of aqueduct were never going to be any better than the one defect in it. "Put it to the test," the chief ordered. Full pressure was to be turned on, and they would see what happened.

In the resulting cataclysm the engineers were given all too spectacular an example of the formidable pressure built up in the flow from Haiwee Reservoir. As the tunnel filled, the fierce pressure forced water through the cement cracks and granite seams. Geysers shot across the canyon. A mountainside began to slip. Suddenly the entire top of the tunnel was lifted upward. The canyon wall erupted and was flung aside. An avalanche descended, shearing off the side of a workshop at the base. The steel connecting pipe at the bottom of the canyon was bombarded with gigantic boulders and buried in debris.

An engineer later estimated that 250,000 cubic yards of rock and earth were displaced by the incredible force. The only thing to do was replace the tunnel with a steel siphon on the surface, Mulholland agreed, after the water had been turned off and the damage assessed.

Because of that break, Los Angeles did not get its water that summer. It was November 5, 1913, when the precious product of Owens River was finally ready to be turned into San Fernando Reservoir. Some 40,000 Southern Californians gathered to celebrate the momentous event. Brass bands blared, flags waved, cannon boomed.

And when the hour arrived for the chief to make a grandstand speech and turn the aqueduct officially over to the city, the throng was far more interested in seeing the flow of water he had brought than in hearing anything he had to say. He arose to make his address just as the first cascade came ripping through the gates. At that moment, as though prearranged, the audience turned tail and joined in a vast stampede from the grandstand to the side of the ditch. Out of the crowd of 40,000, not more than half a dozen heard Mulholland's famous five-word speech: "There it is. Take it."

IX

OF COURSE, EVERY DAY IS FINE HERE

DIED. Walter Edward Scott, 78, legendary California prospector fraud . . . at Scotty's Corner, California. "Scotty" first made headlines in 1905 when he rode into Los Angeles flourishing a fat roll of $500 bills, reported that he had just found a fabulously rich Death Valley gold mine, hired a special train to take him to Chicago, and jovially flung $100 tips to the crew. Thereafter he was a Sunday supplement stand-by. Revelling in his own publicity, he lived in a $2,000,000 Moorish castle in Death Valley, once rode through the streets of Manhattan in a buckboard with a kegful of gold pieces between his knees, left behind a trail of $50 bills whenever he hit town. In 1941 Scotty broke down and confessed that the gold mine was a myth; he had been grubstaked "for laughs" by the late multimillionaire, Chicago insurance tycoon Albert Johnson.

That two-inch obituary in 1954 was one of the most modest press notices Walter Scott ever received. By the fifties, people had begun to lose track of the incomparable practical jokester. Headscratching was called for, even to figure out who this Walter Scott, without the Sir, might be. Ah! but Death Valley Scotty—that rang a bell. Anyone out of his teens remembered *him*.

For almost half a century Death Valley Scotty's newspaper and magazine panegyrics had been reckoned by the column, the page, the yard. The famed race of the Santa Fe Special from the Coast to Chicago in 1905 established a long-standing world's record for rail speed—2,244 miles in 44 hours and 54 minutes—and it also established something of a record in newspaper coverage. It made the front page of every daily in this country and a great many foreign countries, and accounted for enough lineage to pave approximately 2,244 miles with galley proof.

The public ate up the story and called for more. In Times Square restaurants, in Vermont barbershops, in Montana mines, and at Texas ranch roundups, everybody talked about the latest character to crash the halls of American folklore. Temporarily, Paul Bunyan, Davy Crockett and Johnny Appleseed moved over to make room for the newcomer. Folks roared over the picture of Scotty, filthy rich and dressed like a tramp, except for his smart sombrero, guzzling champagne in the cab of a locomotive that was doing 106 miles on hour, while he urged the engineers on to try for 110, 115, 120; and behind lurched a diner, sleeper and coach, practically empty except for the conductor, half-a-dozen lackeys and one passenger, his publicity agent, Charles E. Van Loan, who was far too terrified to record a coherent account of the journey.

Trains were not geared to travel that fast in 1905. West of Chicago, twenty miles an hour was still considered a good average to maintain. "When we were rounding the curves with only two wheels hitting the tracks," Van Loan recalled with a shudder, "and I knew that Scotty was in the engine cab, filled with champagne and offering constant inducement to the engineers to go a little faster, I wondered why I had been so eager to get that assignment." But once they were safely in Chicago the publicity agent did a masterly job of promoting both his client and the Santa Fe Railroad.

It was noised about that Scotty's fare on the special had cost him $60,000. That made fresh headlines. He denied the rumor and hiked the figure to $75,000, and then $100,000. That made more headlines. Years later someone took the trouble to dig up the truth from the Santa Fe books and found that the total figure was a mere $5,500. That made still another story, which no one believed, for by then folks loved Scotty and were sure that someone was trying to debunk him.

Off and on for thirty years and more he kept the public laughing at his antics and agog with his lies about the fathomless gold mine he owned and the incredible riches being drawn from it. In fact, he lived solely to create a string of tall tales for the benefit of a gullible world. Some of them sounded farfetched, but his followers believed them because they wanted to.

Even Scotty's past was obscured in fabrication altered from

day to day. Presumably he was born in Kentucky about 1876. Nobody was ever quite sure of the date or place. Presumably he migrated to Nevada at the age of six, became a cowpuncher at the age of twelve, and a whip for one of the twenty-mule-team borax wagons of the Harmony Company before he was eighteen. The ages and the occupations had to be taken with a grain of salt.

But there was no presumption about his meteoric rise to fame as a daredevil rider with Buffalo Bill's Show. He toured the United States, England and the Continent, billed as the Wild West's wildest horseman and hip-shot artist. He hobnobbed with notables like the Prince of Wales, knew Madison Square Garden and the show arenas of Chicago, London and Paris as intimately as he knew the highway between Death Valley and Mojave.

Through it all his first love was for the sand wastes of California. He came home for good in the early 1920's, began broadcasting more superb tales about the magnificent gold strike, and set up headquarters in Grapevine Canyon at the north end of Death Valley, with multimillionaire Albert Johnson as his grubstaker and patron in the craft of practical jokesmithery.

Johnson was the silent partner, content to keep in the background, be entertained by the extravagant shenanigans, and foot the bill. He got his money's worth. Penniless Scott was his opposite, a colossal egotist and braggart, but good company and a good jester. With Johnson's blessings, Scotty wore the pants of the partnership. Together they decided to turn Grapevine Canyon into a national show place.

Renowned architect Julia Morgan was constructing a marvelous castle for William Randolph Hearst on a bluff overlooking the Pacific at remote San Simeon. Why should not Scott and Johnson build just as fine a castle overlooking the desert? They had heard of a pretty fair architect named Frank Lloyd Wright, as good a headline getter as there was in the business. So Wright got the commission for creating the first desert castle in America.

He drafted plans for a stunning building, a modified Hopi Indian structure that would melt into the background of Grapevine Canyon as if it had grown there. The partners took one look, paid off the architect, and summarily discarded the design. They wanted something that would stand out in the desert, not shrink into the setting—something attractive, more on the order of the Hearst monument. They had no reason to shy away from trappings and ornamentation. Their building had to have eye-catching style.

They got what they wanted—a gaudy pile that did not stop with pseudo-Spanish Mission, but added touches of medieval French, Italian Renaissance, Elizabethan English and Early Hollywood, all set off with Moorish turrets and embattlements and huge ornamental gates. It took five years to build. Into it were crammed such refinements as a $50,000 pipe organ, a swimming pool, a waterfall at one end of an enormous lounge, and a fancy master bedroom for Scotty, costing $185,000.

"There is enough cast iron pipe on the ranch to build a water system for a town," declared a prowler in 1926, before the building was completed. "There are plans for an ice refrigerating plant in that spot where the white sand makes a mammoth reflector, and the sun beats down blistering hot during summer's months. Already there is a two-story building of concrete construction, with screened-in sleeping quarters, luxurious bathrooms and expansive living quarters.

"There is a garage that houses three trucks and two passenger cars and has sufficient empty space to care for a fire department. There is another enormous building that shelters mules used in the development work. And Scotty is building a plant to generate electricity by the use of power that comes from spring water flowing from higher grounds. There are whisperings, even concerning a huge landing field for airplanes. It doesn't do any harm to ask Scotty what it all means; neither does it do any good."

To a worshipful public the edifice was Scotty's Castle, with never a reference to the real owner and bursar, shy Albert Johnson; and for years Johnson appeared more than glad to have the onus for his prodigality attached to the partner. As for Scotty himself, away from home he invariably referred to the Gargantuan pile of masonry as "my shack."

Every detail of the desert household was worth another news story: the three-foot concrete walls; the tiled kitchen floor; the antiqued redwood cupboards crammed with enough canned goods to stock a grocery store; decorated tunnels leading from one section of the castle to another; a music room with two grand pianos, as well as the organ; the lavish fountains and grottoes. The public learned that although Scotty was a talented cook, possessing a wealth of French recipes he had collected in Paris, an old Armenian was the *maître d'hôtel* and a Canadian ex-machine-gunner his assistant.

Scotty went into ranching on a grand scale, raising everything from Rhenish grapes and Algerian dates to American turkeys, quail and pigs. His interest in agriculture and husbandry was good for a feature story. When news slacked off there was always the mysterious mine to fall back on, with a yarn about another $700,000 "just minted." Trips to Los Angeles, Kansas City or Manhattan were interspersed often enough to get pictures in the newspapers again. The story of a $500 breakfast for three was incidental. He had a nervous habit of tearing $50 bills in two when he did not happen to have a twenty with which to tip a bellhop—handing out the half and buying it back next day with a crisp twenty. Somehow those accidents had a way of getting onto the press wires. Scotty was a legend, but also a reality.

By the middle 1920's his shack had become a major tourist attraction in the Southwest. It was on the itinerary of every middle-class tourist and a considerable number traveling first class. People thronged to the castle to sponge on Johnson's hospitality —free meals, free drinks, free beds, and of course a free tour of the buildings and grounds. They also appropriated souvenirs freely.

In his Buffalo Bill days Scotty himself had been an ardent souvenir collector, and delighted in calling attention to the showcase of solid silver spoons he had surreptitiously picked up in dining cars of most of the nation's railroads, aboard ships and in the best restaurants and hotels of Europe and the United States. But he resented this sticky-fingered practice in others—when he was the victim.

After a crowd of guests had departed, the hospitable guides noted the absence of a wide variety of *objets d'art*. Johnson was tolerant, but it made Scotty mad. The tourists were getting to be a damned nuisance. He had to do something about it. Prowling visitors, after a time, were startled by strange posted notices: HAVE JUST POURED FIVE POUNDS OF ARSENIC INTO THIS SPRING. DRINK AT YOUR OWN RISK, OR, EAT ALL YOU WANT. STAY AS LONG AS YOU WANT. BUT DON'T TAKE ANYTHING AWAY. LOOK OUT FOR THE PET RATTLE SNAKE. DON'T KILL HER. SHE WON'T BITE YOU. A few people got the point.

He talked of building a moat around the castle and fortifying the towers and turrets. For three years the grounds were closed to the public altogether. But tourists still flocked to Grapevine Canyon. He had started something he could not stop.

Later on, hard times came to the castle. Perhaps Scotty's humor was wearing thin, but millionaire Johnson spent less time there. He made frequent trips back to Chicago, stayed for protracted periods, and was slower about paying the bills which his "caretaker" ran up. A feeble, white-haired woman named Ella Josephine Scott collapsed on a street in Long Beach, California. She turned out to be the candy store clerk Scotty had married in New York back in the Buffalo Bill days, and had all but forgotten. Now, with the aid of the police and an eager attorney, she was trying to collect maintenance of $1,000 a month and $25,000 in legal fees.

"The castle is open," declared Scotty to the press. "She can come home any time she wants. Gold is the root of all evil. That's what's back of it. Somebody wants to see my hole card."

Then it came to light that both Scotty and Johnson had been negligent in filing a proper homestead entry before building the shack in Grapevine Canyon, and were dispossessed by the President of the United States, who had ideas of turning Death Valley into a National Monument. Only through a special act of Congress was the title cleared, and Johnson had to throw good money after bad in buying the land from the federal government. Moreover, Scotty's story about that famous gold mine was questioned, for the Secretary of the Interior retained all mineral rights.

But even through the hard years there was scant letup in the flow of tourists. Scotty had brought renown to Death Valley. Singlehanded, he had done more to publicize the California desert than any other one living man. Press agents for the Southern Pacific and the Santa Fe had worked on it, too, but not with the flair Scotty possessed. "That inferno of sand would make a gorgeous playground for the public," one of them had hinted. But while they were merely beckoning, the master publicist had brought the crowds and ushered in a new day when the driest of the desert was to be a show place, a tourist Mecca and a popular playground.

Long before the castle was built, however, an entirely different kind of popularization movement had started on the Los Angeles side of the desert. The western fringe had been spotted as a potential Utopia by the first serious American settlers. The climate and the setting were just right. All they needed was water, and that they could easily bring in. Many of the early colonists were farmfolk who were tired of grubbing a living from rough soil in the rugged climate of the East. They were looking for a place where they could have a more relaxed, comfortable existence. Easier living conditions were on their minds. They wanted to mix a little pleasure with work. Though they would have been the last to admit it, theirs was a quest for a playground, as well as a quest for a good livelihood. They found it in the San Bernardino and San Fernando valleys.

"What Holland was to the life of Europe in the fourteenth, fifteenth and sixteenth centuries, Southern California is to the life of the Pacific Coast at the end of the nineteenth century," wrote ecologist William E. Smythe in 1899, after making a brilliant study of arid regions in America.

"The industrial impulse which the men of the Netherlands caught from their conquest of the sea, the men of the southern valleys caught from their conquest of the desert . . . Tempering their superlative instincts with love of home, they developed towns and surroundings of rare beauty and comfort. The land was a desert of sagebrush and cactus, in which a few scattered mission gardens made charming oases—a country which offered nothing to the stranger save climate and scenery. To this barren place came irrigation and the Anglo-Saxon, bringing a new era in their train."

As a typical example, Smythe pictured Riverside, an expanse of marginal desert colonized by farm folk from Tennessee in search of an easier way of life. "With the rare intuition which Eastern men have frequently displayed in going to the West," he remarked, "the newcomers selected a location which seemed quite preposterous to the natives of the country. They deliberately bought lands assessed at a valuation of seventy-five cents an acre. These lands then constituted a sheep pasture of inferior sort. They were similar to the stretch of desert which the transcontinental traveler sees in passing through Arizona. After the winter rains they bore a short-lived crop of wild flowers, but during most of the year they offered nothing more attractive than sagebrush and mesquite."

These escapists from the farms of Tennessee bought the land against the advice of rancheros in 1871, built a canal from the source of the Santa Ana River, planted oranges and more oranges. Then they persuaded State Department officials to stoop to the level of farm agents and import from foreign countries both horticultural information and citrus grafts.

Within twenty-five years the original sheep pasture was producing some of the finest oranges in the world. The first colony tract of 2,000 acres had been expanded to 10,000, and 4,000 carloads of fruit, worth $1,500,000, were being shipped out annually.

The Tennesseans had found exactly the kind of comfortable life they sought. "They are no longer farmers," Smythe suggested, "but business and professional men who have risen above the general level of society. At Riverside at least ninety percent of the total population live in homes that front on beautiful boulevards, presenting an almost unbroken view of well-kept lawns, opulent flower beds and delicate shrubbery.

"Newspaper carriers canter through these streets delivering the local morning and evening dailies. Though this is a farming population, the people enjoy the convenience of free postal delivery. They fill their bathtubs with water piped through the streets. They light their homes with electricity. In the center of the colony they have fine stores, churches, hotels and public halls. Their schools are of the highest standard. A well-patronized institution is the clubhouse and its reading room."

No one denied that a lot of sweat and toil went into the making of a town like Riverside, but after the drudgery endured in sidehill farming of the East, contending with frost and thaws, snow and summer rains, this was holiday agriculture. Here in the temperate semitropics one could relax. There was time and occasion for laughter and enjoyment of life. To be sure, Riverside and Grapevine Canyon had little in common, but here were two prime examples of desert playground living that appeared mighty attractive in the East.

From Maine to Missouri the story of Riverside made alluring farm news in the eighties and nineties. Anaheim, Redlands, Ontario, Pomona and a dozen other lush little towns sprang out of the marginal desert land that had never before been decorated with anything but spring wild flowers, sagebrush and mesquite. "The fruits of this new impulse," recapitulated Smythe, "are seen in the scores of charming communities which stretch eastward to the margin of the Colorado Desert and southward to the border of Mexico. It is pleasant to note that beautiful homes and high average prosperity have not spoiled the simplicity of the homes."

These were the halcyon days of Southern California. Every other literate traveler who took the long trek across the continent seemed compelled or inspired to write an essay and then a book about the glories of the new-found paradise. No North American region had ever prompted such a flux of travelogues in so short a period. The product was biased, contradictory, overdrawn, sometimes cynical, but out of its sum came the indelible impression that Southern California was a happy-go-lucky land of opportunity such as man had seldom uncovered.

Eastern readers could chuckle with Mark Twain, sentimentalize with Mary Austin, travel vicariously and comfortably with J. Ross Browne, get excited about John Spears' picture of the desert, become thoroughly muddled by the six-foot shelf of autobiographical accounts carrying the threadbare titles: *My Two Years in California, My Three Years in California, My Six Years in California, My Twenty Years . . . My Forty Years. . . .*

But if an itchy-footed Easterner wanted the straight conservative dope on this Western Mecca, he read Charles Nordhoff. In edition after edition Harpers kept the bookstores stocked with that best seller, *California for Health, Pleasure and Residence,* "A Book for Travelers and Settlers, Giving Detailed Accounts of the Culture of the Wine and Raisin Grape, the Orange, Lemon, Olive and Other Semi-tropical Fruits, Colony Settlements, Methods of Irrigation, etc., with Maps and Numerous Illustrations."

For thirty years Nordhoff was the true gospel bearer for California proselytes. He tended toward the ecstatic, but he backed his ecstacy with clean, clear fact, unhesitatingly played up the desert borderlands as the ideal retreat for harried, nerve-shattered, consumptive Easterners, and made it clear that this was the work-and-play land of tomorrow—"California, which has so many delights in store for the tourist, and so many attractions for the farmer or settler looking for a mild and healthful climate and a productive country.

"The constant or almost uninterrupted brightness of the skies," he puffed, "has, of course, a good deal to do with the healthful influence of the climate. The southern counties have but little rain. There are no gloomy days . . . All winter the gardens are full of flowers, the grass is green, and Nature is in her

most inviting garb. The whole of Southern California is full of novelties and wonders to the intelligent person. . . .

"For all healthful, open-air enjoyments you will have extraordinary facilities, because the life is free and untrammeled. You are expected to do what you please; horses are cheap; roads are almost invariably excellent; every place has a good livery stable; you can get competent guides; and you carry with you wherever you go fine mountain scenery, bright sunshine—so constant that, when I remarked to a citizen of San Diego that it was a fine day, he looked at me in amazement, 'Of course, it's a fine day; why not? Every day is fine here.' Moreover, at all these places you will meet pleasant, intelligent and hospitable people, who will add to your enjoyment.

"There is no longer any doubt of the very great and often surprising beneficial influences upon diseases of the throat and lungs, of the dry and warm winter climate of Southern California . . . I know myself, not dozens, but hundreds of instances of men and women who would have perished in the more eastern part of the United States, but who after a winter in California found themselves capable of enduring fatigue and exposure with enjoyment, and who had lost that uncomfortable consciousness of 'having a throat,' which is so often the bane of existence among us.

"California offers, in my belief, the best opportunities for men willing to work on land to be found on this continent . . . The rewards for his toil are much greater than anywhere in the East. The mild climate relieves him of a great deal of the drudgery and painful toil of the Eastern farmer . . . I have seen growing, with only common care, on one two-and-a-half-acre lot in Riverside, and all bearing, oranges, apples, lemons, pears, figs, plums, apricots, almonds, quinces, grapes of a dozen varieties, prunes, pomegranates, peaches, English walnuts, and limes. The apples were as fair to view, as juicy and spirited, as though they had grown in New England. It would be difficult to find outside of California such a collection in the same enclosure; but I have seen a dozen and could find a thousand localities there, where, if the owners chose, they could make quite as varied a show.

"It is an admirable climate to work in. After the hottest days of summer follow always cool nights. Moreover, the heat is dry, and therefore far more enjoyable. There are no such muggy and sticky days as we have in July and August . . . He who comes to this state from the Eastern states of America wonders at the fresh complexion of the people; he is pleasantly surprised at their healthful color and the red blood in their cheeks. The forms of the women who have lived some years here are more full and robust than with us . . . I do not remember seeing anywhere in the state a single weakly or what the Yankees call "peaked" looking child. It is a paradise for men who will work with their hands, and the better if they will also put brains into their work."

It was an irresistible come-on, and emigrants responded almost as they had during the gold rush. The railroads, of course, had a proprietary interest in peopling the West, and in the late eighties the Southern Pacific and Santa Fe had set off a fantastic real-estate boom around Los Angeles by staging a rate war.

The standard fare from the Missouri Valley region had been approximately $125. The Santa Fe dropped it to $100. Southern Pacific countered by advertising tickets for $75. Week by week the bargain in rail rides improved until the Santa Fe was down to $12 in March 1887. The Southern Pacific equaled it. In a few hours the rate was scaled down to $6 and $4.

At noon on March 6 the Santa Fe was offering rides to California for a dollar. Meanwhile, lecturers and promoters in the pay of the railroads swept through the East and Middle West, campaigning for California. They organized community tours, offered to serve as employment agents and real-estate agents, airing in their whirlwind recruitment the wildest ballyhoo the country had ever heard.

Land sharks arrived in Los Angeles and San Diego ahead of the crowd. They bought up huge tracts of arid land, subdivided it, marked it off into modest plots, distributed fliers, and with brass bands and top-hatted auctioneers, free lemonade and barbecued beef, went to work on the tens of thousands of gullible newcomers. A "choice residence lot" or a "villa site" was the most modest piece of land any of the barkers had for sale.

In one year the two rail lines, each running three or four trains a day, transported almost 250,000 people to Los Angeles, real-estate transactions topped $200,000,000, and scores of new towns were platted in Los Angeles and San Diego counties. Already people were slowly pushing out into the desert.

The boom died quickly and scores of towns named on the prospectuses never came into existence, but even without them the area was overrun. The railroads readjusted their rates and

THE GREAT CALIFORNIA DESERTS

let the California towns, on which they had dumped thousands of passengers, carry on. Los Angeles and San Diego stepped up the tempo of their boostings. The Chamber of Commerce came into existence. Itinerant lecturers, representing the chamber, took to the road armed with mountains of literature and stereoptican slides.

A special train, "California on Wheels," exhibiting agricultural products, photographic enlargements, home models and statistical charts, set out on a two-year cross-country tour. By 1900, Los Angeles was the best-advertised city in America—and the country's most garish metropolis. By 1915 or 1920, sensitive residents were trying to escape from it toward the desert, and the more conservative tourists were following their trail.

When two adventuresome middle-aged matrons, Edna Brush Perkins and Charlotte Jordan, for example, arrived from the East on the Santa Fe Limited for a Los Angeles holiday in 1919, they took a quick look at the city and decided it was all too bizarre for them. "It is so different from the pictures on the timetables and hotel fliers," they apologized politely.

They took an excursion up the coast and then down to San Diego. That country did not have much of an appeal either. The tourist literature that beckoned them westward had emphasized "charming bungalows with date palms in the doorways and yellow roses climbing the porches, square orange groves brushed and combed for dress parade, picturesque missions, and white towns shaded with feathery pepper trees." They saw all that and still did not get excited about California.

Crossing the country, the one region that had impressed them the most was the long stretch of desert between Needles and the San Gabriel mountains. It seemed strange to them that none of the travel literature had mentioned the Mojave, as though the promoters were rather ashamed to admit it was there.

"Mojave is like a tiger, terrible and fascinating," they had concluded. The sweeps of blue-green brush, leading off to mysterious mountains, blue and red against the sky, the black lava beds, the clifflike rocks, the emptiness and vastness of it had captured their imaginations. The Angelenos and the tourists could have Los Angeles; they wanted to explore the desert.

They checked out of their hotel, rented a Ford roadster, purchased the prescribed water jugs and camping equipment and headed east to survey what they considered the real attraction of Southern California. In newspapers and magazines they had seen a great deal about Death Valley, and now they were not going to be content until they had inspected this "white heart of Mojave."

Raised eyebrows and shocked silence were the only reactions they could draw from their inquiries about routes and road conditions. Two ladies setting out for Death Valley alone! Weren't there enough attractions in Los Angeles to satisfy them? Not until they were in the dying mining town of Randsburg three days later did they find a kindred spirit in a decrepit old prospector who appreciated their passion for desert adventure; he urged them on, but urged them to leave their car behind and take the Tonopah and Tidewater Railroad, like other tourists.

The motorists listened to his advice grudgingly and drove on to the rail line, following the sand ruts made by a broken-down Ford truck. But they had no intention of following the beaten trail to Scotty's Castle. Instead they took the train to Beatty, hired a buckboard piloted by an ancient teamster, and entered Death Valley on foot, the hard way, like the Jayhawkers and the survivors of the Sand Walking Company.

Their first view of it from the rim opposite Corkscrew Mountain was worth all the struggle. "The road turned abruptly around a point of rock," Mrs. Perkins recorded. "Charlotte and I were walking ahead of the wagon. We went gayly to the end of the promontory and were brought to a sudden stop by what we saw. There, without any warning of its nearness, like an unexpected crash of orchestral music, lay the terrible valley, the beautiful, the overwhelming valley."

"Well, that's her," announced their guide, who obviously thought his clients were insane, and admitted that he could see none of the colors and enchantments they pointed out to him.

"We all stood silent then," continued the enraptured Mrs. Perkins. "We were about three thousand feet above the bottom of the valley, looking down over its whole length, an immense oblong glistening with white alkali deposits, deep between high mountain walls. We knew that men had died down there in the shimmering heat of that white floor, we knew that the valley was sterile and dead, and yet we saw it covered with a mantle of such strange beauty that we felt it was the noblest thing we had ever imagined.

"Only a poet could hope to express the emotion of beauty stronger than fear and death which held us silent moment after moment by the point of rock. Before terror and beauty like that, something inside you stands still; for a while you rest in the companionship of greatness."

The two women followed the Jayhawker trail, wandered through the ruins of Keane Wonder Mine, Furnace Creek Ranch and the old Harmony Works, explored Wild Rose Canyon, climbed Mount Baldy for a panoramic view of the highest and lowest points in the United States, saw Skidoo and a great deal of spectacular scenery, gave Scotty's Castle a wide berth, and were still in a seventh heaven when they got back to Los Angeles a month later. To them, as to an increasing number of discriminating travelers, the desert was unquestionably the foremost attraction of Southern California.

As yet, few residents were fully accredited sand hermits; they could not bear to cut off ties completely with the green world. But in the early twenties city folk, as well as choosy tourists, were seeking refuge on the edge of the desert.

A little place called Palm Springs, one of the old stage stations of the fifties and sixties, and more recently noted for its sanitarium, appealed to those who really wanted to get away from it all. It was a delightful desert hideaway, tucked under the shadow of San Jacinto Peak, which towered above for almost two vertical miles and was declared to be "the steepest mountain for its height on the continent."

The railroad had missed Palm Springs by ten miles, and the road to the village was a notorious sand trap. However, a cautious motorist who stayed in the sand ruts and was lucky enough not to have to turn out for cars coming in the opposite direction, could make it all right. And once there, Palm Springs was indeed a charming rural village. "Garden in the Sun," the desert addicts called it fondly.

"Village is a pretty word," one of its spellbound citizens ruminated, "though ambitious settlements are keen to disclaim the implied rusticity and to graduate into the rank of town or city. Palm Springs has no such aims, and is well content to remain far down the list in census returns. We decline to take part in the race for 'improvements.' Rural Free Delivery does not entice us; we prefer the daily gathering at the store at mailtime, Indians and whites together.

"Electric lights are here for those who like them: yet to some of us nothing seems so homelike for the dinner tables as shaded candles, or for fireside reading a good kerosene lamp . . . Telephones? No thanks. We are here to possess our souls and live all day in the open. How can we do that if anybody and everybody who wishes can jerk us back with a telephone wire, as if we were parrots tied to a perch with a string? Cement sidewalks would be to us a calamity: we may be dusty, but dust is natural and we prefer it.

"The village itself is a place of two or three score unpretentious cottages scattered along half-a-dozen palm- and pepper-shaded streets. We do not run much to lawns and formal gardens; we live in the desert because we like it, hence we don't care to shut ourselves away in little citified enclosures. . . Wealth and fashion, as such, are not much attracted to our village. Palm Beach, not Palm Springs, is their mark . . . We're placed together in these Palestine-like surroundings, just a hundred or so nobodies, possibly one or two somebodies, and a few Indians, but all friends.

"Two or three old places which formed the nucleus of the settlement are bowers of bloom and umbrageous greenery. Gray old fig trees lean out over the sidewalk, while oranges, dates, grapefruit, lemons and trees of other sorts for fruit or ornament, flourish. Stores, inns, church and school—of these it is enough to say that they are well up to what would be expected in a community such as ours.

"In 1909 the Desert Inn opened its doors, with a standard of hostelry service that might have been taken to signifiy a new era. In that year our white residents could be counted on one's fingers with a digit to spare, and winter visitors ran from a dozen to a score. Now—1923—white residents number about a hundred, while our winter population amounts to perhaps four times that figure. . . .

"The state highway, which threatened to bring an increasing roar of automobile travel through our quiet streets, has been diverted—averted is the better word—to the north side of the valley, leaving Palm Springs with no more than its quota of traffic racket to put up with.

"I shall not try to forecast the future of our small community; we are content as we are. The less history there is in store for us, the better we shall like it."

There was more unwelcome history in store for Palm Springs than those escapees from the roaring twenties could imagine. But for a few years longer they were allowed to revel in their idyllic solitude. It drew the nature-loving romanticists, the throwbacks and carry-overs from the age of Emerson and Thoreau of New England, adherents of a John Muir philosophy translated into the vocabulary of sand and sagebrush.

Except in natural phenomena, there was not much going on in the town. One could take baths in the warm springs, preferably by moonlight or candlelight. For young and old, horseback riding was the major sport, and it was a morning ritual for bright-eyed botanists and birdspotters to canter off to the canyons and dunes.

There was a periodic stir in the village when Hollywood companies put in an appearance to borrow the dunes or a canyon for a backdrop, and a greater stir for a few weeks every autumn when the local Thespians rallied to put on an outdoor pageant for the benefit of the tourists. For that extravaganza practically every resident in the region was recruited—even the Indians. The dramatis personae and the roster of sceneshifters, carpenters, wigmakers and prompters could take the place of a census-taker's check list.

After the play was over, there was no more man-made excitement until the farewell parties of the following June, when most families prepared to "go inside" for the summer—take off for the Coast. During the winter, residents and visitors alike leaned heavily on nature for entertainment. There were the cliffs and caves of Andreas Canyon to visit. One could go hunting for low-grade precious pebbles in the Garnet Hills. Eight miles to the northwest was the Devil's Garden with a fair, natural display of cactus. The rocky, winding ravines of Palm Canyon, crowded with thousands of statuesque palms, was the most highly touted attraction of the area.

A dozen or more canyons were within a day's horseback ride of Palm Springs, and the soft-spoken publicists for the playground did not stop with nearby points of interest. Places as far afield as the Salton Sea, the foothills of the Orocopia Mountains, fifty miles away, and distant oases which were to become the sites of future towns—all were included among the allurements. But take your trip on horseback, was the advice of anyone from the stableboy to the omniscient postmaster.

If the hurried tourist insisted on tripping into the desert by car, special local instructions were issued by no less an authority than the United States Geological Survey: "Automobile parties should always carry a supply of spare tires and tubes. A vulcanizing outfit for making patches is especially desirable. A tire gauge is useful and an air pump and jack are necessary.

"Sand is the worst obstacle. The average road consists of a pair of wheel ruts, and in sandy places it is essential to stay in these ruts. Leave them only to pass another vehicle and then keep two wheels of the car in a rut if the sand is bad . . . A shovel is useful in short stretches for cleaning out covered ruts . . . and very effective use can be made of two strips of heavy canvas, say 30 feet long and 18 inches wide, laid lengthwise ahead in the ruts to avoid spining of the wheels. Water, oil and gasoline, more than enough for probable needs, should be taken, and it should be remembered that desert roads may require twice as much per mile as pavement."

Although the automobile apparently was to be a permanent affliction, Palm Springs recluses were nonetheless distrustful of it. They did not like the racket and the fumes, and were suspicious of people who habitually depended on that kind of transportation. They wanted to keep their village quiet and sleepy. "Calmness, quietude, restfulness, as a rule very relative terms, here approach the absolute," boasted an early-to-bed resident. "It may seem odd to speak of sleep under the head of 'amusements,' but such sleep as one gets in the desert fairly ranks as enjoyment, so it is much the same. Few people know what night at its best can be; the desert is the place to learn it."

But Palm Springs was due for a rude awakening. Condoning the use of those canyons and dunes as movie sets was a mistake. The studio luminaries, unwillingly dragged to this off-beat setting, took an inexplicable liking to the place—as did their understudies and idols. Hollywood came and Hollywood conquered. Palm Springs quickly lost its kerosene-lamp charm. In little more than a decade it was completely transformed.

"One of the newest playgrounds of rich America," was the label hung on the place by the late thirties. "Today this ultra-smart winter resort for movie stars and for people who like and can afford to live where and as movie stars live, gleams as brightly as a new toy village," ran the popular appraisal. "Its buildings are uniformly of California pseudo-Spanish architecture: the white, lemon or buff-colored dwellings, entered by doors painted bright red, blue or yellow, are surmounted by tile roofs and enclosed by wooden fences, bordered by rows of pink and white oleanders or the green, feathery plumage of tamarisk trees.

"Here are branches of the most expensive New York and Los Angeles shops; golf courses and hotels that range from the palatial to the modestly magnificent; private and public schools, and no lack of masseurs and masseuses; dude cowhands for atmosphere, and branch offices for the bigger businessmen ... Hollywood discovered the climatic and topographical charm of the little village resting on the shelf of the San Jacinto Mountain base at the edge of the desert. A new highway was cut through, Los Angeles and New York promoters got to work, and the modern town sprang up almost with the speed of a movie set.

"Here one finds the desert safely pushed to the borders of a transplanted section of Hollywood Boulevard. Guests sprint about town on bicycles, sip cocktails, play table tennis, explore the nearby desert on horseback, or relaxing in some hotel garden, enjoy the lengthening shadow of Jacinto and the quiet of the land stretching out to the eastern hills. After dark they visit the night clubs, casinos and movies."

And that was only an early beginning. The village that wanted to remain a village boomed into another Los Angeles suburb a hundred times the size and population it quietly boasted in 1923, with motels and guesthouses stretching out end to end for miles into the desert, and meeting more motels and guest ranches reaching in from a dozen towns and cities which sought to emulate the original Garden in the Sun. There was no end in sight for the sprawl of desert playlands.

So fast were choice desert sites being gobbled up for towns, resorts and commercial exploitation, that conservationists, who had never given much thought to the need for preserving barren scenery, leaped to attention. If future generations were to see what California desert was like in its natural state, something had to be done about it immediately, before it was too late. There were wilderness-lovers as keenly fond of dunes, cactus patches and remote canyons as were brother protectors of the giant sequoia and the mountain meadows. Given a chance, private usurpers could overrun and ruin the most attractive desert spots in the same way that lumbermen, miners and sheepherders had laid waste to the Sierra heights.

Responding to pressure from farseeing Californians, Congress was persuaded, in 1922, to establish Palms National Monument as a means of preserving the handsomest surviving groves of native American fan palms. The 1,600-acre tract was to include Murry, Andreas and Palm canyons, the favorite picnic spots for a generation of Palm Springs horseback riders.

But it was necessary also to take into consideration the Cahuilla Indians, who had migrated 400 years earlier from New Mexico and Arizona, settled around San Jacinto Peak, and more recently had been granted official asylum there by the Great White Father—before anyone dreamed that the Caucasian race would ever covet the land.

The Indian reservation actually encroached on the village proper, so Congress tactfully attached a rider to the 1922 Conservation Bill, making the establishment of the monument subject to the approval of the friendly tribesmen. The Cahuillas held a powwow, agreed that they were getting on fine with the local villagers and did not mind their amicable visits, but also agreed that they did not want every Tom, Dick and Harry traipsing into their private back yards. To the astonishment of everyone, the Indians vetoed the bill. Moreover, to make doubly certain that tourists understood whose land it was, they erected a tollgate, built a road, and started charging admission.

With that experience to serve as guide, when Uncle Sam grabbed Death Valley a decade later, the Panamint Indians, who for centuries had regarded the valley as their heritage, were virtually ignored. Here, at least, the desert conservationists could claim a clear victory. In Death Valley there were 3,000 square miles of hot, rugged playground, rescued from the menace of private ownership—except for a few plots staked out in prior claims.

Death Valley was stupendous; it was beautiful and it was awe inspiring, but not exactly representative of California desert and too far removed from coastal population centers. Needed to please the ever-increasing legion of desert-lovers was a more accessible reserve that typified the Colorado Desert. So in 1933, the same year that Death Valley National Monument was dedicated, California became the landlord of Anza State Park, just east of the Coast Range. At first it included only 275,000 acres, donated by local organizations and individual landowners, but Anza grew and grew until it became Anza-Borrego State Park and measured almost 500,000 acres—the largest piece of real estate in the whole California park system.

This playground, extending eastward from San Diego's central mountain ranges into the Imperial Valley lowlands, and south almost to the Mexican border, was large enough and wild enough to satisfy desert addicts of the present generation or of any future generation. Here they could relive, to their heart's content, all the delights and discomforts of desert exploration known to the Spanish padres, the overlanders, coach passengers and gold prospectors.

Big as it was, the area was crowded with history. En route to San Francisco in 1775, Anza and his entourage made three camps there. The Southern Emigrant Trail and Butterfield's mail line both crossed it. Military expeditions, the Mormon Battalion and Kit Carson were all too familiar with the terrain. Vallecito, on the western edge of the park, was the center for desert travelers, gold seekers and the most desperate desperados.

An east–west highway cut the vast tract roughly in half, and a few secondary roads led into it, but aside from these and formal camp and picnic locations, the desert hound was on his own. Vague trails or suggested "routes of travel" were plotted on official maps, but the only maintenance they received was the seasonal scouring from flash floods and winter rains. It was the intention of the park management to leave them that way.

Miles and miles from civilization—and even from park headquarters—one could roam through the wild, dry wastelands of folded hills, alkali sinks, white sands and rolling reaches of cholla and creosote bush, the barren badlands, relieved here and there by a tiny oasis or a fringe of palms at a canyon entrance. Elevations varied from sea level to over 6,000 feet in the San Ysidro Mountains.

Explorers could make their excursions on foot, with pack and saddle animals, and to a few points of interest in an ordinary automobile, but none of these means of locomotion was quite adequate. Anza-Borrego had popularized a new mode of desert travel. The jeep was the thing. This was one of the world's best tilting grounds for the new sport of jeep-jaunting.

As though the state and federal governments were competing in their efforts to play host in the big southern sandbox, three years after Anza Desert Park came into existence the Department of the Interior announced the opening of Joshua Tree National Monument, 200,000 acres larger even than Anza-Borrego, an area more than four-fifths the size of the state of Rhode Island. Its 870 square miles stretched out north of the Salton Sea, overlapping both the Mojave and the Colorado deserts, encompassing a little of everything associated with both and a lot of spectacular Joshua trees.

"Located in beautiful high desert country," read the prospectus, "the Monument preserves a typical California desert where plants and animals have acquired specialized habits in order to survive; where the sand may suddenly be covered with millions of wildflowers; where the oases shelter a colorful and varied bird population; and where the colorful cactuses, the spidery ocotillo and the grotesque Joshua tree are symbols of the desert."

As an entirely different kind of desert playground, another state park was created in 1951 on the north shore of the Salton Sea. For a few years after the great Colorado flood of 1907, the waterline of the sea slowly receded through evaporation, then excess ground water, seeping in from irrigation canals, brought a corresponding rise until a fairly stable shore margin was maintained.

No sooner did the word get around that the Salton Sea was a permanent fixture on the landscape than it suddenly boomed into a popular resort region. The tepid, salty expanse was discovered to be one of the "fastest" bodies of water in the world, ideal for boat racing and water skiing. Since the state had been more than generous in sponsoring mountain recreation for hikers, hunters and pack-trip enthusiasts, it was only fair that some of the largess should be spent for equally enthusiastic boatmen.

They got their docks, launching ramps, campsites and picnic areas on this new 16,000-acre beach, and before the installations were completed, water-sports pilgrims were pouring into the park by the thousands.

Dotted here and there on the desert were other public playgrounds, as varied as Mount San Jacinto, overlooking the sands from the heights above Idyllwild; Joshua Trees Park, east of Lancaster; and Mitchell Caverns, with its labyrinth of chilly limestone chambers and remnants of aboriginal cave dwellers, fifty miles west of Needles.

In Coachella Valley, in Apple Valley, in Imperial Valley, in the towns on the highways across the Mojave, and in fifty other resort centers in and about the living desert, thousands of private inns, lodges and motels catered to the increasing throng of sun-and-sand worshippers. Uncle Sam and the State of California had entered the tourist business, too, and were proving to be the most congenial and democratic desert hosts of all.

X

GOODNESS GRACIOUS, ALL THAT SCENERY FOR CINEMA!

THE gold rushes had beckoned to California just about every kind of crook and criminal known to the constabulary of the world. In the years that followed, the worst of the miscreants were dispersed; they mellowed or went straight; they were rubbed out, forgiven or absorbed in the general populace.

A half century of Western history was so liberally seasoned with outlawry that most sections of the state were tainted. Los Angeles was one of the few places which had been spared. Compared to the rest of California, the City of the Angels was almost worthy of its name. It was puritanical—a dead end for outlaws, so overpopulated with self-righteous Midwesterners that an enterprising scapegrace did not have a chance there.

But respectable Los Angeles was not sufficiently respectable for Horace H. Wilcox, a pious man who, with his wife, was trying to escape the sins of the world and forget the afflictions with which they had been visited. In the search for solace, the Wilcoxes found a big, sandy watermelon patch well outside the city limits in 1887; they bought it, divided in into lots for sale to customers of conservative habits, and established a "temperance colony."

On these acres Padre Junípero Serra, more than a century before, was credited with having celebrated a mass to the Holy Wood of the Cross. So Mrs. Wilcox reverently and appropriately named their watermelon-patch development "Hollywood."

For several years neither Hollywood nor the Wilcoxes prospered. Few prospective tenants could present proper character references to meet the colony standards. Moreover, the amateur realtors were much too heedless of their own material needs; they set aside free land for churches, schools, parks and public libraries, and when a highly desirable homesite candidate—like the distinguished French painter Paul de Longpré—came along, likely as not he would get three or four acres along Hollywood Boulevard for nothing. Commercialism in any form was highly distasteful to the landlords.

Wilcox died land poor in 1892, but his wife kept on with the business and was less selective with her clientele. By 1900, Hollywood's population had swelled to over 400. It was still a very rural community where the excitement of the day was furnished by the arrival of the Toluca stage en route to San Fernando Valley. The village was separated from Los Angeles by a broad stretch of open country, and occupied by so civic-minded a people that when it was incorporated in 1903, one of the first ordinances passed by the 177 voters made it a misdemeanor for a herder to drive a flock of more than 2,000 sheep through the streets. The Wilcox design for a refined residential colony had been accepted: industry was not wanted.

Los Angeles gradually became more worldly and cosmopolitan, but Hollywood shrank further and further into its shell of conservatism. It was known for its fine churches and schools, its charming homes, orange groves, winter flower and vegetable gardens—and its righteousness. To the mother city came dance halls, theatres, nickelodeons, a phonograph and vitoscope parlor, but such dens of iniquity had no place in Hollywood.

The Wilcox watermelon patch at last acquired a look of prosperity. It thrived on wholesome respectability and grew. By 1910 the population had increased to 4,000 and was suffering from growing pains. Too many people were crowding in, and like other towns of Southern California, Hollywood was running short of water. After long and heated debate the villagers decided they would have to stoop to the inevitable. They traded their civic independence for a share in the Los Angeles water supply. But regardless of that concession, they were determined to hold tenaciously to their rural identity. They did not want to be too closely associated with the big city.

This was the Hollywood that a brand new breed of California outlaws discovered about that time. They were chronic violators of patent law, fugitives from Chicago, Philadelphia and New York, where state courts and the attorneys of Thomas A. Edison were making life uncomfortable for them. They needed the protection of the wide open spaces of the West, a quiet business refuge safely removed from the beat of Eastern law-enforcement agents—near to the Mexican border if escape to a foreign country proved expedient, or near to the desert if temporary escape in that direction was indicated.

They were the vanguard of the new profession of moviemakers, and, entirely by accident, they found in Hollywood a climate and a setting far more suited to their trade than New York, New Jersey, Illinois, Connecticut or Pennsylvania.

Two decades before, Edison and George Eastman had perfected the frame-lined celluloid strip that put pictures in motion. In penny arcades and nickelodeons, the kinetoscope had become extremely popular and profitable. Company after company had copied the Edison invention, gone into the moving-picture business and developed a product far beyond any conception of the original inventor.

A group of ten moviemakers finally made peace with the Edison lawyers and agreed to pay royalties on cameras, film and projectors, but the resulting monopoly only made it more difficult for the scores of other fly-by-night producers who still wanted to stay in business. The outlaws sought and found sanctuary in the West, and they brought with them as unwelcome a tribe of gypsy players and hangers-on as ever invaded California. Makeshift studios were set up in out-of-the-way places like Niles, Santa Barbara, Los Angeles and Hollywood. Hollywood was ideal.

Before the gentle community quite realized what was going on, David Horsley and Al Christie, operating under the name of Nestor Company, rented an old barn and a run-down roadhouse smack on the corner of Sunset Boulevard and Gower Street, converted them into a studio, and were filming a story called *The Law of the Range.*

Industry had come to Hollywood, and from Hollywood it was soon to spread into the desert. During the next decades more wealth was to be taken from the desert on celluloid than ever came from all the gold, silver and borax mines. To help stay the insatiable public appetite for cinema, bad men galloped down the canyons before whirring cameras and bellowing directors, the Children of Israel traipsed through the wastelands again and again, foreign legions marched over the dunes, lusty sheiks dragged maidens into desert harems, whooping savages am-

bushed stagecoaches in the arroyos; ersatz blood, bullets and passion thrilled audiences the world around.

The invaders served an uncomfortable apprenticeship at first.
"I knew that spies from the patent companies were circulating
in Hollywood," declared pioneer Jesse Lasky, in partnership
with Cecil de Mille. "We had an approved camera, but, even so,
we were afraid of trouble . . . Cecil was apprehensive enough to
carry a gun at all times."

It was only a matter of time, however, before the legal tussle
with Edison lawyers was resolved, and by then the would-be film
monopolists in New York had decided that Hollywood and environs was a better place for moviemaking than the handy hills
of New Jersey. "Westerns" were the rage, and their manufacturers conceded that even these could be produced in the West
as well as the East. Staid Hollywood was doomed—predestined
to become an industrial capital. The change came quickly.

Film companies were a disreputable, disorderly crowd, and
they proceeded to disrupt the temperance colony and replace it
with a colony of their own choosing. A high board fence, enclos-
ing a city lot and a few jerry-built sheds, trade-marked the first
studios. Behind that shield most of the early film footage was
shot in the open against flapping canvas flats, whether the scene
was a boudoir or a battleship.

But when a pretty house front, a prim garden or a street was
required, the whole company trooped out from its hiding place
and went on location. "Location trips were very simply arranged," explained an early director. "In those days, when we
wanted to show a country church, say, the whole company set out
in search of it. I sometimes rode ahead on horseback, with the
crew and cast following in two cars. When we found what we
wanted, we stopped and shot a scene, then went on to the next
setting. No one objected to our trespassing or charged us for the
use of his property."

That tolerance was broadly misinterpreted. The natives were
soon fed up on these bands of wandering cinema tramps, and it
was more often out of pity than out of gracious hospitality that
they were allowed on lawns and front porches. They were worse
than a plague. Only a few years before, Hollywood had shown
enough spirit to chase sheep off the streets, but no one quite
knew how to get rid of these interlopers.

The police were just as puzzled. Time and again an officer

shoved his way through a hooting throng of spectators to break up the street fight that had drawn the crowd. With club flying, he would separate the pugilists, and then have to suffer the embarrassment of being informed that it was all make-believe for a picture. One company was held up for hours on a charge of attempted arson before the police judge could be convinced that he had spoiled the climax of a photoplay.

From the producer's point of view, the police were a nuisance and the crowds that inevitably gathered wherever a camera was set up were a worse nuisance. Parts of a company often approached a location in stealth from different directions, to mislead the spectators. Directors put a cast through the action in half time, before a heckling mob could gather. They went to the trouble of setting up a dummy camera, with a fake show in front of it, to draw attention from the main event.

The infant industry was completely dependent on the charity of Hollywood property owners. There was neither time nor money for building elaborate sets inside the fences. So great was the demand for pictures back East, that a week or two was all that could be allowed for a new reel. Everything had to be done in a hurry.

"Motorcars rushed up to bungalows and stately dwellings," recalls a witness, "and discharged their loads of heroes, heroines, villains, trained nurses, policemen and society gentlemen and ladies—all with faces painted a ghastly white, save for lips as bright as slices of ripe watermelon—and a man in leather puttees, and with a large megaphone to amplify a voice that seemed to require no amplification, began to shout orders."

David Wark Griffith had notions of developing a new art medium from the chaos, but he, too, was bound by the laws of haste. Cold weather, snow and rain made it impossible for him to keep up with the demand for one-reelers in his Eastern haunts, so in the winter of 1910 he rushed to California with a troupe of thirty actors, half-a-dozen carpenters, a cameraman and a young girl named Mary Pickford. So pinched was he for funds that they could afford only one motorcar; they traveled by train or carriage and had to fashion their properties and scenery on the spot. Yet in sixteen weeks that winter Griffith ground out exactly sixteen pictures.

"Goodness gracious," exclaimed his wife, after sizing up the landscape they had to work with on the Coast, "how could we ever get all the scenic beauty on the screen! It was too distracting, what with missions, desert, mountains, ocean, beaches, cliffs and flowers. We wanted to send enough of it back in our pictures to ensure our coming again."

Griffith proceeded to get it all in. Off the company went to San Gabriel Mission to film *Threads of Destiny* and two moral preachments, *The Converts* and *The Way of the World;* to Hollywood for a romance of the Spanish Dominion, *In Old California,* and *Love Among the Roses;* to Pasadena for *Gold is Not All* and *The Kid;* into the Sierra Madre to do a story of the fortyniners, *The Gold Seekers,* and to feature Mary Pickford in *Romance of the Western Hills.*

The desert was so much nearer to Los Angeles in 1910 that it was not necessary to trek into the Mojave or Imperial Valley. For the first American desert picture, Griffith merely had to go to the outskirts of San Fernando. There a lone miner and his daughter suffered their way across the continent by prairie schooner in *Over Silent Paths.*

San Fernando Mission was headquarters for the company. "The desertion and desecration of the picturesque place was complete," observed Mrs. Griffith. "For more than two hundred years the hot sun and the winter rain had beat upon the mission's adobe walls. Not even a priest to guard it. A few Japs were living in the one habitable room—they mended bicycles. We were as free to move in as were the swallows so thickly perched on the chapel rafters. An occasional tourist with his kodak had been the only visitor until we came."

The whole company lived, camped and cooked like gypsies on the hurried tours. To make *The Two Brothers* they rushed down to San Juan Capistrano, where the only accommodation to be found was a little inn, the Mendelssohn, "an airy wooden structure evidently built under the prevailing delusion that Southern California has a tropical climate.

"The bedrooms were upstairs," reported the tireless scribe. "To reach them you had to go out in the yard, the back yard, climb the rickety stairs to the porch, onto which each little bedroom, by means of its own little door, opened. The bare-floored bedrooms were just large enough to hold a creaking double bed, wash-bowl and pitcher and a chair . . . There were no more than ten bedrooms in the hotel. Actors slept everywhere, two and three to a bed; even the parlor had to be fixed up with cots . . .

The walls were paperthin. Between the creaking of one's own bed, the snores from other rooms down the line, and the footsteps on the shaking porch, of actors going from room to room looking for something better than what had been allotted them, it was not a restful night.

"It was all so weird and spooky that midnight had arrived before I summoned sufficient courage to let myself go to sleep. No sooner had I dozed off than out of the black and silence came a terrific roar, yells, and loud laughter, and pistol shots going zip, zip, zip. These hot-headed Mexicans! Something dreadful was going to happen. I heard horses; and soon horses and riders galloped madly into the back yard, right to the foot of our stairs.

"But it was only our extra cowboys who had arrived feeling good and full of the joy of life. For this picture a bunch of rough riders were to pull some thrillers in the way of horse stuff. No thought had been given to their slumber places, and so, after a look around, they docilely crawled up into the barn."

Four days were enough for *Two Brothers;* then they were off to Ventura to produce *Ramona,* the first Pickford classic and "the most expensive picture put out by any manufacturer up to that time." It took more than a week and cost over $1,000.

Along the San Gabriel River, Griffith had spotted a pigeon farm and decided that photogenic pigeons would make a hit on the screen. A yarn was quickly concocted around the captive birds, and in a day or two they had a reel entitled *As it is in Life.* Oil wells were becoming a conspicuous California landmark, and if an all-inclusive job was to be done on Coast scenery, petroleum had to be included. *Unexpected Help* and *A Rich Revenge* were quickly turned out at Olinda. The Pacific Ocean could not be neglected, so the company hied north to a little fishing village called Santa Monica and completed the winter season with *The Unchanging Sea.*

Sixteen movies in four months, and every one was a success except *Gold Is Not All.* That had been taken on the lawn of a hospitable Pasadena capitalist who did not realize, until he saw the preview, that its sole point was to show up the wide gulf between a grasping, dishonest capitalist and a family of honest paupers. "I just don't like it, that's all," insisted the man who had played gracious host to the gypsies, loaned his uniformed butler as part of the cast, spread an elaborate garden party for them, only to find himself satirized in the film. "You know, a person can have money and still be a respectable citizen in the community," he politely suggested. "Is it absolutely necessary, Mr. Griffith, to release that picture?" '

Discounting *Gold Is Not All,* Griffith's first California venture was enormously successful—so successful that he returned the following winter to produce an even more impressive series and experiment with two-reel shows. The desert fascinated him, and more and more of his pictures called for prairie schooners, pioneers, redskins and sand. "He answered the desert call," explained Mrs. Griffith, "with a big epic of pioneer romance, *The Last Drop of Water.*

"We set up camp in the San Fernando Desert," she continued, "two huge tents, one for mess, with a cook and assistants who served chow to the cowboys and the extra men. Two rows of tables, planks set on wooden horses, ran the length of the tent. There must have been at least fifty cowboys and riders to be fed hearty meals three times a day. The other tent contained trunks and wardrobe baskets, and here the boys slept and made up."

The girls were discreetly segregated in quarters somewhat less informal, and generally heeded the director's admonition: "Girls, stay together when you're not busy, for you're likely to hear some pretty rough stuff if you don't."

Although Griffith was operating on a shoestring, he was becoming increasingly extravagant with personnel and properties. The script for *The Last Drop of Water* took a group of pioneers, burdened with precious family keepsakes, all the way from Mississippi to the California gold diggings. But most of that distance, according to the story, was barren desert. The company carpenters nailed eight covered wagons together on the site, and Griffith assembled scores of horses, dogs and chickens, and dozens of cowboys who doubled occasionally as military escorts and Indians. A herd of cattle was also needed, but one cow was all that could be rustled in the area and she had to do. In grim conflicts with the Indians and the elements, the cherished possessions of the pioneers were gradually left behind and the caravan disintegrated until only a few survivors arrived at the diggings.

It was not much of a story, and there was a heavy play on sentiment, but Griffith was sure he was dealing in "things vital to American life" and was headed in the right artistic direction—so sure that he immediately launched a two-reel, covered-wagon masterpiece with a title that would reach around three sides of a marquee, *Crossing the American Prairies in the Early Fifties*. For this he increased the number of wagons to eleven and rounded up hundreds of extra women, cowboys, horses and cattle.

But this story called for a still more melancholy ending than *Drop of Water*. During the desert crossing, the guards posted for night duty fell asleep, Indians swept in to massacre practically the entire cast, and the bodies were left behind for a sandstorm to bury. Creating the sandstorm was the major technical problem. Wind machines had not been invented, so Griffith settled for great cornucopia-shaped containers—held just out of camera range—to spill sand on the prone bodies.

"Getting covered up was a dirty job for the living corpses," one of them complained. "Little grains of sand gently falling upon one from out the property boys' cornucopias, while unpleasant, could be silently endured; but when the property boys got the storm really started and the sand was being poured upon one thick and heavy, getting into hair and ears and eyes, no matter how protective the position one had assumed, there were heard smothered oaths from the dead people that no wild cowboy had ever excelled."

That sandstorm made theatrical history. Griffith was bringing the geography of the Southwest in all its graphic realism to his public, and he was also working up courage to try for epics like the twelve-reel *Birth of a Nation* and the movie colossus *Intolerance*.

Griffith's company made only periodic visits to Hollywood, but the citizens saw enough of him and his confederates in the business to be shocked and appalled by the intrusion. Not only were the "fillums" a harum-scarum trade, but all the associates seemed to be either loony or immoral—perhaps both. The show people had neither manners nor modesty; they were an abomination to the community. Yet once they had a foothold, they seemed to own the place.

Very soon it was too late to consider any kind of eviction. There were too many. Company after company swarmed into the area with a retinue of actors and a much larger following of heelers who wanted to be actors or writers or directors or scene designers or extras. Hollywood was overwhelmed. Five or six years after Horsley and Christie set up the first studio on Sunset Boulevard, Hollywood had become the film capital of the nation, with all the bureaucracy, social stratification and ostentation expected of such supremacy.

The transformation was starkly delineated by Cosmo Hamilton, erudite British author, who was summoned there to compose a scenario for Cecil de Mille. "In New York," he chuckled, "I had heard many references to 'The Coast,' and I had visualized it as a most bewildering place, built somewhat casually on sand dunes, to which all the world sent stories to hear of them no more. It was, therefore, with great astonishment and interest that I discovered the expression to mean a long, wide and well-laid street almost wholly composed of cafeterias and apartment houses, completely surrounded by villas which sat in each other's pockets from the foothills to the sea, among which, in various spacious corners, minor cities of smart and well-built studios throbbed with activity.

"Gargantuan geranium trees grew opulently on the sidewalks among semitropical brothers and sisters . . . There were more cars of every vintage to the square inch in this place than ever in New York in the busiest of the day.

"The first of my thrills came when, while lunching in one of the uncountable cafeterias, I rubbed shoulders with Charlie Chaplin in his well-known make-up and sat in juxtaposition to Douglas Fairbanks and Mary Pickford, Gloria Swanson, Elliot Dexter, Will Rogers, William Hart, Wallace Reid, Thomas Meighan and hosts of others who had made themselves of greater importance to the peoples of the earth than kings and presidents, prime ministers and politicians, bishops and judges. . . .

"The second of my thrills was caused by the first visit to the Famous Players-Lasky Studios and there to find not the bewilderment and chaos that I expected, but a vast and efficient institution running with the calm deliberation of a military hospital, Kellogg's Sanitarium and Oxford University rolled into one.

"In the long lane of low buildings that faced the street were housed with great comfort and many individual ideas of interior decoration, the managers, directors, architects, art-advisers, editors, financial experts, advertising experts, scenario writers, secretaries, stenographers and an army of clerks. In these also were the large pens in which were herded together daily the growing number of would-be picture actors, who came from every conceivable country and every walk of life. Young, no longer young, not quite old and old, nearly all of them were there, I suppose, because

237

they labored under the wholly erroneous impression that Hollywood was the Mecca of easy money, and that nothing else was required to make them famous in the pictures than the desire to become so. . . .

"Attached to every studio was a little army of workers: the directors either crouching on the floor in riding breeches and gaping shirt, or buried in a canvas chair on which his name was stamped; the camera men and their assistants, all of whom bore a close resemblance to the rough riders of a maurauding force; men with searchlights perched on the tops of ladders; and made-up actors hanging about in listless attitudes.

"As I stood in the studio in which Cecil de Mille was working, hour after hour and day after day, in an endeavor to photograph a little boy in the act of catching a frightened goldfish in a large glass bowl, to the inspiration of a wailing violin, a prize fight was going on before a howling mob to my right, a shrill maiden was being noisily assaulted to my left, and a body of cowboys was shooting up a bar to the complete indifference of Will Rogers behind me. The conglomeration of sounds was overpowering and indescribable, and beneath it all, always, persistently, there crept the muted sweetness of that nerveless violin."

No multimillion-dollar industry in the history of business and the arts had ever become so thoroughly sophisticated in so short a time. Half a decade before, there had been little organization and no engineering; now the high-powered machinery of the studio creaked from the weight of its vital parts. The director was important; the stars were important; the cameraman, the decorators, the architects and the editors were important. And there was one important cog often overlooked in the total assessment—the location man.

To give the screen illusion that the fish snatch was taking place in a palatial residence, that the maiden was being assaulted in a remote mountain cabin, and that the cowboys were shooting it out in Slumgullion Gulch, exterior glimpses of the mansion, the mountain environment and Slumgullion's main street had to be dubbed in occasionally. If expenditure for construction of an incidental set on the lot could not be justified, it was the job of the location manager to find the appropriate building or scenery somewhere within reasonable distance of Hollywood.

Photographing those exteriors meant a junket for the stars, the crews and most of the cast—as well as escape from the regimen of the studio. By train, car, bus or truck, depending on status, the filmfolk headed off on their holiday. They doted on the excursions, and so did the host towns and cities—for one or two visits. The arrival of a motion-picture company about 1918 in a California village was something to remember. It was a bigger occasion than Fourth of July or Homecoming Week. Here were the greatest celebrities of the day suddenly in their midst. No splurge was too much for them.

Everyone in town turned out to greet them, to do a little flag waving, hopefully standing by to be included in the mob scene. Sheriffs and deputies had a heyday clearing the streets and re-routing traffic, as decreed by the movie director—the guest dictator for the day.

Sheltered under a huge umbrella, the cameraman took over the center of the street. Waiting stars and satellites hovered around, looking bored and important. The director's canvas throne was close by, but on location he was usually too preoccupied with his megaphone to spend much time in sedentary repose. The excitement could all be over in a couple of hours, or it might go on intermittently for days—until every rosebush in the town park had been trampled, until every teen-ager had an autograph, and the most resplendent stars had lost luster in the eyes of the public through displays of temper and temperament.

For "quickies," for Westerns, and exotic pictures involving sultans and seraglios, the scenes taken on location grew longer and longer. Directors decided that desert environment could give realistic touches that no studio artifice could provide. Frequently the entire picture, except the interior scenes, was made away from the studio. Location scouts kept returning to places like Victorville, Daggett, Lone Pine, Red Rock Canyon and Palm Springs.

"In the past few years," gloated a Palm Springs resident in 1919, "our village has become headquarters, so to speak, for Algeria, Egypt, Arabia, Palestine, India, Mexico, a good deal of Turkey, Australia, South America and sundry parts of the globe. Wondrous are the sights and sounds the dwellers of Palm Springs are privileged to see and hear when the movies are in town; wondrous the stars that shine in broad daylight on us; wondrous the cowboys; cavalcades and caballeros, the tragedies and feats of daring, the rescues and escapes for which our dunes and canyons provide the setting. The quiet village becomes, in fact, a studio for the time, and the visitor whose ideal is something doing every minute has little reason to pine away with ennui."

Visitors, indeed, were much more inclined to worship the screen idols than were the villagers. Old-timers who loved their desert village for what it had been, rather than for the wondrous glow imparted by celebrities, were soon disenchanted with movieland. Instead of continuing as "headquarters" for Algeria, Arabia, Australia and "sundry parts of the globe," Palm Springs became a holiday headquarters for the moviemakers, and the original escapists sought refuge elsewhere.

Victorville, a run-down desert town on the Mojave River, little more than a hundred miles from Hollywood, had less natural charm to lose from an invasion of film stars. It had seen better days as a booming mine camp of the eighties and nineties. Like Calico, Johannesburg, Skidoo and fifty other gold and silver bivouacs, Victorville had sprung out of nowhere in no time, complete with false fronts, corrals, saloons, shops, sheriff's office and hitching rails—about as near to the Coast as any major mining activity had reached.

The location on the Mojave River, its quarries, cattle ranches and poultry farms had kept it from quite turning into a ghost town. From a heyday population of several thousand, it was down to three or four hundred and dwindling fast, but the false fronts were still intact, and left over from the boom were even a few authentic characters to decorate the porches and street corners.

It had all the trappings of a typical frontier village, and was made to order for Hollywood. William S. Hart, the "good bad man" of the movies discovered it about 1914 when looking for a ready-made Western location. He shot his first "quickie" there, and brought Victorville so much renown that during the next twenty years the town and its environs were the backdrop for more than 200 films.

Bill Hart did not invent the formula for Westerns; he merely eliminated some of the fallacies and distortions and gave his horsemen a more honest character. Westerns had been popular with nickelodeon audiences for a decade—single-reel travesties of the Big Country, shot in the New Jersey woods or along the Palisades of the Hudson River, by men "who didn't know a bowie knife from a bolo."

Hart, who had spent most of his boyhood as a ranch hand in the land of the Sioux and the Blackfeet before turning to Broadway, saw his first Western while on the road in Cleveland. "It was awful," he moaned. "Yet when I talked with the manager of the theatre he told me it was one of the best Westerns he had ever shown. None of the impossibilities or libels on the West meant anything to him—it was drawing the crowds. The fact that the sheriff was dressed and characterized as a sort of cross between a Wisconsin wood chopper and a Gloucester fisherman was unknown to him . . . Here were reproductions of the Old West being seriously presented to the public—in almost a burlesque manner—and they were successful. It made me tremble to think of it. I was an actor and I knew the West."

It was a case of spot conversion. Before he left Cleveland, Hart had made up his mind to show the world what the real West was like. "The opportunity that I had been waiting for years to come was knocking at my door," he exulted. "Hundreds of ideas seemed to rush in from every direction. They assumed form. It was engendered—the die was cast. Rise or fall, sink or swim, I had to bend every endeavor to get a chance to make Western moving pictures."

Armed with that fixation, he turned up in Hollywood in 1914 and went to work. His location scenes took him to the Grand Canyon, to the Sierra and Lake Tahoe, to the Sacramento River —for a Mississippi river-boat sequence, to San Ysidro on the Mexican border, to Topanga Canyon, to the Big Trees of Felton and Ben Lomond, to Sonora and the Bret Harte country.

While carrying out his mission, he camped in every part of California from the heights of Donner Pass to the banks of the Colorado River. But for canyon, desert and frontier shots, he returned to Victorville.

At or near Victorville, Hart rescued more damsels in distress, evened the score with more low-down cowpunchers, shot up more redskins, vaulted more canyons than anywhere else. Between 1916 and 1924 he created an average of two pictures a year there, including *Wild Bill Hickok, O'Malley of the Mounted* and *Tumbleweeds*. And, in the process he kept the town in a constant state of disruption.

One of the principal sets for *Wild Bill Hickok* was Dodge City, Kansas—too far away to transport a whole company. "By building two new streets near the depot, we made Victorville, California, into Dodge City, Kansas," he explained. "At times we had five hundred people on the set, and we got some splendid stuff.

It was most amusing to watch the Overland trains pull in and see the startled passengers jump off with a watch in one hand and a timetable in the other. That sign, 'Dodge City, Kansas,' on the depot was surely official! Some of them became quite panic-stricken and acted exactly like a green goods victim, when he discovers he has been fleeced. And the train crew, from the fireman to conductor, enjoyed the joke."

Nobody enjoyed it more than Bill Hart. And to this day, sexagenarians delight in recounting details of the greatest binge Victorville ever indulged in—while *White Oak* was being filmed. Bill was directly responsible. He and a company of 125 had just returned from northern California where, in line of duty, the hero had picked up a bad case of flu from swimming across the Sacramento River in December. The desert scenes had to be made at Victorville. Hart went to bed with a temperature of 103°, and the rest of the cast, with time on their hands, went on a bender.

As Hart told the story, "A heavy Santa Fe freight was sidetracked at Victorville to allow a passenger train to go through. One of the cars of the heavy freight was, to all outward appearance, an oil-tank car. But it wasn't an oil-tank car. Appearance was all wrong. It was a camouflage.

"I never knew who put it there, nor who was responsible for it, but ninety-seven million gallons of the finest Mexican wine ever made from grapes was in that car. Where it was going, I do not know. I only know it never arrived there, and that through the medium of several short pieces of garden hose, enough wine was siphoned out of that car to irrigate the Mojave Desert. Only it was not used for such purposes.

"At the end of every piece of hose was an endless line of cowboys, each with a receptacle; said receptacle being every movable thing that could hold liquid—wooden buckets, tin buckets, milk pans, garbage pails, horses' canvas nose-bags, washtubs—every repository imaginable or available within two miles of Victorville was on that line. The heavy freight and the sadly depleted oil-tank passed on.

"For two whole days and nights the carnival lasted. The streets of the town became a public dance hall. Innocent and harmless —yes! But to those who knew not the way of the cowboy—menacing.

"The more timid citizens telephoned to San Bernardino, forty

miles away for help. The sheriff and twenty deputies, all armed
to the teeth, arrived on a special train. They did not need guns.
They needed many husky men and many stretchers. The merry-
making had ended. Every foot of space outside and inside at Victorville was occupied by a sleeping cowboy. The courthouse was
full. The jail was full. Nothing was sacred to those Bacchanalian
inebriates.

"There were no 'good Indians.' They were all alike, from the
manager and the director down. I was ill in bed, but I can make
an affidavit that it was good wine, and said affidavit can be supported by a reliable witness—the sheriff was in the room at the
time. The sheriff was a real sheriff; no one had been harmed, no
damage had been done. He returned with his deputies to San
Bernardino.

"I often wonder what some of those old desert-rat prospectors
think when they uncover some of those lost board-covered buckets that were cached during those two days of revelry and the
location forgotten. I'll bet they don't try the contents on the
burro first."

In three days Hart had shaken the flu, and on the fourth he
was raising his glass of choice Mexican wine to the health of his
shaky coyboys. After such episodes, a well-tutored publicity team
protected the image of the "good bad man" from being shattered
in the eyes of a worshipful public. Their fluency was saved to
portray the hero performing the ultimate in daring—leaping
from cliff to cliff, shifting from fleet horse to racing stagecoach,
split-second draws and infallible marksmanship.

Singer Jim McKee, one of Hart's last pictures, called for a
scene in which his horse was shot from under him while he was
riding full speed on the top ledge of a sheer cliff that fell off for
200 feet; rider and animal were supposed to roll hoof over saddle
down the precipice to the gorge below—and remain alive. Hart,
who prided himself in never employing a double or using a
dummy, weakened on this one. He would make the fall, but he
was afraid of injuring his horse Fritz.

For $2,000, expert mechanics at the Lasky Studio produced a
convincing model of Fritz, mane and tail of real horsehair, mark-
ings, weight and stance duplicated, and every joint working on
springs. "It took thirty carpenters and helpers," claimed Hart,
"to get the mechanical horse to the top of the precipice and wire
him in place."

The cameras started to grind, and Fritz galloped along the precarious ledge to the side of the dummy. A cut was called while the hero shifted from live steed to model and the supporting wires were snipped; then down they went.

"The result was such an astounding illusion," Hart asserted, "that I had to go before the board of censors in New York City and tell them my story before they would consent to this scene being shown on the screen. They were positive that it was a living horse and a living man that rolled to the bottom of the canyon. The man was alive, but he didn't breathe much. I was shaken up quite a bit; but we never took such scenes until the end of the picture. The censors kept the faith. No one ever knew."

Drawing from his own memories and experiences, Hart created a new portrait of desert life and the Western frontier, ending forever the New Jersey-Palisades conception. For a long generation he stood as the prototype of the strong, silent adventurer of the West.

He was usually cast as the outlaw who underwent some kind of moral regeneration as the plot unfolded, yet, true to the Western code, he stayed outside the law. In the country which he portrayed, murder was, of course, not too serious a crime—not nearly as despicable as siding with the Indians, horse stealing or claim jumping. He put his message across, was understood, honored and worshipped by millions; he brought to the movies the first authentic representation of the desert and the Old West, fulfilling his self-imposed mission so imaginatively that little room for invention in the production of Westerns was left for his followers.

Hart gave Victorville and a corner of the Mojave a new lease on life. Other producers were quick to recognize the scenic advantages of the locale, and soon a parade of stars like Harry Carey, Tom Mix, Hoot Gibson and Will Rogers, was riding down the streets and canyons he had made so famous.

A hundred and fifty miles directly north, on the opposite side of the desert, Lone Pine put in almost as early a bid for movie fame. Lone Pine itself could not boast of having a made-to-order frontier main street, but there were pretty good replicas in the region around, and variety in scenery that Victorville did not possess—dry hills and green ones, deserts and wasteland, lakes and rushing streams, not to mention the background of the sheerest mountain range on the continent. With the proper props and a little ingenuity, a director could fake or piece together, near Lone Pine, practically any kind of setting he wanted.

Fatty Arbuckle—in the early twenties—with a get-up of coonskins and leather stockings and an entourage of Injuns and gunbristling frontiersmen, was the first movie great to thrill the local populace, and Mary Pickford soon gave a similar treat to the neighboring town of Independence.

After that, Hollywood celebrities were annual visitors in the area, for pictures as varied as *Gunga Din, The Bengal Lancers, Stagecoach, The Light Brigade, Union Pacific, The Westerner, Wanderer in the Wasteland,* Hopalong Cassidy creations and a string of Westerns. Owens Valley environment was passed off as North Africa one year and Afghanistan the next, as Tibet or Texas, as the Andes or the Alps, as Utah or Uganda. For any movie that called for a combination of desert and green country, Owens Valley would do.

Ideal spots for moviemaking were often ignored in the early days because of their relative inaccessibility and their total lack of overnight accommodations for a large cast—and because it was cheaper to make a film on a makeshift location near Hollywood. The shifting sand dunes of Little Valley, twenty miles east of Yuma, were a natural for *The Sheik* in 1920, but it was still a long, hot journey from Sunset Boulevard to the Arizona border. *The Sheik* was not made on the Colorado Desert or any other desert. Rudolph Valentino, his harem and the caravan of camels, were merely transported a few miles up the coast to the unromantic sands of Oxnard Beach.

Of course there was no oasis there, so carpenters hurriedly clipped from canvas something that remotely resembled palm fronds, pasted them onto poles, stuck the poles in the dunes, and —presto—there was the oasis. The slight haze that clouded the picture was no sandstorm or smudge from Arab campfires; it was spindrift from the Pacific. But other companies with exciting scenarios featuring foreign legions and less enravishing sheiks were not long in finding their way to Little Valley.

The overwhelming climax of *Beau Geste* was shot there a few years later. From the desert sands arose the fake façade of Fort Zinderneuf, garrisoned with its twenty-two gallant Legionnaires, and as zero hour for the storming of the fort approached it looked as though all of Hollywood was invading the Colorado Desert. Two thousand horses and 2,000 sweating cowboys, arrayed in the get-up of bloodthirsty Arab tribesmen, assembled on the dunes. William Powell was there, Alice Joyce and Ronald Colman. This was to be one of the most excitingly realistic scenes ever filmed—so important that a dozen extra cameramen were brought in to cover the different angles. Herbert Brenon was master of ceremonies, and what with the blistering heat and all the confusion, he was beside himself.

The order to advance finally came. Twenty-two Legionnaires took their places on the parapet, prepared to hold off the dragoons or perish in the attempt. Two thousand Arabs lined up for the charge. "A ten-dollar bonus to every man who takes a fall!" bellowed Brenon through his megaphone. "Ten dollars to every man who takes a fall!"

That order must have cost him $20,000. In a scene calculated to unnerve the most callous theatregoer, the horsemen came galloping head on down the dunes, furiously striking from every direction. Twenty-two guns puffed from Fort Zinderneuf—and instantly 2,000 cowboy Arabs and 2,000 steeds dropped dead in their tracks. Brenon had never guessed the magic power of a $10 dare. The picture was a sensation—except in college towns where arithmetic mattered. To collegians the felling of all those Arabs from one piddling burst of gunfire was the funniest anticlimax of the decade.

Very early, the role of the desert itself as a major antagonist was recognized, and picture after picture employed the dramatic theme of struggle against thirst, solitude and trackless waste, in one way or another. Cecil de Mille used it in *Heir to the Hoorah*, in which the tattered hero, lost in the desert, carrying an empty canteen and slowly dying of thirst, reaches a water hole only to find it dry. Half-crazed and delirious, he sees a magnificent mirage across the shimmering sands and struggles on until the lone figure disappears over an outcropping ledge. Slow fade-out. THE END.

Thomas Meighan took the title role, and de Mille motored his cast and truckloads of equipment down to Palm Springs. "This was in the days when Palm Springs had not yet been adopted by the movie colony as a desert retreat," commented the director. "The town was only a cluster of weather-beaten dwellings, served by a typical country store—a desert settlement in an Indian reservation. If you walked a few hundred yards from the little oasis of the village, you were in the trackless waste of the desert itself, with all the mysterious sense of loneliness, its mirages, its deceiving distances and its cruel grandeur."

De Mille quickly discovered the handicaps of location work in the desert. At the foot of Palm Canyon, where cameras were set up, thermometers registered 130°. There was no ice within fifty miles. To prevent film from melting in the sun, assistants had to keep wet compresses over both cameras and cases. "The heat was so killing," de Mille reckoned, "that I didn't let Tom play up in rehearsal—just walked him through it to get camera composition and position, and also to be sure that the route he traversed was fairly clear of rattlesnakes, scorpions, centipedes and other items which might take an actor out of the proper mood."

Around a dried water hole the property boys planted the collection of skulls and bones brought all the way from Hollywood, and at last the touching sequence of Meighan's demented wanderings and disappearance was started. "It was really quite an effective scene," gloated de Mille, "with miles of desolation as a background and no sign of human habitation visible."

All went off exactly as the script specified. Tom's figure got smaller and smaller in the distance, to represent "the insignificance of man opposed to the desert's silent power." The director was delighted. "Cut!" he called.

But the order was scarcely issued when a yelp of agony came from the distance into which the hero had faded. Apprehensive over the fate of the irreplaceable star, fearing that he had broken a limb, stepped on a rattler or too closely identified himself with the crazed man he was portraying, de Mille led the rescue rush across the sands.

They found Meighan immobile, sprawled on the edge of a rock ledge, his face contorted with the misery he was suffering. To make a retreat from camera vision at the end of his scene he had vaulted to another shelf, without first surveying the terrain, and had landed bottomside down on a massive cactus plant. Meighan was all but impaled on a cushion of two-inch spikes.

With quantities of prickly pear still adhering to his rear, Tom was cautiously lifted from his perch and laid face down on the sand. The rest of the afternoon was spent out of camera range and out of visual range of starlet admirers as his tattered trousers were clipped away and the needles plucked from his hindquarters with mechanic's pliers. Meighan recovered from the surgery, but never from his embarrassment.

In 1925 the public was given the ultimate in the man-versus-desert theme, straight from Death Valley. The story came packaged in the famed film called *Greed,* and to this day it can provoke such an overpowering thirst in an audience that viewers invariably stampede from the theatre to the nearest bar.

Erich von Stroheim directed it—130 reels of mining, money grabbing, misery and murder from Frank Norris' *McTeague.* But the theme ran away with the director and he did not know when to stop. Eventually he cut the film to twenty-six reels, insisting that they be shown in two installments. Metro-Goldwyn-Mayer ruled otherwise, trimmed the film down to ten reels, and in the process eliminated all but the bare essence of a story.

But left in with every grim detail was the final episode in which the implacable avenger catches up with murderer Mc-Teague on the broad salt flats of Death Valley. In all the heat of the desert the two fight it out, and just before the pursuer is killed he succeeds in snapping handcuffs on Mac. There, a hundred miles from water, against a horizon of endless salt and sand, Mac finds himself manacled to a dead man. In the fade-out he submissively lies down beside the corpse to await his own fate.

Greed was an artistic triumph and a magnificent box-office flop—one of the greatest flops in Hollywood history. Moving pictures of the day, agreed the critics, had to serve up either amusement or entertainment. Von Stroheim's masterpiece offered neither. There was too much avarice, too much aridity and too much Death Valley. For a year or two the picture even helped to scare tourists away from Scotty's Castle.

Though the desert failed to provide a palatable setting for *Greed,* with its complex moral preachment, it proved thoroughly adequate as a location for the string of Biblical extravaganzas that began pouring from the studios in the twenties. Finding just the right spot to look like the environs of Jerusalem, Mount Sinai or the Sea of Galilee, took some doing on the part of location scouts, but in general the Mojave was a fair double for the Holy Land.

The first *Ten Commandments* set the standard for picture testaments that followed. Cecil de Mille traipsed the Israelites halfway across Southern California, with Pharaoh and the Egyptians in hot pursuit. But the filming chronology had nothing to do with Biblical chronology. Moses picked up the Decalogue in Red Rock Canyon; the great scenes of the Exodus and the crossing of the Red Sea were shot on the sand dunes at Guadalupe, near Santa Maria; while Muroc Dry Lake—now Edwards Air Force Base—bore witness to some of the more chilling plight of the wandering Children.

At Guadalupe a huge tent city was set up, with a compound for 2,500 people and 3,000 animals. And it was there that a major crisis of the screening developed. De Mille was sure that he could get the best performance out of a cast of orthodox Jews, and he scoured Los Angeles for them. Eager to re-enact the critical events in the annals of their fathers, they assembled at Santa Maria in hundreds, trusting that they would be properly provisioned during their acting debuts.

De Mille had the right intentions, but there was some oversight in the commissary department, and the Israelites from Los Angeles walked between the parted billows of the Red Sea as famished as their forebears. For lunch they had been offered nothing but ham. A few made an unfilmed exodus before the cameras started grinding.

For the biggest scene of all, Muroc Dry Lake was chosen. Down the rugged hills to the north, Pharaoh's horses and chariots were supposed to charge and chase the Children into the Red Sea.

The Muroc sequence was so stupendous that there were not enough horses and horsemen in all Los Angeles to fill the bill. A hurry call was sent to the Presidio in San Francisco. Responding cheerfully to the emergency, the commanding general dispatched an entire cavalry brigade. And that sparked another crisis.

The Army had nothing but contempt for the Hollywood cowpunchers who had previously been engaged, and behind scenes they hatched a plot that was not in the script. In the precipitous descent to Muroc Dry Lake, the San Francisco campaigners intended to show up the screen professionals and ride them down. The plot leaked to the opposing camp, and half the cowboys refused to get into the melee at all. Nevertheless, that charge into Muroc Dry Lake was one of the all-time spectacles of the screen.

On *Ten Commandments* de Mille sunk almost $1,500,000, to the dismay of his employers in New York. It was an unprecedented expenditure for a film of the early twenties, but as an indication of the market value of California desert scenery in terms of celluloid, the picture eventually earned over $4,000,000.

To eliminate some of these expensive filming safaris the big cinema companies soon had their location "ranches" spotted in the canyons northeast of Hollywood or on the edge of the desert. There the same settings could be used over and over in turning out adventure epics or cowboy quickies.

When talkies came in, everyone in Hollywood assumed for a few years that Westerns and magnificent outdoor spectaculars were washed out. The day of the soundproofed studio had arrived, and technical problems of reproducing authentic sound in the wide-open spaces were insurmountable.

Because the microphone was considered to be immobile, the free-flowing action of the silents was abruptly displaced by static, staged presentations. Pictures were studio bound and the desert less frequently visited. But it did not take long for producers to catch on to the technique of intersplicing close-up recordings with long-range scenes and dubbed-in sound effects.

Talkies such as *In Old Arizona* and *Cimarron* paved the way for bigger and better desert epics. Over the years they came in a steady flow: *Stagecoach, Jesse James, Treasure of Sierra Madre, Broken Arrow, High Noon,* and desert-made Westerns—long regarded by the first-run theatres of the big cities as box-office poison—proved as popular there as they had everywhere else.

Then came television, with a demand for mass production of Western serials. Places like Red Rock Canyon and Fairview Valley were busier than ever with the influx of Hollywood idols. Although the movie ranch at Corriganville, only 30 miles from the film capital, would fall short of complying precisely with either the tourist's or the geographer's conception of desert, its 2,000 acres of canyons, bold rocks and parched highland, easily satisfied the screen criterion.

Corriganville catered to the rubberneck crowds and the kids, as well as to studios. Open to them were such familiar sets as Fort Apache, the Burma Road, a Corsican Village, a Mexican border town, and the typical Wild West street. And its proprietors could boast that over 3,000 pictures had been made there in 20 years.

That movie ranch was headquarters for TV series like *Bat Masterson, Wyatt Earp, Gene Autry, Cisco Kid, Kit Carson, Gunsmoke, Have Gun, Will Travel, Tales of Wells Fargo, Wagon Train, Rin Tin Tin* and *Robin Hood.* For flatter, sandier scenes to fill out the continuity, the Mojave and Colorado deserts were just over the hills.

Over the years, of course, many a good desert location of the past had been lost to the real-estate developers. Palm Springs was sold out, Victorville had turned into a modern metropolis, and scouts had to go farther and farther afield to find sand dunes where a golf green or the roof lines of a smart ranch house did not spoil the site for a panoramic shot of old Araby.

More and more the moviemakers were depending on public lands and even military reservations in the search for desert locations. For the opening scenes of *Spartacus* the cast traveled all the way to Death Valley's Zabriskie Point, and *X-15* was filmed at Edwards Air Force Base. Still, the desert's most profitable industry was far from doomed. There were enough wasteland settings left so that young fry would not need to worry for awhile about discontinuance of their favorite bang-bang telecasts, or their elders about future Foreign Legion, Wild West and Holy Land screen entertainment.

XI
WHAT DID I DO TO DESERVE THIS, SERGEANT

IF worst came to worst and the desert had to be defended against a paratroop invasion from Mars or Muscovy, the Mojave could put up some very stiff resistance. The Army is there. The Air Force is there. The Marines are there. The Navy is there. No other desolate area in the world shelters such a concentration of military might.

Over the course of a century and a quarter the desert has seen some weird and wonderful defenders marching across the sands: leatherstockings scouting a passage for overlanders, armies of occupation patrolling the Mexican border, vengeance-seeking posses on the trail of outlaws, veterans campaigning against the Piutes and Yumas, even an Army camel brigade plodding West to subdue unidentified foes of the Republic.

But none of these parades of militia was half as weird, wonderful and sinister as the forces that began assembling in the desert when World War II was shaping up. And the encampments have been swelling ever since.

Down near Twentynine Palms, tubas and trumpets blare across the parade grounds of the Marine Corps Base and echo against the bleak, hot hillsides. Field-dressed troops of the Fleet Marine Force are on parade. In precise formation, units clomp past the reviewing dignitaries, responding like robots to the barked orders. They click, stomp, swivel, shoulder arms, by the right flank march, halt, present, parade rest. Overhead the colors flutter against a dry, cloudless sky. Leatherneck musicians ump and clarion their martial harmony, casting the reverberations far out into the once-silent wastelands.

In the broad expanse between the Bullion Mountains and Joshua Tree National Monument the Marines have broken that silence alarmingly. Out of earshot of the band is heard the rumble of distant guns, and the earth trembles underfoot. The thunder and rumble come at any hour of the day or night, and at night the far-off flashes are like heat lightning. Somewhere out in the desert, gunners of the First Field Artillery Group are ramming projectiles home, hard at work in their war games.

Then there are three Light Antiaircraft Missile battalions, whose pet plaything is the devastating guided missile Hawk, designed especially to lambast low-flying targets, traveling close to the speed of sound. The blasts come from fixed positions or from tactical points far afield, where carriages and equipment were dropped by whirlibirds only minutes before.

And supporting the attack units is "D" Company, Seventh Engineer Battalion, with giant vehicles and massive machinery, ready to tackle any kind of construction job, whether it is bridging a canyon on a new road to a firing area or paving another runway for a landing field. All belong to Force Troops, Fleet Marine Force, Pacific.

The vast military complex at Twentynine Palms is the largest Marine Corps Base under the United States flag. The combined areas of better-known Quantico, Camp Pendleton and Lejeune could be multiplied by two and fitted inside the base boundaries. Sprawling Los Angeles and a like-sized twin could be chucked into place there, with space left over for a few more moderate-sized cities.

Actual military installations, gun parks, warehouses, motor pools and quarters occupy a mere 20 square miles, while the undeveloped land used for unrestricted training and impact areas stretches out over more than 900 additional square miles—a total of more than 500,000 acres.

The Marine Corps dates back to 1775, and Quantico to 1917, but the biggest home of the corps was not staked out until 1953. For a few years prior to that the site had been used by an Army glider and training school, and by General Patton for training his famed tank corps. The Navy also shared it briefly as an aerial gunnery range.

Among Marines of the fifties, Twentynine Palms is still remembered as a tent city pitched alongside a dry lake bed in the middle of the Mojave. There was no air conditioning to temper the 120° flights of the thermometer. Billowing canvas and dilapidated buildings left over from the days of Army control were the only shield against rip-roaring sandstorms and chill winter nights. Comforts and conveniences were unknown, and so was the usual gung-ho spirit. In hollow commendation, the early tenants of Twentynine Palms Base were known as "pioneers," and orders to the desert outpost were welcomed with the same kind of enthusiasm as assignment to the outer Aleutians or Tierra del Fuego.

But the pioneer period was of short duration. Within two or three years the base was as perky as a gate sentry's salute. Neat concrete buildings took the place of the tents. Fourteen miles of surfaced road linked a half-dozen identical semi-independent units—each complete with air-conditioned barracks, mess hall and administration building, warehouses, vehicle and equipment parks. Life was pretty tolerable, even when sixty-mile-an-hour winds whipped up the sandstorms, when summer temperatures climbed to 110°, 115° and 120°, or when the thermometer dipped 10° or 15° below freezing in January.

Along with Honest John, the Hawk, the Terrier, the latest in flame throwers, Howitzers and 155mms., Twentynine Palms got the refinements of a deluxe family summer camp—officer housing that would bespeak status in suburban Palm Springs, clubs, theatre, gymnasium and swimming pools.

"The Theatre is on distribution for the very latest film releases," boasted a slick, four-color brochure advertising the attractions of the camp. "Admission is ten cents for all Marines and their dependents . . . The Enlisted Club is one of the finest service clubs at any military installation in Southern California. Facilities of the club include game room, dining room, snack bar where beer and ale are dispensed, and a patio.

"The dining room serves outstanding meals, and a sandwich grill and short-order counter prepares many tasty and inexpensive sandwiches. Special activities, dances, parties, movies, etc. are conducted on a continuing basis for the pleasure of all . . . The Base Beauty Shop is located on the service road to the old area . . . It is operated by fully trained and qualified beauticians, and prices are quite reasonable. For appointment call 7392. . . ."

Nor were intellectually inclined leathernecks shortchanged. At the education center they could sign up for courses in anything from philosophy to flute playing, and at the library browse through a display of books that would be the envy of many a small college. Plugged the corps circulars: "A large selection of well over 10,000 volumes in all categories, plus magazines and newspapers, is available for your reading pleasure. There is a good stock of reference material and space for letter writing and studying. In addition the library has a special room for artists where they may work on current projects."

Churches? Tailor shop? Bank? Western Union service? Radio station? Nursery school? Dental clinic? Bowling alleys? Golf? Hobby shop? The Marines had them. The intramural athletic program of thirteen major sports was as "well rounded" as that of any institution of higher learning. Extracurricular dramatics? "To appeal to the fancy of would-be Thespians, there is an amateur theatrical group . . . If you would like to gain some interesting experience in make-up, costuming, set construction, property, stage management, lights, publicity, acting and directing, keep this in mind when you report aboard."

And as far as general entertainment was concerned, all the enticements of the Southwest were within an easy day's drag. "Twentynine Palms is centrally located in the Southern California recreation area," advised the publicists, "and playtime pursuits of almost any variety may be satisfied. Two and a half hours' drive to the east is the Colorado River, Lake Havasu and Lake Mohave, where boating, fishing, waterskiing and camping can be enjoyed.

"Two hours to the northwest you can climb into the mountains around Big Bear and Arrowhead for all types of winter sports and summer fun. Twenty minutes to the south is the Joshua Tree National Monument, a wonderful area for hiking, camping and picnicking. Farther to the west is Los Angeles, Long Beach, Oceanside, San Diego, the beaches, Disneyland, the Angels and the Rams. Four hours' drive to the northeast is the glamour and glittering night life of Las Vegas. Recreation unlimited is available for the pursuit of your hobby or pleasure."

Join the Marines! See the desert! Why pay $35 a day for lodgings and entertainment at Desert Palms when they come free under the auspices of the United States Marine Corps?

The brochure writers could make the desert sound mighty alluring, but most of the enlistees responding to the appeal were well aware that holiday maneuvers took a remote second place to harsh military maneuvers. Nevertheless, after release from service that had included a hitch at Twentynine Palms, it was amazing the way ex-Marines in civies drifted back to the area to talk business with local realtors and architects. In large measure they and their friends were responsible for the boom all through the high desert of Morongo Basin—at Joshua Tree, Yucca Valley, at Palm Wells, Morongo Valley and Twentynine Palms itself.

Inadvertently the Marines were developing into some of the best publicists the desert had. But the Army? Its spokesmen were perhaps more reserved. Compared to the array of niceties advertised for the corps at Twentynine Palms, Fort Irwin—150 miles to the northwest—was rather Spartan. The Army made no attempt to play it up as a resort or vacation center.

Fort Irwin had its library and educational opportunities, its crafts shop, gymnasium, theatre, swimming pool, beer bars, bank and beauty shop, but the barrens, 37 miles north of Barstow, were not portrayed as a recreational retreat. The command did not try to decorate the truth.

"Fort Irwin is located in the Mojave Desert in San Bernardino County, the largest county in the United States," buck privates were bluntly informed. "It is thirty-seven miles northeast of Barstow (road distance) and thirty-seven miles south of Death Valley (crow distance) . . . The road to Irwin is a stretch of black top known as Barstow Road at Fort Irwin and Fort Irwin Road at Barstow. You'll get used to it.

"A word of caution: the last service station between Barstow and Irwin is located at the corner of Route 91 and Fort Irwin Road. The road runs through country that is best described as barren wasteland. In case something should go wrong while you are on Irwin Road, four emergency telephones are available to summon aid from the post. They are mounted on telephone poles along the route, and their locations are well-marked by yellow arrow-shaped signs."

Then, in one of those rare outbursts of official Army humor, the soldier was warned: "Your first sight of Fort Irwin will come at the top of the hill four miles from the post. The first appearance of military life is a sign nine miles from the post proper, which marks the southern boundary of the reservation. Your reaction on this first sight may be, 'What did I do to deserve this?' "

"It isn't really that bad, and most of us really like it," comforted the Fort informant. "It is our proud boast that Fort Irwin is probably the friendliest post at which you will ever be stationed. This is the result of remoteness. . . ."

Getting down to the dry facts, the military exile learned: "There is little grass on post, and none off it . . . The desert itself is made up of small pieces of eroded rock, washed down from the five mountain ranges that border the desert. Except for Joshua and greasewood trees, most of the vegetation grows no more than two feet high. The Mojave is characterized by bright sun, low humidity, infrequent rain and occasional high winds. It is recognized by its many dry stream beds, canyons, arroyos, hills and ranges, but few sand dunes. The desert is full of peculiar and seldom-seen wild life, including jackrabbits, coyotes, wildcats, snakes, lizards, spiders, field mice, owls, large crows, hawks and eagles.

"Yes, the weather is hot and cold, to an extreme in either case. During the summer months the days are hot. In winter from about 0900 to 1600, it is a warm spring day; from 1600 on, in a matter of minutes, you may be in the arctic, and you'd better have a coat ready.

"The sand and wind can do considerable damage to your private vehicle, particularly on paint and glass. It is advisable to consult your insurance agent in this respect prior to reporting for duty. There are no garages available at Fort Irwin. One of the nicest features of the post is the year-round sunshine. It is unfortunate that this can also cause sunburn, heat stroke and heat exhaustion . . . The other threats to your welfare include spiders, snakes and scorpions. The obvious solution is to studiously avoid spiders, snakes and scorpions."

Fort Irwin is the United States Army Armor and Desert Training Center—larger even than the Twentynine Palms Marine Base, so big that a 90mm. tank gun can be fired at maximum elevation in any direction near its center without overshooting the bounds of the 1,000-square-mile reservation. Isolation is what the Army required for that kind of target practice, and the Mojave was one of the few spots left on the continent that offered enough of it.

According to Irwin legend, the desolate 1,000 square miles first made Army news back in 1857. That was the year when Secretary of War Jefferson Davis talked Congress into appropriating $30,000 for importing a herd of dromedaries to form the Army Camel Corps. The beasts arrived from the Middle East,

reluctantly padded down the gangways at the little port of In-
dianola, Texas, and set out, caravan fashion, on a five months'
march to the West Coast.

In charge of the camels was a heterogeneous squad of Syrian,
Turkish, Arab, Greek, Mexican and Pennsylvanian mercenaries,
under the command of veteran desert trailbreaker Lieutenant
Edward F. Beale. As scribe, Beale took on a young adventurer
named May Stacey, who jotted in his diary at the end of the first
day, "It is my decided opinion that these camels will prove a
failure." Stacey's opinion proved to be prophetic.

Fort Irwin historians hint that the expedition paused in the
Barstow area long enough to investigate the virtues of the site
as an Army post, before proceeding to Los Angeles. Once they
had reached their destination, however, neither Lieutenant Beale
nor the Secretary of War seemed to have any definite plan of
action for the Camel Corps, least of all setting up headquarters
near Barstow.

The foreign mercenaries gradually deserted. There were few
unemployed camel drivers in California to take their places, and
the bewildered dromedaries sooner or later found their way into
circuses, zoos, private barnyards and Western folklore. The episode was never regarded as one of the more glorious triumphs of
the United States Army. Nevertheless, Irwin proudly boasts that
it is "the only army post that can trace its history from camels
to tanks."

The modern history of the fort dates from August 8, 1940,
when President Roosevelt, by executive order, created Mojave
Antiaircraft Range. For five years during World War II, planes
with targets in tow shuttled back and forth over the range. Guns
sputtered during the day; tracers lit up the night skies; and bursts
of ack-ack were heard overhead at any hour of the day or night.
As a name, Mojave Antiaircraft Range lacked distinction com-
mensurate with the high order of training provided there, so in
1942 the place was redubbed Camp Irwin, in honor of the distinguished World War I field artillery commander, Major General LeRoy Irwin.

By late 1944 the camp had served its purpose and was inacti-
vated. For seven years the desert winds and sandstorms did their
best to wipe it off the map. But there was enough left to patch
up in 1951 when the Korean trouble broke out. Camp Irwin
came back to life with military emphasis switched from antiair-

craft to armor. It proved its worth as a training center, continued to grow, and ten years later was designated as a permanent installation and accorded the added nominal dignity of "Fort" rather than "Camp."

The most vicious-looking vehicles in the Army's cavalcade of armor have been groaning across the sands ever since, walloping shells into the void, scaring the hide off the jack rabbits, the coyotes and human intruders imprudent enough to disregard the CLOSED TO THE PUBLIC signs.

Fort Irwin means business—very serious business; as deadly a business as there is in the United States of America. "The mission of the U.S. ARMY Armor and Desert Training Center," recites the post commander in grim earnestness, "is to provide the command, operation, training, administration, service and supply to (a) complete the individual and unit training of tank units involving firing of the main armament which cannot ordinarily be carried out at home stations; (b) familiarize tank units with the operation and employment of special armor equipment; (c) familiarize tank units with the operation and employment of the latest types of tanks and related equipment; and (d) conduct combat firing and tactical exercises as time and facilities permit."

In effect, Fort Irwin offers a postgraduate as well as undergraduate curriculum in heavy armor. Indoctrination comes in big doses, highly concentrated. It is not the "remoteness" alone that keeps morale at a high pitch and life on the rugged side. The desert-club recreation refinements are there, but in the interests of national defense they sometimes get neglected.

America's Armageddon is as likely to be fought on a desert as anywhere else, so there was military foresight in selecting the Mojave as a training ground for soldiery. But ordinary civilian logic would have to exclude the Navy. The desert is no place for sailors. Davy Jones in the sand hills would be as incongruous as a burro and prospector on the thwarts of a rowboat in mid-Pacific. Yet there the fleet arm is, and not merely a token force. Including Marine contingents, the Navy representation in the Mojave and Colorado deserts is larger than Army and Air Force combined, and the biggest establishment rubs shoulders with Fort Irwin, plumb in the middle of the northwest Mojave.

The only Navy-commanded metropolis in the continental United States is not where one would expect it to be—say, on the north or south shore of Boston, on the Virginia coast, on the outskirts of San Diego or Bremerton. It is 150 miles inland, stranded in the desert—a city of 12,000 where everything from kindergarten to commissary is Navy owned and Navy operated.

China Lake is the place, but no cruiser, PT boat or captain's gig will ever be launched on the lake. The city is incongruously named for a borax colony of Chinese coolies who decamped three-quarters of a century ago, and for a lake that is not there. The lakesite is bone dry and has been, within the memory of man.

Nudging Fort Irwin on the east is a vast naval estate of 2,000 square miles, 1,250,000 acres, one of the most complex and vital defense installations in the country—the Naval Ordnance Test Station, NOTS for short. In fact, there is not a United States submarine, destroyer or carrier afloat that does not owe a debt in armaments to the laboratories and firing ranges of NOTS.

The details of what goes on at China Lake are "classified." None of the 12,000 residents and employees may enter or leave the city without presenting authentic credentials to the Marine guards at the municipal gates, and ordinary rubberneck tourists are looked upon askance, except during the exciting Armed Forces Day celebration and the annual open-house Wild Flower Show which the station puts on. Roads and trails which once crossed the station proper are "permanently closed," and on adjoining Randsburg Wash Test Range they might as well be, though the parlance used is "restricted travel."

The reservation boundaries fence in a lot of history, as well as naval confidences. Across these grounds trudged early trail blazers like Joseph Reddeford Walker, overlanders like the jay-hawkers, and a host of gold prospectors heading into the Coso, Argus and Panamint ranges. Only with a Navy pass can one hope ever again to retrace the old twenty-mule-team road between Death Valley and Mojave.

The vast quadrangle of the main station sprawls halfway between the Sierra Nevada and Death Valley, and Randsburg Wash stretches from a few miles north of Barstow to the Panamints. All this unlovely country is out of bounds to ordinary civilians, and few of them begrudge the Navy's appropriation of it. No land anywhere could suffer less from the scars of gunnery demolition.

The Navy first began investigating the region during the early years of World War II. At that time the California Institute of Technology in Pasadena was engaged in a hectic race to develop motors for a family of brand-new rockets desperately needed on the fighting fronts. The rockets had to be tested somewhere, so the professors were taking the experimental projectiles into Eaton Canyon, just back of Pasadena, where they fired away, much to the discomfort and danger of themselves and the neighbors.

Old Faithful, Minnie Mouse, Holy Moses, and Tiny Tim were then in their infancy, as was the whole science of rocketry. To exemplify the youthful status of the science, one of the pioneers recalled: "Temperature data was recorded by crouching behind a sandbag barricade and reading the gauges by means of a telescope poked between the bags, and the human eye was used as a documentary camera."

The institute scientists sorely needed space for their experiments—uninhabited space, clean air for photographing rockets in flight, and a place where weather changes would not constantly be interrupting test schedules. Goldstone Dry Lake near Barstow filled the bill for a few months, and there the first rocket-driven depth charge, the "retrobomb," was fired on July 2, 1942.

But Goldstone soon proved to be totally inadequate. The Army had a nice, secluded airport sheltered by the Sierra at Inyokern—Harvey Field. It was surrounded by an expanse of land mostly in public domain, a small area owned by the state and a few parcels filed as homestead claims. It was a perfect setup for the Navy program.

In some high-level dickering, the Army agreed to swap Harvey Field for Navy-owned swampland in Louisiana; the state agreed on another property trade; the public domain went to the Navy; and the parcels owned by twenty-six homesteaders, who were having a hard time eking a living out of the desert anyway, were condemned. By November 1943, nine hundred square miles of high desert had been set aside for a rocket and related-weapons facility, and the Naval Ordnance Test Station was born.

The war tot grew as only a favored offspring fed on a multi-million-dollar diet from Washington could grow. Before the end of the war some $55,000,000 had been poured into NOTS' upbringing. The United States had been caught napping in its rocket development, trailing a poor fourth to Germany, Russia and England. At China Lake, rocketry had to be pushed through infancy and youth to full maturity in less than half a decade. The miracle was very nearly accomplished, and unlike other defense projects that were allowed to atrophy after V-J Day, NOTS kept growing.

Actually, most of the station's maturing has been since 1945. The California Institute of Technology dropped out, and the Navy assembled its own teams of scientists. Armitage Field replaced Harvey. The original 900 square miles were more than doubled with the addition of Randsburg Wash and other plots.

Millions upon millions in defense dollars went into the physical plant during the next fifteen years. On the construction of a single laboratory, roofing ten acres of floor space, $10,400,000 were expended, and the scientific equipment it shelters cost an equal amount. Nowhere in the country is there another technical and research institution that could begin to match it in size and equipment.

If an academic tourist, unaware of what the Navy was up to in the Mojave, had wandered into China Lake, he would have jumped to the conclusion that he had stumbled onto the campus of a great university in hiding. The place had the look and atmosphere of a college town. Aboard were more Ph.Ds than senior naval officers, and commanders and captains probably had advanced engineering degrees, as well as rank. China Lake lacked the stamp of a typical naval establishment. Civilians outnumbered military personnel better than three to one. The city had a true cultural tone. It was a place where crowds turned out for a concert or an erudite lecture, where the library was always busy, and baby sitters were in great demand, because parents insisted on attending evening classes in mathematics, linguistics or fine arts.

Nowhere in the confines of the desert was there a more attractive, orderly oasis. Streets were shaded with thousands of trees that had spread out lush foliage in fifteen short years. Unpretentious homes were set off with groomed lawns, patios and gardens. The shopping plaza and recreation center were as tidy as they were immense. Half-a-dozen religious denominations amicably shared the handsome community chapel on Sundays. Even the schools—kindergarten through high—accredited with one of the finest educational programs in California, seemed to reflect the serious attitude of science-oriented parents. And just outside the station fence, congenially sharing its religious, community and business services, was the twin civilian town of Ridge-

crest which had miraculously grown up in the same disciplined atmosphere.

Yet from this pleasant oasis emanated some of the deadliest weapons known to generals and admirals. NOTS cut across defense-department demarcations and served the Air Force, NATO and the Army, as well as the Navy and Marines. In the laboratories and test ranges of China Lake originated the vicious Sidewinder, most widely used air-to-air guided missile in the free world; the Zuni rocket, produced with interchangeable war heads, so that it could be used either in air-to-ground or air-to-air combat, a lethal weapon when turned against vehicle convoys, tanks, troops concentrations, gun emplacements, trains or small ships; the Mighty Mouse, a folding-fin aircraft rocket designed for salvo firing, so destructive and in such demand that over 14,000,000 were produced in one decade between 1952 and 1962.

These were only samples of the hardware perfected at China Lake. Of no less significance were such products as antisubmarine rockets, scanning devices for transmitting pictures from outer space, satellite monitors, solid and liquid propellants for rocket motors.

The propulsion laboratories alone included 150 buildings scattered over thirty-two square miles. Just about everything that could be contrived to fuel missiles and space vehicles was carried on in those 150 structures—mixing, casting, extruding, curing, machining, inhibiting and testing. And included in the works was a gigantic stand dubbed Skytop, where rocket motors with as much as a 1,000,000-pound thrust could be tested statically, and where the vitality of smaller ones could be proved in a vacuum chamber simulating conditions outside the earth's atmosphere.

Spread over 1,000 square miles of desert were more than a dozen ground and aircraft ranges. For testing rockets and guided missiles there was one free-flight range 37 miles long. On NOTS' four miles of test track, as precisely engineered as a Swiss watch, vehicles zipped at supersonic velocities of 3,700 feet per second to try out the thrust of a missile motor or the effectiveness of a plane ejection seat. And far out on Randsburg Wash, in an isolated valley, mammoth B-29's and B-47's were hoisted aloft from 360-foot towers, merely to be blown to bits as targets for fuse tests.

Designing weapons simply and reliably was the key objective

at China Lake. Within one organization was seen the whole ordnance process—research, development, evaluation, production engineering. The cost was fantastic, but even frugal politicians who had to vote the funds, back in Washington, conceded that the achievements were worth the price.

Still more costly and still more diversified were the activities of the Air Force, less than 50 pigeon-flight miles south of NOTS. Known to the world as Edwards Air Force Base, here was the one and only flight test center of the Air Force for manned air and aerospace craft. Compared to the 1,250,000 acres occupied by the Navy, the flight test grounds were modest, only 301,209 acres. But the acreage was ample, and on it were crammed more technical wonders of the twentieth-century jet age—and the twenty-first—than were concentrated anywhere else in the Americas.

To the casual taxpayer it would appear that many of the expensive mechanical behemoths were unnecessarily duplicated at both camps, that Navy and Air Force were each trying to outdo the other in thinking up outsized gadgetry for tests and trials. Both had extensive flight ranges and airfields; both had long precision-built tracks for supersonic ground runs; NOTS had its mighty Skytop for static tests of Polaris, and the test center its stands for the Minuteman, Thor, Atlas, and other rocket engines; the Navy's 360-foot towers for hoisting planes were matched by the Air Force's Whirl Tower at El Centro that could fling a gondola or parachute around in a circle at speeds of 400 and 500 miles an hour, not to mention the main aircraft control colossus, the tallest single-structure tower in the United States.

But when the facilities were sized up, it became increasingly evident that the functions of the two sets of similar equipment were different. The Navy station was primarily concerned with shooting hardware; the Air Force base with vehicles of flight. And for properly putting those vehicles to the test, Edwards could boast of possessing the world's longest runway—a paved strip stretching out for 15,000 feet and continuing on across hard-packed Rogers Dry Lake for 15 miles or more.

It was the dry lake that first attracted the Air Force to the Mojave. Here lay a prodigious natural landing field covering some 65 square miles, practically made to order. During ten months of the year the sun kept the clay-and-silt lake bottom baked in a crust hard enough to hold up under pressures of 250 pounds per square inch, and driving winds swept it clean. During the other two months—usually January and February—a few inches of rain accumulated on the bed; winds washed it back and forth, obliterating tracks and ripples from the previous season. By March or April the water was gone, the lake bed packed, smooth and resurfaced—a leveling process that would be prohibitively expensive without the assistance of nature.

Actually the Army discovered Rogers Lake long before a separate Air Force existed. As the nucleus for a bombing range, a camp was first set up on the east shore in 1933. All the Army Air Corps found there at the time were the Santa Fe tracks, a watering station named Yucca and the little village of Muroc, founded by Clifford Corum and family.

The homesteading Corums had made hard work out of naming the place. Other dots in the desert commonly bore the names of the first settlers, but the practice seemed a little immodest to Clifford. He realized that not capitalizing on an opportunity to perpetuate the family name would be considered disrespectful by the rest of the clan, so he compromised by turning it around and spelling it backwards. By 1933 the population of Muroc had swelled to 44, yet even the modest Corums were ready to grant that the desert around their oasis was about as good for bombing as for raising crops.

The Corums moved over and the Army Air Corps moved in. For nine years groups of lonely enlisted men held down Muroc Bombing and Gunnery Range, while P-38 Lightning Fighters, B-24 Liberators and B-25 Mitchells dumped bombs around them.

To give zest and incentive to the sport, after Pearl Harbor, an all too realistic 650-foot model of a Japanese heavy cruiser, Mogambi class, was erected near by. The project cost the startling sum of $35,819.18, and was officially carried on the base books as "T-799, Japanese Battleship, Plan No. 944/41 W-509-ENG 4239," but pilots and bombardiers playfully called it the *Muroc-Maru* and went after it with a vengeance.

As a target it was such a success that it had to be made still better. Mounds of sand were skillfully packed around the ship to simulate ocean waves. Someone raised the Rising Sun on the aftermast. That did it. Many a passing motorist, unaware of the Army's caprice, rubbed his eyes at what he hoped was only a mirage, and hurried on, half expecting the Japanese Navy to open fire before he could get out of range.

Legends of an oriental Flying Dutchman cruising the desert

circulated far and wide. "The sun's reflection on the dry lake created a mirage that made the area appear under water," explained a contemporary. "Then heat waves in the middle of the day caused the simulated ocean to shimmer so that the *Muroc-Maru* actually appeared to move."

The mock-up, riding the undulating billows of sand and heat haze, was strafed, high bombed and skip bombed for years before it began to lose its realistic look. When the ship was finally scuttled, because it was becoming a flight hazard, her "lower decks" were so strewn with duds and unexploded bombs that Army engineers risked their lives in dismantling her.

Within a year after the war another better use had been discovered for Rogers Dry Lake. It was just the spot needed for testing the new jet family, so Muroc Bombing and Gunnery Range became Muroc Air Base and chief contestant for the title of air-speed center of the nation.

Here the first turbojet had taken flight in 1942. Four years later a rocket test sled was clocked at 1,019 miles per hour. On December 9, 1946, the X-1 experimental rocket plane hit 550 miles per hour in the first flight under its own power. The next June, Muroc and the United States regained the world speed record by zooming over a 1.86-mile course at the rate of 623 miles per hour in a Lockheed F-80 Shooting Star.

Four months later Air Force test pilot Captain Charles Yeager broke the sound barrier in the X-1. In September 1948, another world's speed record of 671 miles per hour was chalked up in the F-86 Sabrejet. The following spring the X-1 set an unofficial record of 1,100 miles per hour, and the rocket-boosted jet experimental XF-91 became the first combat-type aircraft to exceed the speed of sound in level flight.

But in this steady accumulation of records there were setbacks too. On June 5, 1948, Captain Glen W. Edwards took off in the boomerang-shaped YB-49. Nothing quite like it had ever been flown before. It was a batlike flying wing with a drag-producing fuselage, a revolutionary bomber powered by eight jet engines producing 32,000 horsepower. Everything about it was super: its cost—$3,000,000; its wing span—172 feet; its bomb load—fifteen tons; its top speed—500 miles per hour or more; its operating altitude—over 30,000 feet.

The Air Force attached a lot of importance to YB-49, and impressive delegations of gold braid assembled to witness its performance. They watched Edwards take off and swiftly gain altitude. Then something went wrong. YB-49 suddenly went into a dive and plunged to earth. It scythed through desert sagebrush and greasewood, and under a billowing cloud of dark smoke burned to a black skeleton.

The bodies of the five-man crew, including Captain Edwards', were gathered up from the wreckage. So baffling was the cause of the disaster that the Air Force could explain only that the plane "ran into difficulties in the air." But the hero of that flight, a captain who had flown fifty World War II combat missions in the European theatre before becoming a test pilot, was not forgotten. Muroc Air Base was renamed Edwards Air Force Base.

The list of records tallied at Edwards continued to grow. The F-86 Sabrejet did 698 in 1952 for a new world record. The F-100 Super Sabre topped that with 755 in 1953 and a supersonic 822 in 1955.

Meanwhile, new generations of X planes were evolving. Breaking the sound barrier with them was routine, yet no one knew how planes would hold together as pilots sped faster and deeper into the unknown. Stress and strain could be figured out theoretically in the drafting rooms, but the accuracy of the figuring had to be tested in the air.

On December 12, 1953, Captain Yeager climbed into the X-1A —designed, claimed the engineers, to fly stably at twice the speed of sound. Yeager had faith in the engineers. He gave the plane full throttle and watched the meter needle move from Mach 1 to 1.5 and then to Mach 2. The engineers were right. But Yeager tried for more. The X-1A rode smoothly at Mach 2.435—nearly two and a half times the speed of sound.

A slight yawing motion startled the pilot. Then abruptly the plane went completely out of control, porpoising wildly. It virtually tumbled end over end, weaved, flipped on its back, appearing to gain momentum as it somersaulted over and over, streaking across the sky in a crazy pattern of motion.

Obviously the plane was doomed. Harnessed in his seat, Yeager fought back, desperately trying to overcome the tumbling. It was useless. Under the frightful pressure and the brutal buffeting he lost consciousness.

"Inertial coupling" the experts called the gyrations of the plane. It came on when the demands placed upon an aircraft exceeded the design limits, and all stability was lost in the violent speed. The X-1A had been overwhelmed. Yeager had called for too much, and now there seemed to be no escape for him. In 1953 it was still assumed that seat ejection at supersonic speed would be suicidal. Yeager's canopy was locked from the outside. He had to stay with the plane.

Cameras mounted at the rear of the cockpit recorded everything that was happening to the pilot and to the instrument panel. The crushing force of 14 g's wracked him. He was hurled from one side to the other, forced deep into his seat, flung out of it, mauled on every side, pounded against the instrument panel.

The fuel of the rocket motor burned off and the X-1A started to fall. It had dropped 10 miles, to 25,000 feet, when Yeager regained consciousness. The plane was spinning upside down like a gyropropellor. But somehow he pulled himself together, broke the spin, and two minutes later glided onto the floor of Rogers Dry Lake.

He was so nearly beaten to death that he had to be carried from the cockpit. Yeager survived. The X-1A was not doomed, but it was another pilot who took it to the record height of 90,000 feet six months later.

Its offspring, the X-2, bettered those marks in 1956 with 1,900 miles per hour and an altitude of 126,200 feet, nearly 24 miles up, and then registered a speed of 2,094 before a crash in September of that year. New X descendants took its place.

On the ground the rocket sled was shot down the tracks at a velocity of 1,560 miles per hour in June 1956, and three years later at 2,050—the fastest two-rail run ever made anywhere. And new Edwards' milestones, just as notable, were being made with missile recovery, with supersonic fighter bombers, with all-weather interceptors, with jet vertical take-offs and guided missiles.

The X-15 was ready for an historic flight by mid-June of 1959. Imperturbable Test Pilot Scott Crossfield leisurely finished a breakfast of bacon and eggs early that morning, struggled into a skintight pressure suit, and was soon strapped into the cramped cockpit of a needle-nosed plane, locked beneath the right wing of a B-52 bomber.

Sharp on the dot of eight o'clock the B-52 roared down the Edwards runway and lifted. Crossfield, in the X-15, and Pilot Charles Bock, at the controls of the B-52, were well aware of the significance of the mission. The X-15 was the first United States aircraft built to carry man to the edge of space. It was designed to do 4,000 miles an hour and reach altitudes of 100 miles or more. But it had never been tested in free flight. Six times the crucial test had been postponed because of bad weather or failures in the telemetry and electrical systems.

As the giant mother plane with the odd-shaped nursling clamped underneath soared above the Mojave, lay ground observers were not as confident of success as was Crossfield. They were quoting odds that the X-15, its wings little bigger than 1959 Cadillac tail fins, would plummet down like a dead pigeon when released.

At 38,000 feet the tense moment came. In the B-52, Bock checked his air speed—450 knots, and queried Crossfield on the intercom to make sure that he was set. "Ready when you are, buddy," Crossfield fired back lightly.

Bock went through a five-second countdown, and pushed a red button on his control panel. With a resonant click, a locking device opened and the X-15 dropped on a long, swift, powerless swoop toward the desert floor. The gibes about the amputated wings proved ill conceived at that moment. The X-15 glided as prettily as a bird and responded agilely to the controls.

"Wish I could do a roll on my way in," squawked Crossfield over his radio at 14,000 feet. But he settled for a lazy S-turn, and zeroed in on Rogers Lake bed, cutting his air speed from 285 miles per hour to 185 with three nose-up porpoising maneuvers. The X-15 touched down effortlessly, slid almost a mile to a dust-raising stop, and its pilot casually commented as he eased out of the cockpit, "I hope all my landings are as smooth as that one."

The X-15 had been in the air 38 minutes, and its first powerless flight had lasted just over 5 minutes, but in those brief minutes man had moved many, many miles closer to space.

The Edwards' records still kept piling up. Before Christmas of 1959, the F-105 Thunderchief fighter bomber set a new world mark of 1,217 miles per hour. The F-106 Delta Dart jumped it to 1,525, and the F-104 Starfighter zoomed 103,395 feet up for still another ground take-off altitude record. And almost monthly during 1960, 1961 and 1962, important paragraphs were added to the annals of conquest over air and space. Included in the flight center tests were vehicles as diversified as the Minuteman, new parachutes, experimental helicopters and rockets.

The X-15 kept breaking its own speed records: 2,196 miles per hour, 2,275, 2,905, 3,074, 3,603, 3,920, 4,093—and altitudes that edged up from 25 miles to over 50. Edwards Air Force Base was the starting point for some of the epoch-making transcontinental flights. From its runways a supersonic T-38 Trainer took off on February 19, 1962, and angled to a height of over 6 miles in a minute, to break four time-to-climb records in one performance.

The base was intricately involved in the space race, looked forward to the day when Dyna-Soar, the space glider, would swoop across the continent in perhaps 6 minutes, when the long-delayed RS-70—fastest, hardest-punching aircraft in the world—would be ready for a test flight, and when Rogers Dry Lake would serve as a land space-recovery center.

All this activity was focused into the future, and to make sure that there would be no shortage in space-oriented specialists to test the planes and space ships of the future, every eight months a new class of 16 hand-picked pilots was graduated from the Experimental Test Pilot School operated by the base. Whenever and wherever aviation and space history were to be made in the United States, Edwards Air Force Base and the Flight Test Center would, in all likelihood, be in on it.

An elite flying fraternity of less than 50 test pilots were the peers of the Edwards flight program. They were the ones who made the headlines, won the citations and awards for their exploits—and occasionally the prominent obituaries. But backing up that little fraternity was an army of some 12,000 base employees—military and civilian, including the representatives of thirty or more commercial aircraft companies and contractors who maintained facilities there.

Altogether, Edwards made up one of the largest communities in the Mojave Desert. With an annual pay roll of almost $26,000,-000, it was doing much to bring economic stability to the desert. As at the Navy, Army and Marine bases, civilian residents and personnel in uniform at Edwards had all the living refinements that could readily be lugged into the barren land—clubs and clinics, shopping center and swimming pools, libraries and laundromat, schools and snack bars, Capehart homes and a hospital, even an animal clinic in charge of a base veterinarian.

Perhaps the armed services were tardy in discovering the virtues of the desert as a training and testing ground, but they were fast making up for lost time. Twentynine Palms, Fort Irwin, China Lake and Edwards were hardly more than representative of a dozen other military centers like the enormous Marine Corps Supply Base at Barstow; George Air Force Base for pilot training at Victorville; the Radar Station atop Mockingbird Hill, north of Kramer, a major link in the Western Air Defense Command; the Joint Parachute Test Facility of the Navy and Air Force at El Centro, where spectacular drops and recoveries were carried on as though they were part of an industrial routine; the Salton Sea Bombing and Gunnery Test Base; Chocolate Mountain Aerial Gunnery Range; the Navy's Dive Bombing, Rocket Firing and Air-to-Ground Machine-Gun Firing Ranges of Holtville and Sand Hills.

In keeping with swiftly moving defense developments, military units moved into the desert with a flourish, and occasionally left with a similar flourish as they were superceded by some new program. Old landmarks such as Camp Dunlap, east of the Salton Sea, and the vast Marine Air Station at Mojave, are no more, but desert dwellers were not complaining about inadequate garrisoning of their purlieus. So many military reservations were crowded into the area—all with restricted air space above them —that piloting a plane across Southern California was like threading a route through a maze. After all, there were only 15,-000 square miles in the whole Mojave, and a third of the area was already occupied by the armed forces.

XII

THE DESERT SHALL REJOICE
AND BLOSSOM

THE wonder of spring bloom in the Mojave was not wasted
entirely, even on leathery characters of the boom-and-bust borax
days or the gold era. In the right company a flinthearted old prospector could be pressed into acknowledging that the flowers he
was wading through were "sort o' fetchin' "; skinners and swampers were known to have interrupted their sparring long enough
to exchange blasphemous exclamations about the stunning spectacle; and there were hardy derelicts who actually relapsed into
a mood of civilized sentimentality for a brief period during the
height of the April bloom.

The dazzling display, stretching to the horizon and beyond,
brought out the poet in a man. One hell-roarer, under the influence of the Muse—or something else—was reported to have
paused over his canteen in midmorning and startled his companions with the observation, "God Almighty outdone Himself on
that rug." And to another was ascribed the rash utterance: "Holy
Mackerel, look at all that screamin' yeller and red. Take a whiff,
Josh. Like a powdered-up hussy."

Early explorers tucked into official reports vague suggestions
of the floral splendor. Overlanders and forty-niners wrote home
about it. Globe-trotting journalists, scientists and artists tried
to describe the spectacle in their notebooks or on their sketch
pads. Eastern naturalists heard tell of the incredible displays and
came to catalogue the species. Their count of different varieties
ran into the hundreds.

All agreed that there were few places on earth where there
was a greater profusion of bloom than in the deserts of the South-

west. But it was unpredictable and very short lived. The most glorious of the flowers might appear any week from March to May, depending on the rain and the season. And after a dry winter there might be no blossoming at all. Seeds could lie buried in the sand for a decade and never sprout. Then one year would come a rainy February, and in a few weeks the whole desert would be ablaze.

In assessing the total scene, the splurge of color in the backdrop had to be taken into account too. "Every peak, every face, every ledge, every declivity, every gorge, every stratum, every rock has a color of its own," claimed John Spears, in characterizing the borax mountains in the 1890's, "and there are no two breadths of color exactly alike. They vary from marble white to lava black, from the palest green to the darkest carmine, from the faintest cream to royal purple—there is every tint and every brilliant or dull body of color, and all mingled, contrasted and blended, and all piled up in such magnificent masses as are beyond description."

Add the riot of floral radiance to the background shades, and here indeed was something beyond description. What an overlander saw in the fifties, a botanist in the seventies, or a silver prospector in the nineties, was not very different from what naturalist Donald Culross Peattie saw from the yard of a Mojave ranch in midtwentieth century. "Not even in the Alps in full summer," he exclaimed, "had I ever beheld so dancing a carpet as on that April morning when I stepped out into the Mojave in bloom . . . As anyone will cry out involuntarily at an unexpected sharp pain, so there was no stopping the laughter that rose in the throat at the sight.

"Not just the first time, and not just on my lips. Everyone at the ranch, each time he stepped out into the dazzling profusion of color and dancing shapes, laughed again, a pure enchanted laugh."

Peattie marveled at the sea of ankle-deep bloom, big, blazing flowers perched on tiny stems scarcely an inch tall—desert gold, desert stars, tiny tim, golden poppies. And above this undercarpet rose other displays, tier on tier: golden glow, desert dandelions with canary-yellow heads; white tidytips; pink sand verbena, pervading the whole desert with fragrance; royal-purple lupine everywhere; brilliant blue scabiosa sages; desert mallows with chalices of fiery flowers varying from apricot to deep grenadine;

lilac larkspur, asters, thistle sage, fragile, perfumed gilias and more gilias. "Every day, every hour you saw the gilias, but you could never get used to the sheer improbability that anything so dainty could be put forth by the Mojave . . . once in many years a million of them like this.

"What brought delight," he rhapsodized, "was the sheer abundance of the carpet, the feeling that we were actually besieged by an army of little flowers. The bees were drunk with them; they came in thousands from only the Mojave knows where. I saw hummingbirds flock by in such a state of excitement that they looked as if they had been shot sideways out of a cannon with a twisted bore. They seemed unable to settle their scattered brains on anything . . . We used to wonder at the ranch how far this flood of rare flowering stretched across the desert floor. You couldn't tell; you only knew it was on to the rim of the horizon. And you knew it was brief. It must be loved while you had it."

The fantastic bloom was real, but also symbolic. It was a perennial reminder that the desert wanted to burgeon, produce, come to life. For perhaps one month of the year the land seemed to rejoice and be filled with Biblical gladness; for the other eleven it was a forbidding barrens. Eons before, the Mojave—like the Colorado Desert—had been an arm of the Pacific. The sea had given it latent fertility; the Colorado River had spilled over and fed it too. Once, before the coastal mountains were brought forth to curtain off the ocean rains, the whole area had been an expanse of green. To become productive again the desert needed only to have its thirst quenched.

Mere men could not make up for the Pacific rains. With pumps and conduits they could help a little in reviving the sands, though never could they hope to bring a permanent material bloom that would measure up to the seasonal floral bloom. Ground water was not that quantitative. Besides the spotty subterranean reserves, there were three principal sources within possible reach: the shed from the east side of the Sierra Nevada—which Los Angeles had appropriated; the Mojave River, meandering northeastward from the San Bernardino Mountains for a hundred miles, mostly underground, but here and there gushing to the surface and flowing on until finally lost in the sands; and the mighty Colorado. The Colorado was the best prospect, but the greed for the waters of that river was so great all through the American Desert that three Colorados would not go the rounds.

There was never a chance of giving year-round bloom to much of the upper California desert. The best that could be done was to broaden existing oases, create a few others, and salvage more of the Mojave River.

Down in the Imperial Valley the planters were better off, but in less than ten years after Rockwood and Chaffey had dug their ditch the beneficiaries were not at all satisfied with it. Particularly they disliked the long loop through foreign soil and the endless political complications the detour brought them. In return for the right of way, a large share of the canal's flow had to be given up. It was too high a price. Moreover, the river—riding on its delta cone in Mexico—kept breaking over the banks, growing more threatening every year.

The Imperial Irrigation District directors had found it necessary to maintain a standing army of river crews, and the Mexican authorities were anything but cooperative when an emergency arose and men had to be rushed to the scene of a new break. The valley farmers lived in suspense, never knowing when they might be flooded out of existence, never knowing what the whim of their foreign neighbors might next decree.

They wanted a canal entirely on United States soil, one that would tap the Colorado above Yuma and carry water through the sand hills north of the border. The present supply was erratic—flood one year and drought the next. By 1919 everyone was convinced that the only relief from the recurrent rampages and shortages of the river would come from a great controlling works in the Colorado channel itself. They needed a big dam at Boulder Canyon, but—come what may—they at least wanted an All-American Canal.

Arizona demanded its share of that water, too, as did the eastern California towns bordering the river—and Nevada and New Mexico and Utah and Colorado and Wyoming, where the headwaters gathered. So began the bitterest interstate water wrangle of the century. It went on for fifteen years. No state was going to concede to a sister state a cubic foot of water that was not won on a political battlefield.

Yuma was flooded disastrously in 1921, Palo Verde Valley worse the next year. And always the threat of inundation hung over Imperial Valley. Year after year the flow of the life-giving Colorado was wasted while the interstate arguing went on. Compacts and hard-won agreements were drawn up only to be nullified when one party backed out.

In despair, Secretary of Commerce Herbert Hoover—world renowned for his mediation as European Relief Administrator—was called in as umpire. For years he made little headway with the disputing factions. Campaigns in the war of water were fought successively in Washington, in Salt Lake City, in Denver, at Riverside, Santa Barbara, San Diego, Phoenix, Santa Fe and again in Washington. The struggle went on and on through the twenties.

The dispute was not only over who was going to get how much water. Caught up in the confusion of squabbling was the question of where a controlling dam would be located—in Boulder Canyon or somewhere else. Was it to be a high dam or a lesser dam? Built by the federal government, by states concerned, by one state, or by a private corporation? To conciliator Hoover and men of broad vision a high dam, constructed with federal funds, was the answer that made sense, but the long view was obscured in regional interests.

Meantime, Los Angeles was again on the prowl for water. In 1924, little more than a decade after San Fernando Reservoir had been filled from the detoured Owens River, tenacious William Mulholland, still carrying the colors in the Los Angeles battle of the faucet, filed for 1,500 cubic feet per second from the Colorado River—four times the capacity of the Owens River Aqueduct. He was worried about how much longer the supply from the Sierra would hold out, and the city fathers were just as worried.

The next year a cluster of nearby towns joined Los Angeles in organizing what they called the Metropolitan Water District, with the specific objective of erecting a dam in Boulder Canyon, if no one else did, and bringing the water clear across the 400 miles of intervening desert.

By 1928 the Metropolitan Water District was a powerful organization of thirteen communities reaching from Long Beach and Santa Ana on the south to Pasadena and Burbank on the north, and its constituted aims had gained legislative approval. The lobby for Greater Los Angeles joined the general free-for-all in Washington. It carried the message that the whole future prospect for continued expansion and future development of Southern California depended on Boulder Dam, on a Colorado Aqueduct and an All-American Canal.

On December 21, 1928, Congress brought an abrupt end to the long war. Boulder Dam Project was approved and Calvin Coolidge signed it into law. As cagey Mulholland had calculated, Los Angeles and its satellite towns were to be the prime beneficiaries. Southern California would get most of the electric power generated at the dam; Imperial Valley and the adjacent desert country would have their All-American Canal; Arizona and other contesting states would get a more modest share of the Colorado's flow. An old Scriptural text had become the Golden Rule of the Southwest: "Unto everyone that hath shall be given."

The urgency of getting the Colorado River under control had been all but forgotten during the long years of interstate wrangling. Imperial Valley was existing on borrowed time. Since the great flood of 1906, observers maintained that the Colorado had been building up its delta bed at the rate of almost a foot a year. It could therefore be assumed that the bed was close to twenty feet higher than when Harriman had poured millions into plugging the breach. Many additional miles of levee had been built, but the banks were now so high that engineers agreed it would never be possible to stop another break like that of 1906. Salton Sea might spread out over Imperial Valley and millions of adjacent acres below sea level, if Boulder Dam were not built in a hurry.

Even with this threat, it took Congress until July 1930, to appropriate the first $10,000,000 for the dam project. Then, disregarding the procrastination, rigid demands in construction haste were placed upon Six Companies, Inc. to whom the Boulder contract was awarded.

Their bid was $48,890,995.50, and the completion date was set for April 11, 1938. The contractors were given just seven years to finish one of the most enormous construction jobs in history, and for every day occupied in construction after April 11, 1938, a penalty of $3,000 would be exacted.

For the engineers it was a race against time, with the threat of financial disaster for Six Companies hanging over their heads, as well as the ever-present threat to Imperial Valley from an untamed river.

Everything about Boulder Dam was in terms of precedent-shattering dimension. In 1930 it was the most massive dam proj-

ect ever undertaken; it would stand 727 feet high and block a sheer gorge of one of the world's greatest rivers for a width of a quarter of a mile. The incomprehensible quantity of 5,000,000 tons of concrete had to be poured into the void. And all this would create a lake 115 miles long and up to 8 miles wide, impounding 30,000,000 acre feet of water—not only the largest man-made sheet of water in existence, but also one so tremendous that it would affect the climate of the immediate environs, and so massive a body that its very weight on the earth's crust would produce earthquakes.

An army of 4,000 men had to be assembled to tackle the project, and for them and their families a city built, complete with schools, churches, recreation facilities, stores, hospitals—and air conditioning to make life bearable in the merciless heat of the Nevada Desert. Roads and rail lines had to be constructed. And before Boulder Dam itself could begin to rise, giant diversion tunnels, fifty feet in diameter, two on either side of the gorge, had to be blasted through the rock to by-pass the site. It took dams to build a dam, and jumbo-sized ones had to be built upstream and down, to wall off the work area.

Belatedly it was decided that Boulder Dam was not going to be placed in Boulder Canyon after all. Nearby Black Canyon was chosen instead, as a more feasible location and to avoid public confusion, as well as to honor the man who had knocked heads together to make any dam possible. The Secretary of the Interior announced at the outset: "The dam which is to be built in the Colorado River at Black Canyon is to be called Hoover Dam."

Merely getting ready to start building Hoover Dam took two years. The Colorado inconveniently chose 1932, when blasting of the tunnels was at its height, for a series of spectacular flash floods. Tunnels and drilling equipment were swamped repeatedly, trestles destroyed, and crews had hairbreadth escapes from unheralded onslaughts. But despite the resistance of the river, work was kept on schedule and ahead of schedule.

For the yawning holes in the rock banks of the Colorado an entirely new system of boring was devised. A huge framework of platforms was mounted on a truck, faced into a heading, and— in an earsplitting clatter such as human ingenuity had seldom contrived—thirty power drills attacked the face simultaneously. Given the right conditions, the men could complete three rounds of drilling, firing and mucking every twenty-four hours, extending the tunnel as much as 45 feet.

The most exciting event of the whole project came on November 12, 1932. The first by-passes were done, and the engineers were ready to throw across the river the cofferdam which would send the water into the tunnels. For the occasion they borrowed a trick Harry Cory had used a quarter of a century before in the battle for Imperial Valley—the same trick employed by Goethals in 1910 for halting the Chagres in the construction of the Panama Canal: dumping rocks into the river from a high trestle, faster than the surge of water could sweep them away.

The only difference in Black Canyon was that trucks instead of railroad dump-cars would be used. This was the key contest with the Colorado.

On the evening of November 12 a line of trucks stood bumper to bumper for a mile along the road that wound down to the trestle, all heavily loaded, all with idling motors. The signal came for the the charge. Instantly, a hundred trucks inched forward in close formation. One after another they dumped their cargoes into the river and roared away for a reload.

The line was endless. Reloaded trucks were taking their place in the rear before the first hundred were emptied. All through the night and into the next day the assault continued without interruption. Every fifteen seconds, for fifteen hours, a truck spilled its haul into the abyss below.

The river rose steadily. It tugged fiercely at the trestle pilings; it rolled ton-and-a-half boulders aside like playthings; it boiled through and under the slowly mounting barrier; it frothed over the top. Never before had the implacable Colorado faced such opposition. The dam held. Just before noon on November 13, the river level had been raised ten feet and the torrent was ripping over the crest of the barrier. A booming explosion tore open the levee guarding the tunnels on the Arizona side. Sluggishly, the river turned and rolled into its trap. The Colorado was licked.

Not until the following March were the companion tunnels on the Nevada side completed, and by that time a solid earth dam, ninety feet high, anchored on a rock core, securely steered the river where the engineers wanted it to go. The downstream cofferdam was completed, too, and between the two barricades was a bared, dry site where Hoover Dam was to rise. From that point on construction of the great monolith was mostly a monotonous routine of pouring concrete and more concrete.

Buckets running on a confusion of overhead cableways were the most conspicuous vehicles at the scene. Every time one of them was tripped, sixteen tons of concrete plummeted below. So much concrete was going into Hoover Dam that the curing of it would generate fiery temperatures deep inside, if it were laid as a solid mass; engineers estimated that it would take 125 years for such a block to cool, and in the process the interior would inevitably crack and crumble unless a cooling system was made a part of it.

What amounted virtually to a refrigeration plant had to be built in, with miles of water pipes, shafts, ventilators and corridors. But these were minor engineering details of little interest to laborers whose job it was to plant 5,000,000 tons of wet concrete, layer on layer, form on form, until the mass reached a height greater than that of the Washington Monument.

Two and a half years ahead of the schedule set for Six Companies, Inc., Hoover Dam was dedicated on the last day of September, 1935. A succession of six United States Presidents had concerned themselves with the harnessing of the Colorado River and the reclaiming of adjacent desert—Theodore Roosevelt, Taft, Wilson, Harding, Coolidge and Hoover—and it was a seventh, Franklin D. Roosevelt, who finally made the bows at the dedication ceremony before the largest audience ever to assemble in the American desert, an eager throng of some 12,000.

The most enthusiastic participants at that ceremony were the delegations from the Metropolitan Water District, from Imperial and Coachella valleys. Hoover Dam was going to give them a brand-new surge of life. Four years before, the citizens of Greater Los Angeles had voted to expend $220,000,000—more than four times the cost of the vast concrete barrier in Black Canyon—to convey Colorado water across the desert. Their dam—the Parker —was under construction 155 miles south of Boulder City, and a new 240-mile aqueduct was snaking its way over the sands.

The builders of that second aqueduct to Los Angeles could draw from the experience Mulholland had gained in running the conduit from Owens Valley, but they had to do a great deal of pioneering too. Mulholland's ditch ran downhill all the way.

For the new one, water had to be pumped over intervening mountain ranges— a total rise of 1,600 feet—involving engineering problems entirely unknown on the parent project.

The Colorado conduit would cost nearly ten times as much as the Owens Valley system. Plans called for 148 of those giant inverted siphons, a series of mammoth pumping stations, 42 tunnels. A third of the distance had to be tunneled, and a single bore under San Jacinto Mountain extended for over 13 miles.

From the Colorado River the aqueduct had to climb uphill for 125 miles to Hayfield Reservoir, a halfway point east of Coachella Valley. All this was through the most rugged of empty deserts, far from rail lines, supply roads, water, electric power and any communication system. On this stretch the water would pass successively through tunnels, siphons and open canals.

Westward from the Hayfield pump lift, the course would be downhill at an average grade of 3½ feet per mile, through an entirely closed conduit of tunnels, siphons and concrete pipe. That 117-mile section paralleled Coachella Valley, wound into San Gorgonio Pass, skirted Banning, passed under San Jacinto, and terminated at Lake Mathews, south of Riverside. From there the water would be distributed to the coast and valley cities as far west as Santa Monica, 392 miles from its source.

Since the days when Mulholland was toying with his clumsy Caterpillar tractors, a new age of heavy machinery had dawned. Replacing the mule teams were powerful trucks. Bulldozers, scoops, cranes and a dozen other giant earth movers and levelers had found their way into construction camps. Thanks to these, the aqueduct was well along before Hoover Dam was dedicated, and most of the engineering problems had been surmounted. Even the greatest economic depression in American history served the builders in making it easy to recruit a legion of some 11,000 laborers, ready to work for a minimum wage in the relentless summer heat of the desert.

Placing the sidehill siphons was no less formidable an undertaking than it had been in 1910, but marvelous new inventions made the ditchdigging a spectacular mechanical sport. Bulldozers grubbed out a path for the 55-foot width of the open canals; huge dragline cranes followed close behind to do most of the excavating; then came the "canal trimmer," a gigantic framework of moving machinery, straddling the ditch and riding rails on either bank. Designed especially for the job, it fitted the profile of the canal, cut it to a precise shape, and was such an efficient device that it could creep forward at the rate of a foot a minute. Against the desert background the monster looked like a spidery carry-over from the age of megalosaurs.

Trying to keep pace with the trimmer was an army of laborers doing the one major item of handwork—fixing the skeletons of re-enforcement rods. And pushing them was a monstrous mechanical relative of the trimmer, the "canal paver," which spread and tamped the concrete lining into place in one operation. Such fantastic giants had never been used before, and though they demonstrated their worth in the desert, they were so cumbersome that they were never used again.

But the greatest obstacle in the path of the aqueduct proved to be the very element it was being built to convey—water. Scarcely had the blasting of the long thirteen-mile tunnel under San Jacinto Mountain started when veins of water were pierced, and then fault lines from which veritable rivers gushed. San Jacinto was saturated with water.

For a time it appeared that reaching all the way across the Colorado Desert for water was unwarranted. The precious liquid was right there in the nearby mountain, pouring into underground chambers, where it was least wanted, at a rate of 10,000 and 15,000 gallons a minute—36,000,000 gallons a day.

Again and again men were driven from their diggings by the floods. Machinery was swamped. Drillers and muckers had to wade out of the tunnels in hip-deep and chest-deep water. An 800-foot shaft was filled almost to the top before batteries of pumps with adequate drawing capacity could be installed to contend with the flow.

Ironically, the worst part of the struggle to bring water across a desert was boring through that underground rainstorm. Intermittently, for weeks and months, the battle against the subterranean deluge continued. Crews entering the shafts and tunnels looked like firemen en route to a blaze—rubber boots, rubber hats, waterproof pants and waterproof jackets. And even in that habit they often came out at the end of their shift soaked to the skin.

As a mucker described it, it was like working under a fire hose played through a sieve. Men stood in water, sloshed through water as they loaded muck, operated drills and handled dynamite blasts under a constant spray and splash. Holes at the bottom of the face had to be drilled under water, and to get dynamite sticks into place they had to be strapped to the ends of poles and wedged into the drill holes to keep the powder in place until it was fired.

Along with the water they encountered "heavy ground"—rock under such pressure that every foot of it had to be shored up to keep it from collapsing. Nor would ordinary lumber and iron support it. Huge timbers were crushed like matchwood, and heavy steel bent and twisted into grotesque shapes. Larger and larger shoring was used, until clear timber cut sixteen inches square became the standard material used for supports.

Handicaps which seemed as insurmountable as these, however, were not allowed to stand in the way of rushing the aqueduct to completion. A side shaft was drilled into the mountain, so that excavation could be carried on at two additional headings.

Despite the underground rain and the above-ground heat out in the desert, despite the remoteness of the canyons that had to be bridged, the mountain flanks to be scaled, the enormous desert distances over which the conduit had to be laid, the work continued without interruption.

Water was delivered to Pasadena on June 17, 1941, and after that, in rapid succession, to other cities of the Metropolitan Water District. Southern California had the greatest domestic aqueduct in the world, and from the generating plants at the foot of Hoover Dam a dependable supply of hydroelectric power.

Meanwhile, those who had first started the rush for Colorado water—the planters of Imperial Valley—were the last to get their All-American Canal under way. It was not a popular cause in the East, and in the West there were a great many honest opponents who maintained that any canal built across the "walking" desert of southeast California would be drifted over with wind-blown sand within months after it was dug. The last political snags in Washington were not removed until October 1933.

With an allotment of $6,000,000 from the Public Works Administration, the project was finally authorized, and the engineers could challenge the transient desert. For the job they had to have a contraption no less impressive than the machinery devised for the aqueduct, and they very nearly outdid their competitors. Their invention was a 650-ton dragline crane, so enormous that its knocked-down parts filled 20 boxcars, and so ponderous that no wheels could support it in the soft sand. Instead of wheels, it was designed with 2 mechanical "feet," weighing over 20 tons apiece, and mounted eccentrically on an axle, so that they actually paced the desert, 7 feet at a step.

This towering Gargantua strode across the Colorado Desert, scooping up seven tons of sand in a bite and spewing it out on high embankments which were to form a barricade against the shifting sands. Then, as fast as the monumental banks were contoured, oil was sprayed over them or plantings established. Within a few months after the work had started, the most pessimistic dissidents had to admit that the canal was well defended against the walking desert.

But even with the services of an efficient monster, it took six years to carve the 80 miles of unlined ditch through the sand hills from a new dam above Yuma to the foot of Imperial Valley. Not until March 1942, were the planters entirely independent of the old ditch that dipped into Mexico. World War II called a halt to canal construction at that juncture, and Coachella Valley had to wait until 1948 for its 119-mile branch.

The water performed wonders in Imperial Valley. Year after year the green area expanded until 500,000 acres were under cultivation. The mileage in canals increased to 3,172—a far greater network of waterways than roadways. Valley promoters adopted the slogan "Breadbasket of the world" and farmers backed it up by shipping out an annual $150,000,000 worth of agricultural products, ranging from cucumbers and carrots to pork and poultry.

In little more than three decades the population of a community like Brawley—altitude -115 feet—had jumped from a few hundred to 12,000; and El Centro—52 feet below sea level—from 8,000 to 18,000. Imperial, the valley's oldest city (-67 feet), did not grow quite as fast as it neighbors, but could brag of a "trade-territory population" of 7,000.

But all this enlargement of the Breadbasket had not occurred without accompanying afflictions, trials and mortal annoyances. The spirit of fraternal joy and generosity was not the most conspicuous trait of those who were coaxing bloom from the sands.

Violence of the worst sort disrupted Imperial Valley in the middle thirties at the height of the depression. It was called the Lettuce Strike. Stoop labor claimed that the average compensation was 56¢ a day, and that the daily income for a working family of ten seldom amounted to more than $2. They were starving. So they struck, pleading for a living wage and tolerable working conditions.

Asserted an official investigator: "We found filth, squalor, an entire absence of sanitation and a crowding of human beings into totally inadequate tents and crude structures built of boards, weeds or anything that was found at hand to give a pitiful semblance of a home at its worst. Words cannot describe some of the conditions we saw."

The trouble came from bumper crops of lettuce—too much for a depression market to absorb. Everyone concerned, except the bankers and the landowners, was losing money. Carloads of lettuce shipped East were rotting on rail sidings, because housewives were not shopping for salads. And ultimately the pinch was felt hardest by the swarms of Mexicans, Filipinos, Japanese, Negroes, and Hindus who had been drawn to the valley as harvesters, and then displaced partially by a flood of unemployed from Oklahoma, Texas and the Deep South.

Attempts of the workers to organize were foiled, so unions tried to do it for them. All that the field hands were asking was 35¢ an hour, a work day of at least five hours, palatable drinking water and free transportation to the fields. The demands were disregarded, and to suppress the strike, armed vigilantes, supported by legionnaires, took up arms. Shacks were burned, defending attorneys arrested, organizers kidnapped, beaten and deported.

Said the farmers: "We suffered the torments of hell to make this region productive. Why, now, should we let a lot of outsiders dictate to us? We'll do what we damn please in the valley."

And they did.

Wired a spot reporter after an abortive attempt to size up the situation: "I asked questions of everybody I could get hold of—for the brief period of less than three days. Then the blow fell. I was a very aggrieved reporter when the sheriff's deputies, after keeping me incommunicado overnight in the El Centro jail, escorted me across the line into Arizona.

"The Imperial Valley is a fascinating hell-hole and I hated to leave it. I wanted to talk at length with the pea-growing sheriff who arrested and deported me. I wanted to talk to the vigilantes, the automobile salesmen and bank clerks who beat up liberal lawyers, strike organizers and journalists like myself. I wanted to talk to the gentle, fine-featured Mexicans whose present servitude is not very different from that imposed upon them by the conquistadors and the padres. And finally I wanted to talk with the growers—the 'patriots,' as they call themselves."

"To those who have watched the movement of recent events in California," added another reporter, "it is apparent that the modern farmer is no friend of the laboring man . . . The old-fashioned farmer has been supplanted by a type to which the term can no longer be applied with accuracy. The new farmer is a grower. He is only semi-rural. Often he regards his farm as a business and has it incorporated. He belongs to a number of wealthy produce exchanges; he is director of several 'protective associations.' Moreover, he has a hand in state politics. He employs a book-keeper, and, in sober truth, he looks like a banker . . . He will never be an ally of labor."

The growers did their best to disprove that charge, but the violence of the vigilantes and the hunger of the stoop labor finally settled the strike. In the process the nation's impression of Imperial Valley became an ugly one that took a long time to wear off.

Then, in 1940, there came to the desert a kind of disaster which no human law and order could control—an earthquake that was ranked at the time as the fifth most destructive convulsion in American history. It shuddered across Imperial Valley at 8:36 on Saturday night, May 18, when half the population was in movie houses, at dance halls or gathered for weekend gossip on vulnerable street corners. Unaccountably, only eight lives were lost in the valley, but the count of injured ran into the hundreds.

As theatre walls and floors groaned under the impact, crowds stampeded for exits and lights went out. The Imperial Theatre happened to be empty when it collapsed. Sidewalks and the Saturday-night shoppers on them were pelted with bricks and tiles. John Moore of Heber watched the firewall of the El Centro Hotel sway and pivot outward from its foundation before it thundered to the ground. He could not get out of the way in time. Abel Portillo of Brawley was struck down with more falling bricks.

Standing by his car on the curb in front of a grocery store in Imperial, Ralph Mullins impatiently watched his wife, two daughters and a neighbor, through the plate-glass window as they strolled up and down the aisles of the store, doing the family weekend shopping. He was still watching when the shock came and leveled the building. None of his family survived.

"Brawley and Imperial appear to be the worst damaged cities in the valley," wired an A.P. reporter next day. "At least half the buildings in Brawley's main business district of eight square blocks will have to be entirely reconstructed. The earthquake shook scores of homes from their foundations and toppled almost every chimney. With its chief main snapped in two, Brawley will be without gas for an indefinite period. Holtville, like Imperial, lost its water tank, a tower nearly 100 feet high and storing 100,-000 gallons . . . Police and city engineers estimate the damage at $2,500,000."

They underestimated it. Bridges throughout the district were twisted and broken. One span on the highway between Brawley and Westmoreland was dropped four feet. Paved roads everywhere were buckled and cracked, with such dangerous fissures in some places that all traffic had to be rerouted.

A typical fault near Brawley showed a lateral displacement of 12 feet and a change of 3 feet in ground level. Imperial's city hall, which housed both the fire and police departments, was a pile of rubble. Telephone lines were disrupted. Fires raged through Calexico and Mexicali.

The most expensive damage was along the banks of the canal that made the detour into Mexico. Water was pouring out from a half-dozen breaks. It would take weeks to make repairs, and meantime, farmers could expect to lose heavily on their crops of peas and watermelons. Even on the All-American Canal, still under construction, tremendous damage was done. A construction engineer measured one break where a concrete outlet channel had been moved 8 feet out of place. When the total damage had been assessed it was nearer $6,000,000 than the estimated $2,500,000.

To add to the troubles of the low country, a new, shocking, preposterous malediction was cast at Imperial Valley and its environs a decade later from an entirely unexpected quarter. It came from old, reliable, impartial *Harper's Magazine* and the pen of free-lancer Alfred M. Cooper. A CATACLYSM THREATENS CALIFORNIA, screamed the title of a prominent article in the monthly, and the first paragraphs spread the alarm that 100,000 Californians were in dire danger of being drowned at any hour.

that both Imperial Valley and Coachella Valley were about to be wiped off the face of the earth.

"Since 1935 a series of events has set the stage for the inundation of three million acres of Southern California's best farm land and the destruction of twenty-five towns and villages," ran the portentous disclosure. "Irresistible forces of nature have joined with titanic man-made formations to make possible a catastrophe compared to which the San Francisco earthquake and fire of 1906 will be remembered as but a matter of brief inconvenience."

Before Hoover Dam was built, explained Cooper, 500,000 tons of silt were daily cargoed down the Colorado River, to be added to the delta. But the dam had upset nature's balance; the silt was now impounded upstream and the delta deprived of its needed re-enforcement.

Cooper ominously warned that the tidal bore of the river, sometimes as high as fifty feet, was eating away at the delta barrier faster than it could now be built up. He asserted that the Gulf of California had already moved inland eighteen miles in less than a decade, and theorized that the San Andreas fault, cutting directly across the area, could at any time promote an earthquake which would upset the silt beds and let the sea in. Seismologists agree, he claimed, that "A disastrous movement of the San Andreas fault might occur tomorrow.

"It is but a question of time," chided Cooper, "until the low earth barrier, no longer re-enforced by silt from the harnessed Colorado, must be sufficiently dissipated to permit the waters of the Gulf of California to flood Imperial Valley . . . Any opening above or below the surface that would permit the flow of ocean water into the low valleys of California must rapidly widen until, within a matter of hours, the silt barrier will fail to function as a dike. The Gulf will then swiftly reclaim all its ancient bed.

"The head of this Gulf will then lie somewhat north of where the town of Indio now stands, a hundred miles north of the Mexican border, and its eastern and western shores will extend far into California, bordered by the mountain ranges to the west and the above-sea-level ground around Yuma to the east.

"The property loss from such a calamity will result in the certain destruction of more than three million acres, including some of the most valuable farm land in the United States, together with the annihilation of a score of cities and towns . . . Engineers are in accord to this extent: that the erection of an earthquake-proof concrete levee one hundred miles in length is called for if the waters of the Gulf of California are to be permanently contained south of the border . . . At this writing, the odds appear to favor the Gulf of California in its race against time."

Alfred Cooper was trying his best to make a little Holland out of Imperial Valley, and put the desert farmers in a more precarious situation than the Dutch. The dikes of the Netherlands were buttressed with basalt and granite and wooden pilings: Southern California had nothing but heaps of silt and sand to fend off imminent destruction. Holland's tulips were a mere 20 feet below sea level, while some of the lettuce and tomatoes of Imperial Valley were cultivated at depths of almost 200 feet.

The *Harper's* article sent chills down the spines of a great many readers and was a damaging blow to the pride of California publicists. It may even have terrified a few valley residents, but old-timers were unperturbed.

"Piffle!" responded a chorus of scientists. Dr. Carl L. Hubbs of Scripps Institution of Oceanography at La Jolla spoke for all of them: "Studies and surveys of the Colorado River delta region by geologists, geographers, ecologists and engineers," he rebutted, "instead of supporting, utterly refute the reasons that Mr. Cooper advanced to support his fantastic idea that the Gulf of California, by breaking down its delta may soon inundate the enormously rich below-sea-level agricultural districts of southwestern California.

"The barrier is longer than Cooper contended and much higher . . . Gulf water will not seep through to create a break. Instead of retreating northward eighteen miles since Hoover Dam was built, the head of the Gulf has scarcely changed since the survey of 1873–75."

Nevertheless, Dr. Hubbs failed to guarantee quite a 100 percent safety margin. "Though the cataclysm predicted by Mr. Cooper is not foreseeable and though the dangers stressed by him are non-existent," he hedged, "the remote possibility remains that a great flood from the Colorado River may again swing across the delta to wreak incalculable loss of life and property. It behooves the American and Mexican authorities to make doubly sure that the river banks are adequately protected at all canal headings, that the present and future levees are kept in good condition, with provision for any hasty repairs that may be needed, and that other engineering precautions be taken, with a wide margin of safety to forestall the danger of a disastrous flood."

If all the scare talk had any effect upon occupancy of the land that had once been a sea bottom, it was not apparent. Imperial Valley continued to grow phenomenally—defiantly—and the transformation of Coachella Valley, after the completion of its branch canal, was even more dramatic.

Indio, just 22 feet below sea level, quickly doubled its population and became the trading center for some 40,000 people and the date capital of America. Where the map had been blank a decade before, towns and cities appeared along the canal shores. The postwar town of Palm Desert, for instance, could claim an area population of 5,000 and a peak wintertime community of 8,000. Its chamber of commerce boasted that the town was "within twelve minutes of twelve golf courses," "the tropical agriculture center of the United States," and "the smartest address on the Great American Desert."

But Palm Desert was being given plenty of competition in the acquisition of smart addresses. No disaster, no threat of disaster, was going to stem the migration into the dry lands. People now differentiated between "high" desert and "low" desert—between barren lands with cooling altitude and the hot sea-level or below-sea-level bottom lands. But the two were equally in demand. Fast new highways, clean sunshine, the prospect of pumping plenty of water for lawns, swimming pools and golf courses, made both high and low desert attractive, and all that was needed to defy the most torrid heat wave was a good air-conditioning system.

The appeal was not limited to any one class or age group. Rich and poor, old and young, active and retired, responded with like enthusiasm, but to the oldsters the desert call sounded particularly alluring, and more and more senior-citizen communities were dotting the sunland of Southern California.

"You're the last person I'd ever expect to see living in a desert," charged a New Englander on finding a long-time Yankee associate contentedly sunning himself in Lucerne Valley.

"I know," replied the ex-Yankee. "I can't explain it myself. The desert got us. Once it has a grip on you, it doesn't let go. Now I could never be satisfied anywhere else."

The developers, the realtors and the soft-sell salesmen were the real missionaries, carrying the migratory gospel. Down on the shores of the Salton Sea, far, far below sea level, land developer M. Penn Phillips took a long gamble, purchased 19,000 acres along the west shore, and in 1958 announced plans to create a "resort." Within three years Salton City was a reality, with 300 miles of roads, Venetian canals, paved airfield, a business district, yacht club, marina, a luxury hotel, a hundred new homes and a great many more going up. Thirty million dollars had been invested in building lots there, and none of the new owners could understand why this magnificent site had been allowed to go unoccupied for half a century. They talked seriously of making the Salton Sea into one of the greatest spas in the West, and visualized the whole sea rimmed with homes in a few years.

The most hard to believe real-estate spectacle anywhere lay between Victorville and Twentynine Palms. It had to be seen to be accepted. There, for a distance of 75 miles, a sweep of valleys, 20 or 30 miles wide, was dotted with desert cottages—unpretentious buildings for the most part, thousands upon thousands of them—and the great majority dependent on tank trucks for water. Anyone who ever doubted the authenticity of the appeal of desert living was obliged to abandon his skepticism after witnessing that display. It was the driest of wasteland, but the rolling hills and the mountains on the horizon supplied a barren beauty. People took to it in the same way that their fathers crowded to lake shores, ocean shores and mountain heights, to build recreation cottages.

To the north, the Mojave was bursting with a vitality no less amazing. Transcontinental motorists, who remembered the gritty little railroad town of Barstow in the twenties and thirties, rubbed their eyes in the fifties and sixties at seeing a sprawling metropolis of 12,000 occupying the old site—still a railroad center, but a thriving agricultural, industrial and tourist center too. Broad Mojave River bottom lands of the region were green with alfalfa, highways were jammed, surrounding hillsides breaking out with a pox of new developments. Three miles to the west, where semiarid ranches existed a few years before, lay the handsome little town of Lenwood, a model suburb for desert living, and more communities like it were appearing rapidly.

The desert's namesake, Mojave, once a rendezvous for twenty-mule teams and the supply depot for the first Los Angeles aqueduct, was booming into a major industrial center where everything was reckoned in terms of multimillions—multimillion-dollar cement factories, multimillion-dollar plants for aluminum, borax, graphite, potash, chemicals and the reconditioning of railroad cars. Fifty trains rumbled through town every day, the swish of thousands of cars and the overhead roar of planes demonstrated all too audibly that the remote desert community had long since lost any claim to isolation.

The thirties had brought another gold stampede to the upper desert when prospector George Holmes exposed a promising vein and borrowed, from three aging Bakersfield schoolteachers, $1,000 apiece with which to finance a probe. Holmes introduced the West to fabulous Golden Queen. He made financial history by selling out for $3,500,000, and added a warm paragraph to human history by paying back to the schoolmarms their $1,000-dollar antes—which they had never expected to see again—along with interest of $297,000.

The operators of Golden Queen netted $9,000,000 in gold and silver, while others were digging even richer ore concentrate from the nearby Cactus Queen. Gold-digger's luck seemed much more durable in the desert mountains than in the Sierra.

In the 1940's, Mojave minerals went to war—tungsten and potash, manganese and antimony, lead and zinc, hematite and borate. The mines brought a stir of prosperity to barren regions that had scarcely been explored before, and it did not end with V-J Day. The borax industry adapted itself to the pace of the jet age and the space age. A hundred new uses for borates had been discovered, and among them was its use in jet and missile fuel. Mojave's magic crystal was indispensable to the new mode of intercontinental and interplanetary traffic.

The world's largest known borax reserves were not in Death Valley, after all, but in a desolate spot named Boron, halfway between Barstow and Mojave. For years the deposit had been mined in a labyrinth of underground tunnels, but to get the mineral out in the quantity needed for the space age the whole "lid" of the mine had to come off. In a stupendous earth-moving project, 9,000,000 tons of overburden were dug away, and the tunnel operation converted to open-pit mining. The craterlike hole finally exposed was over 300 feet deep and broad enough to hide a small city in its depths.

The town of Boron, with its $8,000,000 processing plant, was only one of the unexpected wonders to bloom in postwar Mojave

Desert. New mines dotted the landscape, and huge new manufacturing complexes belched smoke. And the most sanitary-looking operation of all was at Saltdale on the edge of an expansive brine lake where mountainous quantities of salt were produced by solar evaporation. By the sixties, the industrialists had lost interest in the search for silver and gold; they were after the rare earths—the chemical salts and irons in which the desert abounded.

Mojave's business leaders had learned to take reverses in stride too. Economic calamity loomed over the town in 1958 when the Marines announced that they were going to close their base because of air-space conflict with the planes of Edwards Air Force Base. For years the Marine Corps had meant the difference between prosperity and something less for Mojave, and its departure could be a stunning blow to the town's economy. But instead of accepting a slump, the mammoth station, including a runway of 9,500 feet, was taken over as a modern "Industrial Air Park" and corporations were soon clamoring for space there.

The population explosion kept pace with the industrial expansion. The town of Mojave liked to remind people that geographically it was located in Antelope Valley, in company with Lancaster, Palmdale, California City and some twenty smaller communities—a sort of valley capital, responsible in part for the growth of the area. That growth was something to cheer.

California City, a dozen miles to the northeast, was the most fantastic stepchild. Where patches of cotton and alfalfa had been growing on an 82,000-acre expanse of desert one year, California City stood the next, with 8,500 homesites recorded. In a few months $14,000,000 had been expended on real estate alone by prospective residents and commercial investors, 10,000 trees planted, and $1,000,000 spent on a community park. Golfers were going the rounds of an 18-hole golf course, and sailboats were skimming over the surface of a 20-acre man-made lake. Moreover, California City was conceived merely as the nucleus for a complex of seven other adjacent desert communities.

Lancaster, to the south, already claimed a population of 20,000. An entirely new town, North Edwards, was putting in a bid for some of the 12,000 workers at Edwards Air Force Base, had a multimillion-dollar shopping center in operation, apartment projects under way and homes sprouting on three great housing tracts.

Crystalaire started frankly as a country club, with seven artificial "lakes," 176 acres of fairways, a luxurious clubhouse, a swimming pool and a few private apartments, and was such a success that it was expanded into a development. Eighty half-acre lots were put on sale. Within a few months most of the eighty were spoken for and swank $50,000 residences were being erected on them.

Palmdale, the southern metropolis of Antelope Valley, boasted 14,000 residents and had adopted the nickname of Jet-town, home of the RS-70. In its Air Force Production Flight Facility, 400 men were employed one year, 4,000 the next. Lockheed, Convair, North American, Douglas, Hughes and Northrup were all doing production testing of advanced jet aircraft there.

Comparable industrial development was shaping the future of the low desert country to the south. In addition to the agricultural enterprises, there were sugar factories, electronics and airplane plants, big mining activities, the largest cotton gin in the world, and the largest plasterboard plant. Few areas in the nation could boast of such diversity.

Desert dwellers could undoubtedly count on setbacks—natural and man provoked—in years to come. The geography, the precipitate growth, the unremitting competition for more water, and the very nature of the restless generation which was taking refuge in the desert, set the stage for turbulent pageantry. Suspense belonged to the desert. A brooding element of excitement had always hung over it—a kind of drama not found in more prosaic regions. New emigrants carried urban refinements with them into the dry country, but the refinements failed to obscure or displace the theatrical atmosphere already there.

Promoters were playing it up for all it was worth, and the public was responding. Every town was trying to outdo its neighbor with a come-on. The community slogan was as vital to progress as a set of statutes. Chambers of commerce attempted to impress even the passing motorist with an image of local status.

Imperial Valley had the climate that "the rest of the Southwest claimed to have." There were more "capitals" than counties. Indio was "The date capital of the United States of America," Palm Desert "The vacation golf capital of the world," Niland a tomato capital, and Holtville. "The carrot capital of the world."

Westmoreland modestly described itself as "Rather than a place to retire, a place for people of any age to begin to live." Less modestly, Salton Sea was advertised as the future "Riviera of North America." Calexico was "The doorstep to Mexico." Barstow, in the middle of the Mojave, was "The intersection of opportunity," and Mojave itself "The heart of the industrial empire of the upper desert." Brawley liked to be referred to as "The cattle and sheep headquarters of the West." Banning was "The gateway to the desert," Baker its "Hub," while Calipatria, 184 feet below sea level, proudly declared herself to be "The lowest-down city of the Western Hemisphere."

No up-and-coming desert town could exist for long without a recurrent "unique tourist attraction." And the lures were becoming *more* unique annually, with midwinter fairs, rodeos and cattle calls, date festivals, cotton carnivals and carrot carnivals, lettuce tournaments and lettuce festivals, world championship sheep shearing contests, camel races and turtle races, gem and mineral shows, aquacades and water-skiing contests, sky diving, dune buggying and drag races, treasure hunts and an endless string of anniversary celebrations—all highlighted with enough queen crownings to supply pulchritudinous royalty for the capital cities of another planet.

The public fell hard for the showmanship, and the real-estate kings thrived on it. Nothing drew crowds to future homesites like a little carnival spirit. The flow of land-hungry escapists angled out from the crowded coastal cities in every direction. They converged on gleaming new California City and newer Sunland City, on Yucca Valley, Lucerne Valley, Antelope Valley, Apple Valley, Borrego Valley; they took another look at Palm Springs, where a realty corporation had managed to get a 70-year lease on a parcel of Indian land and planned another residential-recreational community to the tune of $50,000,000.

The earmark of a new development was a golf course. The golf course came first, and homeseekers soon crowded in around it. There was a town being built to suit every taste, though the tastes were amazingly similar: La Quinta, Indian Wells, Palm City, Bermuda Dunes, Desert Hot Springs, Hesperia, Palm Springs Panorama, Alpine Village.

"Southland deserts are blossoming with construction," counseled the real-estate editor af the Los Angeles *Times*. "The tempo, both in low and high desert areas heralds a new growth era, one that beckons residents now in summer as well as winter months . . . Water is a factor of some importance worthy of consideration at some desert locations. But sunshine is to be found in great abundance. Recreational opportunities abound. Retired persons are finding the deserts to be new havens of hope and happiness. Thousands seeking refuge from crowded cities are casting glances to the desert."

It is getting to be an old story after two decades of desert migration, but the ever-increasing throng headed in the same direction continue to keep it a live one. "You'll never leave the desert, if you stay long enough to wear out a pair of shoes," runs an ancient saw of the Southwest. Sales in new footwear are keeping pace with the sales in real estate. The invaders are standing the test. They intend to stay.

Each spring the desert sends forth its gaudy token bloom that does not last. Folks are bringing in a much more permanent kind of bloom. And year by year the California deserts are getting smaller and smaller.

QUOTATION SOURCES

Chapter I. P. 19—Ghost Mountain retreat: Marshall South, "Desert Refuge," *Saturday Evening Post*, Mar. 11, 1939, p. 36; reprinted by special permission of the *Saturday Evening Post*; copyright 1939 by the Curtis Publishing Co. P. 21—Desolation beyond conception: W. L. Manly, *Death Valley in '49** (San Jose: Pine Tree and Vine Co., 1894), pp. 132, 136. P. 22—Noon: G. W. Parsons, *A Thousand Mile Desert Trip* (Los Angeles, 1918), p. 15. Pp. 22–23—Corcoran's recollections: Bourke Lee, *Death Valley* (New York: Macmillan, 1930), pp. 152–54. P. 26—Thirstiest trail: Parsons, *op. cit.*, p. 13. P. 26—Bullfrog drinking bout: Lee, *op. cit.*, pp.136–37. P. 29—Death Valley Scotty's story: George F. Putnam, *Death Valley and its Country* (New York: Duell, Sloan and Pearce, 1946), pp. 4–5. P. 33—Highest thermal honors: "Hottest Known Place is Death Valley, California," *Science News Letter*, Aug. 24, 1940, p. 126. P. 34—Stanza: Parsons, *op. cit.*, p. 16. P. 35—Prediction: "Mojave Transformation," *Fortune* Magazine, Jan. 1959, p. 105. P. 36—Permanent home: Joseph Wood Krutch, "Lure of Sun, Sand and Stars," *New York Times Magazine*, Nov. 8, 1959.

Chapter II. P. 39—Bolton's statement: H. E. Bolton, *Anza's California Expeditions*, Volume III, Preface (Berkeley: University of California Press, 1930). Pp. 39–40—Font's text: *ibid*. Vol. IV, p. 20. P. 42—Weather: *ibid.*, Vol. I, p. 309. P. 42—Watermelons: *ibid.*, p 288 Pp. 42–43—Indian affability: *ibid*. Vol. IV, p. 96. P. 43 —Plaster City: *ibid.*, Vol. III, p. 53. Pp. 43–44—Snowstorm: *ibid.*, p. 57. P. 44—Unpalatable meat: *ibid.*, p. 61. P. 45—Wordy defense: *ibid.*, p. 67. P. 48—Assemblage: H. E. Bolton: *Kino's Historical Memoir of Pimería Alta* (Berkeley: University of California Press, 1928), pp. 251–52. P. 49—Serra's disability: Francisco Palou, *Life and Apostolic Labors of the Venerable Father Junípero Serra*, G. W. James, Editor (Pasadena: 1913), p. 65. P. 50—Font on Garcés: Bolton, *Anza's California Expeditions*, Vol. IV, p. 121. P. 50—Garcés' trials: Elliott Coues (Editor), *On the Trail of a Spanish Padre* (New York: Francis P. Harper, 1910), Vol. 1, p. 241. Pp. 52–53—Trappers' desert crossing: David H. Coyner, *The Lost Trappers* (New York: Hurst, 1847) pp. 167–68. P. 53—Californians: *ibid.*, pp. 195, 197. P. 54—Smith's letter: *Letterbook*, Superintendent of Indian Affairs, Kansas Historical Society. Pp. 54–55—Governor's reception: S. A. Coblentz, *The Swallowing Wil-*

derness (New York: Yoseloff, 1961) p. 17. Pp. 55–56—Pattie's account: Timothy Flint (Editor), *The Personal Narrative of James O. Pattie of Kentucky* (Chicago: Lakeside Press, 1930), pp. 255–57, 263. Pp. 57–58—Leonard's account: John C. Ewers, *Adventures of Zenas Leonard, Fur Trader* (Norman: University of Oklahoma Press, 1959), pp. 126–28. Pp. 58–59—Frémont's commentary: J. C. Frémont, *Memoirs of My Life* (New York: Bedford, 1887), pp. 365 ff.

Chapter III. P. 64—Mrs. Brier's experience: Carson, Nevada, *News,* May 27, 1913. Pp. 65–66—Manly's side trips: Manly,* *op. cit.,* p. 132. P. 67—Manly's sentiment: *ibid.,* pp. 254, 259. Pp. 70–71—Mine report: *Alta California, September* 4, December 17, 1863. Pp. 73–74—Cerro Gordo furnace: Inyo *Independent:* July 1, 1871. P. 75—Panamint desperadoes: W. A. Chalfont, *The Story of Inyo* (Published by the author, 1922), p. 260. P. 78—Dalenguela case: Inyo *Independent,* August 17, 1872. P. 78—Rojas case: *ibid.,* August 8, 1870. P. 78—Graveyard: Chalfont: *op. cit.,* p. 261. P. 79—Anonymous obituary: Inyo *Independent,* July 13, 1872.

Chapter IV. P. 87—Proof: *Texas Almanac,* 1859, Galveston, Texas. Pp. 89–90— Washington circular: Sacramento *Daily Union,* September 3, 1857. Pp. 90–91— Sixth mail: San Francisco *Bulletin,* October 31, 1857. P. 91—Advertisement: San Francisco *Herald,* November 1, 1857. Pp. 91–92—Report on ships: *ibid.,* November 4, 1857. Pp. 95–97—Banning report: Captain William and George H. Banning, *Six Horses** (New York: Century, 1930), pp. 121–25. Pp. 98–101—Ormsby reports: New York *Herald Tribune,* September 26–November 19, 1858. P. 99— Apology: San Francisco *Bulletin,* October 11, 1858. P. 99—Second coach: *ibid.,* October 16, 1858. P. 101—Thanks due: *Alta California,* October 21, 1858. Pp. 110–02—San Diego resolution: San Diego *Herald,* Extra, May 9, 1859. Pp. 102–03 —Browne's description: J. Ross Browne, *Adventures in the Apache Country* (New York: Harper, 1869), pp. 47–50. P. 104—Huntington's comment: S. P. Daggett, *Chapters on the History of the Southern Pacific* (New York: Ronald Press, 1922), p. 119. P. 104—Explanation: *ibid.,* p. 135.

Chapter V. P. 115—Shadley grave: C. B. Glasscock, *Here's Death Valley* (New York: Bobbs-Merrill, 1940), Copyright 1940 by C. B. Glasscock; reprinted by special permission of the publishers, the Bobbs-Merrill Co., Inc., pp. 141–42. Pp. 115–16 —Interment: *ibid.,* p. 157. Pp. 121–22—Desert hay: John R. Spears, *Illustrated Sketches of Death Valley and Other Borax Deserts of the Pacific Coast** (New York: Rand, McNally, 1892), pp. 118–19, 111–12.

Chapter VI. *Pp.* 131–32—Carson and Colorado: Spears, *op. cit.,** *pp.* 122–30. P. 132—Greater results: Chalfont: *op. cit.,* p. 322. P. 135—Browne's trip: Browne, *op. cit.,* pp. 47–48. P. 135–36—Antagonist: D. A. Hufford, *Death Valley— Swamper Ike's Traditional Lore* (Los Angeles: Hufford, 1902). P. 136—Van Dyke: John C. Van Dyke, *The Desert* (New York: Scribner's, 1902), pp. 57–59. P. 137— Wídney: J. D. Widney, "Colorado Desert," *Overland,* Jan. 1873, pp. 44–50. P. 140 —Railroad station: R. A. Nadeau, *The Water Seekers* (Garden City: Doubleday, 1950), copyright 1950 by Remi A. Nadeau; reprinted by permission of Doubleday

and Co., Inc., p. 154. Pp. 143–44—Flier: *Imperial Press,* Dec. 21, 1901. P. 151—
Rock supply: George Kennan, *The Salton Sea* (New York: Macmillan, 1917), p. 88.

Chapter VII. Pp. 155–57—Weather reports: Sacramento *Daily Record,* July 27–
29, 1874. P. 157—Inyo report: Inyo *Independent,* August 1, 1874. Pp. 161–65—
Randsburg: H. G. Tinsley, "A Desert Mining Town," *Harper's Weekly,* March 6,
1897, p. 234; Charles L. Greene, "The California Rand," *Overland,* May 1897, p. 559.
Pp. 167–69—Butler's story: S. P. Davis, "Nevada's Safeguard for Mine Buyers,"
Harper's Weekly, April 11, 1908, p. 16. Pp. 171–79—Goldfield: P. V. Mighels,
"When Mammon Makes a Camp," *Harper's Monthly,* April 1905, pp. 719–728; S. P.
Davis, *op. cit.*

Chapter VIII. Pp. 181–82—Shrader's observation: E. Roscoe Shrader, "Ditch in
the Desert," *Scribner's Magazine,* May 1912, pp. 538–550. Pp. 183–84—Lippincott's
assertions: Joseph B. Lippincott, "The Los Angeles Aqueduct," *Review of Reviews,*
July 1910, p. 65. P. 184—Roosevelt's statement: *Complete Report on Construction
of the Los Angeles Aqueduct* (Los Angeles: Dept. of Public Works, 1916), p. 68.
P. 184—Titanic struggle: B. A. Heinly, "Carrying Water Through the Desert," *National Geographic* Magazine, July 1910, p. 568. P. 185—Desert description: Shrader,
op. cit. P. 190—Bonus results: *Complete Report on Construction of the Los Angeles Aqueduct, op. cit.,* p. 151. Pp. 191–92—Easterner's observation: Shrader, *op.
cit.* P. 193—Meal: *ibid.* Pp. 194–96—Caterpillars: *ibid.* P. 196—Failure of caterpillars: *Complete Report on Construction of the Los Angeles Aqueduct, op. cit.,*
p. 97. P. 197—Siphons: Shrader, *op. cit.* P. 198—Steam shovel: *ibid.* P. 200—
Tunnels: *ibid.* Pp. 200–01—Magnificent heritage: Remi. A. Nadeau, *op. cit.,* p. 56.

Chapter IX. P. 207—Scott obituary: *Time* Magazine, Jan. 18, 1954, p. 88. P. 205
—Van Loan recollection: E. A. Vandeventer, "Death Valley Scotty," *Sunset* Magazine, March 1926, p. 22. P. 207—Prowler's observations: *ibid.* P. 209—Scotty's
reply to wife: *Newsweek,* Jan. 16, 1937, p. 12. Pp. 210–12—Smythe's study: William E. Smythe, *Conquest of Arid America,** (New York: Harper, 1900), pp. 92–94,
98, 102–105. Pp.212–15—Nordhoff's commentary: Charles Nordhoff, *California for
Health, Pleasure and Residence** (New York: Harper, 1882), pp. 78–88, 161–68.
Pp. 216–18—Death Valley tour: Edna B. Perkins, *The White Heart of Mojave**
(New York: Boni and Liveright, 1922), pp. 14–15, pp. 93–95. Pp. 218–19—Palm
Springs in 1923: J. Smeaton Chase, *Our Araby* (Palm Springs and New York: Pri-
vate printing, 1923), pp. 17–21, 40–41. P. 221—Hints on auto travel: *ibid.,* pp. 111–
12. P. 221—Sleep: *ibid.,* p. 61. Pp. 221–22—Palm Springs in the 1930's: *Califor-
nia, A Guide to the Golden State,* American Guide Series (New York: Hastings
House, 1939), p. 628. P. 225—Prospectus: *Joshua Tree National Monument,* U. S.
Dept. of Interior, 1961, p. 1.

Chapter X. P. 230—Spies: Jesse L. Lasky, *I Blow My Own Horn* (New York:
Doubleday, 1957), copyright 1957 by Jesse L. Lasky and Don Weldon; reprinted by
permission of Doubleday and Co., Inc. P. 230—Location trips: *ibid.,* p. 96. P. 231
—Hollywood haste: Benjamin B. Hampton: *A History of the Movies* (New York:

Covici-Friede, 1931), by permission of Crown Publishers, Inc., p. 79.   Pp. 231–32—
Exclamation: Mrs. D. W. Griffith (Linda Arvidson), *When the Movies Were Young*
(New York: Dutton, 1925), p. 158. Pp. 232–33—On location: *ibid.*, p. 161, 163, 164.
Pp. 233–34—*Gold Is Not All: ibid.*, p. 160.   Pp. 234–35—San Fernando Desert:
ibid., pp. 197–99. Pp. 236–38—Hamilton's comment: Cosmo Hamilton, *Unwritten
History** (London: Hutchinson, 1924), pp. 264–69. Pp. 239–40—Palm Springs:
Chase, *op. cit.*, pp. 49–50.   P. 241—Hart's first Western: W. S. Hart, *My Life East
and West* (Boston: Houghton, Mifflin, 1929), by permission of the Board of Super-
visors, County of Los Angeles, Calif., pp. 198–99.   Pp. 241–44—Hart at Victorville:
ibid., pp. 319, 305–06, 322.   Pp. 246–47—Meighan at Palm Springs: William C. de
Mille, *Hollywood Saga* (New York: Dutton, 1939), pp. 215–16.

Chapter XI. Pp. 254–55—Marine Base refinements: *Twentynine Palms* Marine
Corps Base (Riverside: Armed Services Publishers). Pp. 256–59—Fort Irwin descrip-
tion: *U.S. Army Armor and Desert Training Center Information Pamphlet* (Fort
Irwin, Jan. 1962).   P. 261—Temperature data: *Rocketeer*, Official Weekly, U.S.
NOTS, Nov. 8, 1958.

Chapter XII. P. 274—Backdrop: Spears, *op. cit.*, p. 134.   Pp. 274–75—Peattie's
view: D. C. Peattie, *The Road of the Naturalist** (Boston: Houghton, Mifflin, 1941),
pp. 12–14; also *Natural History Magazine*, March 1941, pp. 122–25.   P. 287—Official investigation: James Rorty, "Lettuce—With American Dressing," *Nation*, May
15, 1935, pp. 575–76.   P. 287—Farmers' stand: Carey McWilliams, "The Farmers
Get Through," *American Mercury*, Oct. 1934, pp. 241–44.   Pp.287–88—Spot reporter: *New York Times*, May 20, 1940.   Pp. 289–92.—Cataclysm: A. M. Cooper,
"A Cataclysm Threatens California," *Harper's Magazine*, April 1950, pp. 66–69.
Pp. 291–292—Response of scientists: C. L. Hubbs, letter, *ibid.*, July 1950, p.14. Pp.
297–98—Editor's observations: Al Johns, Los Angeles *Times*, May 28, 1961.

* Note: In order to present more readable text, deletions of material not pertinent
to a subject have occasionally been made without insertion of ellipses, and in some
instances sentences have been juxtaposed for clarity or unity.

INDEX